The Introductory Guid to Art Therapy

The Introductory Guide to Art Therapy provides a comprehensive and accessible text for art therapy trainees. Susan Hogan and Annette M. Coulter here use their combined clinical experience to present theories, philosophies and methods of working clearly and effectively.

The authors cover multiple aspects of art therapy in this overview of practice, from working with children, couples, families and offenders to the role of supervision and the effective use of space. The book addresses work with diverse groups and includes a glossary of key terms, ensuring that complex terminology and theories are clear and easy to follow. Professional and ethical issues are explored from an international perspective and careful attention is paid to the explanation and definition of key terms and concepts. Accessibly written and free from jargon, Hogan and Coulter provide a detailed overview of the benefits and possibilities of art therapy.

This book will be an indispensable introductory guide for prospective students, art therapy trainees, teachers, would-be teachers and therapy practitioners. The text will also be of interest to counsellors and other allied health professionals who are interested in the use of visual methods.

Susan Hogan is Professor of Cultural Studies and Art Therapy at the University of Derby, UK. She has written extensively on the relationship between the arts and insanity, the role of the arts in rehabilitation and on women's issues in art therapy.

Annette M. Coulter is a British-trained and Australian-based art psychotherapist specialising in children, adolescents, families, groups and couples. She has pioneered art therapy training and professional development in Australia and Singapore. Through the Centre for Art Psychotherapy, she provides consultation, supervision, education and customised training.

The Introductory Guide to Art Therapy

Experiential teaching and learning for students and practitioners

Susan Hogan and
Annette M. Coulter

 Routledge
Taylor & Francis Group

LONDON AND NEW YORK

First published 2014
by Routledge
27 Church Road, Hove, East Sussex, BN3 2FA

and by Routledge
711 Third Avenue, New York, NY 10017

Routledge is an imprint of the Taylor & Francis Group, an informa business

British Library Cataloguing in Publication Data
A catalogue record for this book is available from the British Library

Library of Congress Cataloging in Publication Data
Hogan, Susan, 1961–
The introductory guide to art therapy : experiential teaching and learning for
students and practitioners / Susan Hogan and Annette Coulter.
      pages cm
   1. Art therapy. I. Coulter, Annette. II. Title.
   RC489.A7H64 2014
   616.89´1656–dc23   2013027593

ISBN: 978-0-415-68215-2 (hbk)
ISBN: 978-0-415-68216-9 (pbk)
ISBN: 978-1-315-84918-8 (ebk)

Typeset in Times New Roman by
HWA Text and Data Management, London

Printed and bound by CPI Group (UK) Ltd, Croydon, CR0 4YY

Contents

Figures

About the authors

Annette M. Coulter studied fine art in Australia (Queensland College of Art, now Griffith University) before travelling to England, where she completed a postgraduate diploma in Art Therapy (Hertfordshire College of Art and Design, now Hertfordshire University) and a Master of Arts in Art Education with an art therapy specialisation (Birmingham Polytechnic, now Birmingham City University). She is a registered art therapist practitioner with the Australian and New Zealand Arts Therapy Association (ANZATA), the American Art Therapy Association (AATA), and the Korean Art Therapy Association (KATA). As a clinical family therapist she is also registered nationally with the Psychotherapy and Counselling Federation of Australia (PACFA), and the Australian Register of Counsellors and Psychotherapists (ARCAP).

In England, she served on the Council for the British Association of Art Therapists, (BAAT), as secretary and newsletter editor. Motivated by working in professional isolation, she drew on this experience to co-found both the Australian National Art Therapy Association (now ANZATA), and the International Networking Group of Art Therapists (INGAT).

She has worked as an art therapy clinician since 1976. Her clinical experience includes adult mental health, a therapeutic community, day hospitals, intellectual disability, child psychiatry, juvenile detention centres, child guidance clinics, community welfare, education and supervising art therapy students on clinical placement. Ongoing professional development includes analytic group work, family therapy, psychodrama, sand play and child and adolescent psychoanalytic psychotherapy. She has also completed training as an Interactive Drawing Therapy (IDT) practitioner and is an endorsed IDT teacher and supervisor.

She specializes in working with children, adolescents and their families and for eight years conducted ongoing individual, family and group art therapy in a residential hospital setting for emotionally-disturbed children and supervised art therapy students from overseas. She worked in a residential school for marginalized, conduct-disordered, male youth; coordinated adolescent and family counselling services in regional Australia for thirteen years; and was a clinical coordinator for Relationships Australia.

She has worked as an art therapy educator since 1983, initially coordinating an undergraduate art as therapy elective at Queensland College of Art. In their first years of establishment, she was clinical coordinator and course coordinator for the Master of Arts in Art Therapy at Edith Cowan University, Perth, and the University of Western Sydney. For over twenty years, she has taught a one-year foundation studies in Art Therapy course through the Centre for Art Psychotherapy which pre-dates the establishment of Australian art therapy training. More recently, she was the programme leader on the first Master of Arts in Art Therapy in south-east Asia at LaSalle College of the Arts, Singapore. Currently, she works in private practice in the Blue Mountains, Australia, offering individual, couple, family and group art psychotherapy consultation, supervision and education.

Annette's recent publications include: 'Contemporary Art Therapy with Transient Youth' (in H. Burt, *Art Therapy and Postmodernism: Creative Healing Through a Prism*, 2011); '"Came Back – Didn't Come Home": Returning from a War Zone' (in M. Liebmann, *Art Therapy and Anger*, 2008); 'Couple Art Therapy: Seeing Difference Makes a Difference' (in E. Shaw and J. Crawley, *Couple Therapy in Australia: Innovative Approaches*, 2007); and 'Art Therapy in Australia: The Extended Family', *Australian and New Zealand Journal of Art Therapy*, October 1(1): 8–18 (2006).

Susan Hogan has a BA degree in Fine Art, a postgraduate diploma in art therapy, a master's degree in Arts Administration (Arts Policy and Management) and a further master's degree in Social Science Research Methods (Social Policy and Sociology). Her PhD was in Cultural History (looking at the history of ideas around madness and the use of the arts) from Aberdeen University, Scotland. Susan has also undertaken further training in group-analytic psychotherapy. She served for six years as a Health Professions Council (UK) 'visitor'. She is a former vice-president of ANATA (Australian National Art Therapy Association, now ANZATA) and has twice served as a regional co-ordinator for the British Association of Art Therapists (BAAT). She has been instrumental in setting up several art therapy training courses.

Susan qualified as an art therapist in 1985. She has a particular interest in group work and experiential learning, following early employment with Peter Edwards MD, an exceptional psychiatrist who had worked with Maxwell Jones, a psychiatrist who is associated with the 'therapeutic community movement' in Britain. She is currently a professor in Cultural Studies and Art Therapy at the University of Derby, where, for many years, she facilitated experiential workshops and the closed-group component of the art therapy training. This training is based on the group-interactive approach described by Professor Diane Waller (summarised in this book). Now most of her time is spent supervising and conducting research.

Susan has also undertaken work with pregnant women and women who have recently given birth, offering art therapy groups to give support to women and an opportunity for them to explore their changed sense of self-identity and sexuality as a result of pregnancy and motherhood. She has published extensively on this subject.

Susan has worked in academia since 1990 for a number of institutions, including The University of New South Wales, The University of Technology, Sydney, Macquarie University and the National Art School, Sydney.

Her major intellectual work is *Healing Arts: The History of Art Therapy* (2001), described by the late professor of psychiatry, Roy Porter, as 'sure to be the definitive monograph on this subject for the foreseeable future'. Her other books comprise *Feminist Approaches to Art Therapy* (as editor, 1997); *Gender Issues in Art Therapy* (as editor, 2003); *Conception Diary: Thinking About Pregnancy and Motherhood* (2006); *Revisiting Feminist Approaches to Art Therapy* (as editor, 2012); and *Art Therapy Theories* (in press). She is currently co-writing on women's experience of ageing with sociologists from the University of Sheffield and on the arts and humanities in mental-health rehabilitation with scholars from Nottingham University. Additional to all the above, she has also published a number of both scholarly and polemical papers on women and theories of insanity.

Particularly influenced by the anthropological work of her late mother-in-law, Dame Professor Mary Douglas, Susan's work has been innovative in its application of social, anthropological and sociological ideas to art therapy and her unwavering challenge to reductive psychological theorising.

Foreword

Judith A. Rubin, PhD, ATR-BC, HLM

That an American art therapist is contributing a foreword to a book by authors from the UK and Australia is indeed remarkable. Although there have been chapters by colleagues from across the Atlantic in books edited on both sides of the ocean, a foreword is additional evidence of respectful collegial relationships. For me, being included in this way is a further confirmation of art therapy's increasing maturation. I am not only honored to be invited, but am also pleased that the field in which I have spent a half century has achieved sufficient security to be able to reach comfortably across borders, whether geographic, political, or theoretical.

As I reflect upon art therapy's "coming of age," I am also reminded of how greatly my own work has been nourished by inspiration – not just from within the US – but from abroad, and especially from the UK. Susan Hogan asked that I write "a foreword, which perhaps focuses, in an inspirational way, on some of the art therapy highlights of your career." I have therefore looked back as well as ahead, and it has been a personally rewarding journey that I hope the reader will find informational, if not inspiring.

When I first entered this embryonic profession in 1963, there were only a handful of books written by anyone calling him or herself an "art therapist," all of which I read eagerly, feeling virtually "starved" for information. Two were by a pioneer from Britain, Adrian Hill (1945, 1951); four were by two Americans, Margaret Naumburg (1947, 1950, 1953) and Edith Kramer (1958). Having been an art teacher before becoming a therapist, I had already been inspired by the writings of art educators who viewed their work as therapeutic – authors like Viktor Lowenfeld (1939, 1957), Florence Cane (1951), and Seonaid Robertson (1963). Scouring the library stacks in search of more such nourishment, I will never forget the thrill of discovering *On Not Being Able to Paint* by British analyst Marion Milner (1957), or of reading Australian psychiatrist Ainslie Meares (1957, 1958, 1960) whose "shapes of sanity" had a lasting impact on me.

These writers were the first "kindred spirits" I found in my quest for understanding and, I believe contact, though they were merely vicarious acquaintances from one-way meetings on library shelves. Yet because I was then the only art therapist in the city of Pittsburgh, discovering people who articulated in print what I was groping to conceptualize for myself in this new and challenging work was helpful in a way that is difficult to convey in an era where art therapy is so well known.

Perhaps the intensity of my response to my newfound literary "friends" was related to the emotional meaning for me of art therapy at that time in my life. It is no exaggeration to say that its discovery had been like finding my true self, reflected in the title of a chapter I contributed to *Architects of Art Therapy*, "An Ugly Duckling Finds the Swans" (Rubin, 2006). In fact, I have always felt that becoming an art therapist "fit" me in a way that being an artist, art teacher or art historian (another career I had contemplated) had not. Thus, meeting others with a similar passion for "image magic" (Kris, 1952) – even on the printed page – evoked a deep sense of kinship, and helped to alleviate my feelings of isolation.

It is no surprise, then, that meeting people in person was even more thrilling. In 1968, I had lunch with a delightful fellow from Scotland who had just given a stimulating paper on "The Psychology of Ugliness," Ralph Pickford (cf. Pickford, 1967). As one of the hundred people who attended the first conference of the American Art Therapy Association in 1970, I felt like I had found my professional family. I felt an immediate bond with my roommate for a week-long seminar (Rubin, 1972), British art therapist Diana Halliday, probably because her work with children was so like my own. At the next seminar I fell in love with Seonaid Robertson, a Scottish art educator whose book I had already read and admired (Robertson, 1963). Soon afterward I met Michael Edwards and Edward Adamson, also from the UK, also kindred spirits.

As I recall the pleasure of meeting these colleagues from across the Atlantic, I also remember that for many years I found myself wondering why the literature from Great Britain seemed so rarely to refer to anything written in America and vice-versa. Of course there were exceptions, but for the most part it seemed that art therapy was growing relatively independently in each of the two places where it was also developing most extensively. Whatever the reasons, I am pleased to see that over time, especially during the past decade, that situation has definitely begun to change. This healthy development, while due mainly to the maturation noted earlier, has also been facilitated by the truly remarkable global blossoming of the field in recent years.

This growth, reflected in a proliferation of international organizations and websites, was also the motivation for a recent film with contributions from colleagues on every continent – "Art Therapy: a Universal Language for Healing" (Rubin, 2011). A related film project in 2011 was accomplished with the help of volunteer translators and monetary support from art therapy associations around the world – a DVD of "Art Therapy Has Many Faces" (Rubin, 2004) with subtitles in 12 languages. The idea came from Liona Lu and the Taiwan Institute of Psychotherapy, who had created a version of that same film with subtitles in both simple and complex Chinese a few years earlier. We are indeed learning from and helping each other, and it is very good.

Collaborating across the miles on both of these recent films was made infinitely easier by the existence of the worldwide web. The Internet has surely transformed our lives in many ways, the email exchange of chapters involved in the creation of this book being one small example. I am convinced, however, that even without that ease of interchange, the current international blossoming of art therapy would still be happening now. Just as developments in psychology and art in the beginning of the twentieth century made "art therapy an idea whose time had come" (Rubin, 2004), so "globalization" has made its evolution as a worldwide phenomenon inevitable in the 21st century.

The therapeutic value of the arts has, after all, existed from the dawn of human history. Art therapy – a profession that deliberately harnesses that healing power for change – is but a recent reflection of that phenomenon. While the discipline has so far developed most extensively in the US and the UK, in many other cultures the arts are even more central, inextricably woven into the fabric of society. It is therefore no surprise that art therapy is growing in a wide variety of ways around the globe, compatible with the specific cultures in which it is taking root.

Hopefully, those of us from the Anglo-American community will, when consulting or teaching abroad, be as sensitive to cultural issues as we are to individual, familial or group dynamics in our clinical and educational efforts. As with knowing ourselves in order to best help others, we need to be culturally aware, sensitive, and competent in order to help support local pioneers in the global development of art therapy. Knowing our own inevitable biases is nicely acknowledged in this book.

One of the most enjoyable things about reading the chapters by each of the authors is that both of them are refreshingly frank about the convictions they have developed over their professional lifetimes. Although the reader might not agree with everything they have written, he or she will surely be stimulated as I was to think long and hard about the topics, some of which are not usually considered in such detail.

For example, the complexities and benefits of doing co-therapy are the subject of an entire chapter, and are elaborated in a way that should be helpful to any art therapist who collaborates with a colleague, student or teacher in offering art therapy to a family or group. Working with a co-therapist can be extraordinarily rich and beneficial to clients, but it also presents serious challenges to the workers. Remaining aware of the delicate transference and counter-transference issues that are inevitably stimulated for each clinician is vital, but is also frequently overlooked.

This book addresses other issues that are rarely discussed or – if treated – not in such useful detail. One of these is the art therapy space, the room in which the healing power of art is made possible; this is a topic that every worker needs to take seriously in order for true transformation to occur. While art therapy can of course be offered under less than optimal conditions – like a crowded hospital ward or homeless shelter – making the space as safe as possible is absolutely essential. If there is a separate room, then making sure that the physical environment provides a "framework for freedom" (Rubin, 2005) requires the most thoughtful attention from the art therapist.

Another welcome aspect of this volume is the fact that no fewer than four chapters are devoted to the nitty gritty of teaching – from single workshops to extended courses – and deal with educating art therapy students, allied health professionals, and art therapists at all levels of experience. A similarly substantive contribution is the inclusion of three chapters devoted completely or partially to supervision. Like those detailing teaching methodologies and rationales, they will be most helpful to art therapists who train others in supervisory sessions as well as in classrooms.

Both authors, having been clinicians as well as educators for many decades, bring their considerable expertise to bear on topics with which they are intimately familiar. I hope that everyone who reads this book – from interested beginners to experienced practitioners – will be inspired by its contents to enhance his or her own efforts to provide and to promote the incredible healing power of art.

Bibliography

Cane, F. (1951). *The Artist in Each of Us*. London: Thames and Hudson.

Hill, A. (1945). *Art Versus Illness: a Story of Art Therapy*. London: Allen and Unwin.

Hill, A. (1951). *Painting Out Illness*. London: Williams and Northgate.

Kramer, E. (1958). *Art Therapy in a Children's Community*. Springfield, IL: C.C. Thomas.

Kris, E. (1952). *Psychoanalytic Explorations in Art*. New York: International Universities Press.

Lowenfeld, V. (1939). *The Nature of Creative Activity*. London: Routledge and Kegan Paul.

Lowenfeld, V. (1957). *Creative and Mental Growth*. Third edition. New York: Macmillan.

Meares, A. (1957). *Hypnography*. Springfield, IL: C.C. Thomas.

Meares, A. (1958). *The Door of Serenity*. London: Faber and Faber.

Meares, A. (1960). *Shapes of Sanity*. Springfield, IL: C.C. Thomas.

Milner, M. (1957). *On Not Being Able to Paint*. New York: International Universities Press.

Naumburg, M. (1947). Studies of the "Free" Art Expression of Behavior Problem Children and Adolescents as a Means of Diagnosis and Therapy. *Nervous and Mental Disease Monograph*, 1947, No. 17.

Naumburg, M. (1950). *Schizophrenic Art*. New York: Grune and Stratton.

Naumburg, M. (1953). *Psychoneurotic Art*. New York: Grune and Stratton.

Pickford, R.W. (1967). *Studies in Psychiatric Art*. Springfield, IL: C.C. Thomas.

Robertson, S. (1963). *Rosegarden and Labyrinth*. London: Routledge and Kegan Paul.

Rubin, J.A. (1972). A Framework for Freedom, in M. Perkins (ed.) *International Seminar on the Arts in Education*. Lancaster, MA: Doctor Franklin Perkins School.

Rubin, J.A. 2004. *Art Therapy Has Many Faces*. VHS/ DVD. Pittsburgh, PA: Expressive Media, Inc.

Rubin, J.A. (2005). *Child Art Therapy*. Second edition. Somerset, NJ: Wiley.

Rubin, J.A. (2006). An Ugly Duckling Finds the Swans, in M.B. Junge and H. Wadeson (eds) *Architects of Art Therapy*. Springfield, IL: C.C. Thomas, pp. 105–21.

Rubin, J.A. (2011). *Art Therapy: a Universal Language for Healing*. Pittsburgh, PA: Expressive Media, Inc.

Rubin, J.A. (2011). *Art Therapy Has Many Faces, with Subtitles in 13 Languages*. Pittsburgh, PA: Expressive Media, Inc.

Acknowledgements

Annette M. Coulter

Most of the material for my contribution comes from short courses that were developed for the promotion of art therapy in Australia and south-east Asia. Throughout this time, my clinical supervisors, in particular, Peter Blake, Brian Cade and Mee Mee Lee, played pivotal roles in the synthesis of my thoughts and ideas through challenging clinical and teaching experiences.

Dr Marcia Rosal introduced me to the practical experience of North American art therapy by inviting me to assist her PhD research in Australia, and Shirley Riley significantly influenced my work with adolescents, families and couples. I would also like to acknowledge gratitude to Maureen Crago, Elizabeth Burns, Dr Maralynn Hagood, Dr Marcia Rosal and Dr Nancy Slater who contributed to the final editing of my chapters, as well as David Brazil for his technical assistance with images. I am especially grateful to Dr Maralynn Hagood and Liz Sheean for their ongoing wisdom and interest.

Art therapist, Jean Eykamp had an original vision for this book and encouraged me to write for publication. Other art therapists who have directly and indirectly contributed to this research include: Janie Stott, Sheila Murugiah, Elizabeth Aylett, Dr Susan Joyce, Claire Edwards, Jennifer Pitty, Jessica Koh, Nancy Caldwell, Melissa Strader, Susanne Calomeris and Dr Donna Betts.

Thanks also go to my partner Boudewijn Maassen, and my family, in particular my parents Pauline and Neil, and my grandmother Margaret Springgay, for their understanding, interest and encouragement.

Finally, I am very grateful to my colleague, friend and co-author, Dr Susan Hogan whose publication experience, belief in my contribution and patience to critique my chapters has been tirelessly supportive. There are also the many clients, students and colleagues with whom I have worked over the years who have extended my skills, challenged my knowledge and stretched my experience.

Susan Hogan

Earlier versions of chapters three and four were published in the ANATA Newsletter several years ago; the chapters have been substantially revised. An earlier version of the Overview of Models of Art Therapy (Chapter 8) appeared in Inscape: The International Journal of Art Therapy; this version has been significantly re-written, partly in view of subsequent feedback. Thanks again to Dr Andrea Gilroy, Michele Gunn, Dr Susan Joyce, Rosy Martin and Nick Stein for their original comments; I'm particularly indebted to Michele for her excellent and detailed critique, to which I hope I responded adequately. Thanks also to Michele for the elegant rainbow analogy. I would also like to thank the Inscape critical reviewers for their thought-provoking remarks, to which I attempted to respond in the original version. Tim, as editor of Inscape (IJAT), also made some helpful critical suggestions that I appreciated and which improved the piece. My chapter on supervision was scrutinised by university colleagues in one of our peer-review sessions, so thank you to all those who contributed to the critique. Regarding Chapter 9, I would like to thank Gary Nash for alerting me to the work of Lofgren, and for making me think harder about this topic.

General thanks too is required for all those who have been prepared to engage with me intellectually on these topics, especially my colleagues Jean Bennett, Jamie Bird and Shelagh Cornish. Final thanks to Annette for her initial suggestion that we do something together.

Routledge have a rigorous production process, which entails soliciting critical comment on the manuscript at various junctures during its development, and this is an important reason why we wanted to publish this book with Routledge. We would both like to acknowledge the hard work of our editor Joanne Forshaw and her assistant, Susannah Frearson. Thanks to Holly Knapp for the excellent layout and design.

Figures 2.1 and 2.3 are copyright of The London Art Therapy Centre and photographer Peter Lurie (lightworkerarts.com) (2012), and are reproduced here by their kind permission.

Figures 9.1 and 9.2 originally appeared in D. Lofgren (1981) Art Therapy and Cultural Difference, *American Journal of Art Therapy* 21, 25–32, and are used here by permission.

Figure 15.1, The Reflective Cycle, first appeared in G. Gibbs (1988) *Learning by Doing: A Guide to Teaching and Learning Methods* (Oxford: Oxford Further Education Unit, Oxford Polytechnic), and appears here by permission.

Chapter 1

Introduction

The scope of the book

Susan Hogan

I try not to forget that each painting is a unique expression of the individual who painted it – no one else could have done it. It has to be honoured as a unique creation.

(Elizabeth Colyer, *c*.1986)

Scope

This book is an indispensable introductory guide for prospective students, art therapy trainees, teachers, would-be teachers and therapy practitioners. The text will also be of interest to an increasing number of counsellors, and other allied health professionals, who are interested in the use of visual methods. The overall aim of the book is to serve as a well-rounded introduction to the subject.

The Introductory Guide to Art Therapy is intended to be a key text for trainees, a handbook for professional art therapists and a resource for other practitioners wishing to use art in their work. The text has been written so that it can also serve as a preparatory text, with careful attention being paid to the definition of key terms and concepts. The philosophy and main styles of working are elucidated without one particular model being promoted above others, thus giving an essential, and previously lacking, even-handed introductory overview of the subject. The lucidity of the prose makes complex topics easily comprehensible. The book presents the principles of experiential learning and reflective practice in an art therapy context. It moves on to explore professional and ethical issues with an international perspective.

As a good all-round introduction to the subject, it is useful for other professionals wishing to get a sense of what art therapy is and how it is used. A would-be employer could pick up this book and, after digesting it, have a clear understanding of the potential role of the art therapist within their organisation. The volume is therefore useful in a range of contexts.

The Introductory Guide will cover all aspects of essential practice. Written with a self-conscious absence of jargon and 'psycho-babble', this book aims to demystify art therapy. Therefore, this text should be useful for those coming new to art therapy. In particular, we hope that trainee art therapists will want to turn to this book as their starting point, but it should also be of interest beyond a trainee readership.

The two authors have distinctive voices and points of view; both are mature practitioners able to offer different, but complementary, perspectives. We may not always agree, but there is mutual respect apparent.

Outline of content

The book explores the context and definition of art therapy. Then chapters which explore experiential learning and teaching (useful equally for the art therapy trainee and the art therapist who is thinking of running workshops) follow. The book then goes on to explore art therapy theory and aims to give an overview before examining art therapy with different populations in several chapters. This is followed in the last chapters by an examination of the supervisory issues, then finally concludes with a consideration of professional issues in a global context.

Defining art therapy

This introductory chapter will outline the scope of the book and present a summary of the book's contents as follows.

2. What is art therapy? The art therapy environment: managing and using the space

The chapter will give an overview of the term 'art therapy'. It moves on to describe the art therapy room, and explores ideas about managing the art therapy space, including the storage of art works. The basic principles of good practice will be articulated regarding the importance of confidentiality. The implications of sharing a room with other therapists or other art therapy practitioners will be explored, especially with regard to the pros and cons of being able, or not able, to put art work up on walls. The disposal of group art objects will also be discussed.

The context of art therapy will be articulated. Different client groups and work settings will be outlined, from prisons to palliative care. Finally, a brief section on the history and development of art therapy is also included.

Art therapy – teaching and learning

3. Reflections on experiential learning

This chapter explores the concept of 'experiential learning' in detail. The chapter is based on the author's experience of teaching structured introductory courses in art therapy since 1990, and will discuss how to teach art therapy experientially. It looks at the role of pictorial symbols, analogies and metaphors, and also at the overall structure of art therapy sessions. The configuration of the workshops, the ability to compare and contrast different formats and then how these different formats influence the dynamics of the group is discussed; techniques which can be used to help participants to start to reflect upon this are described and analysed.

4. An introduction to art therapy: further reflections on teaching directive art therapy at an introductory level

This chapter elaborates in detail on the content of an art therapy workshop series. The aim of the workshops is to present participants with a variety of quite different formats so that they can see the scope of 'directive' art therapy; all the sessions are structured. It is possible that participants may discover one particular way of working they enjoy, or they may go on to employ a range of group formats with clients if they study further in the subject and become practitioners. The different techniques are described in detail.

The chapter also presents a basic analytic 'tool' for students to help them to reflect on their experience of group work and get full benefit from the experiential group work. An analytic tool, or aid, is useful because reflecting on the multi-levelled nature of group work is complex. Students can use the tool as a starting point for their own detailed analysis of the group work in their reflective diaries; it is hoped that it won't be used as a reductive checklist. The concept of 'reflective practice' is elaborated.

5. Becoming an art therapy practitioner

On completing their training, art therapy graduates begin a new phase of their career: the process of finding employment. This chapter covers important topics for practice, from negotiating a job description to suitable attire.

There is also a section on commonly used art therapy assessments. The aim of art therapy assessments varies. Assessment can include assisting in the establishment of a diagnosis (particularly in those countries in which private health-care insurance dominates). Assessment can also be used to determine the suitability of an individual for art therapy (and the chapter outlines several such art-based evaluations). Assessment also refers to the evaluation of the progress of therapy, as well as the evaluation of outcomes. In Britain, standard measures of effectiveness have been developed which focus on the outcome of therapeutic interventions. Clinical Outcomes Routine Evaluations – Outcome Measure (CORE-OM) – for example, is being used to try to produce cohesive global evidence of clinical effectiveness. However, Gilroy, Tipple and Brown (2012) note the presence of a 'heterogeneity of assessment practices' in clinical practice (p. 219).

6. Teaching art therapy to other allied health professionals

Some of our work is about running educative consultation training for established clinical teams, or professional groups or individuals who want quick instruction about using art more effectively in their work. These allied health professionals do not want to complete art therapy training, but often claim to be already 'doing art therapy' in their clinics and just want to expand these skills further. This chapter addresses ways an art therapist can sensitively advise about their profession in this context and demonstrate that just using art materials in a clinical setting is not necessarily 'art therapy', despite that what may be happening can have therapeutic aspects to it.

7. Innovative teaching strategies

This chapter addresses current training practices when teaching art therapy techniques to therapists and counsellors who are already experienced practitioners in their own right and who wish to make more effective use of art in their clinical work. Some innovative teaching strategies are discussed that incorporate current art therapy teaching practices with the skills and experience of other therapist practitioners who wish to make use of art more effectively in their work. Qualified art therapists can be over-protective of their skills and unprepared to share their expertise with non-art therapists. The realities of being part of a clinical team and involving interested colleagues with effective art therapy practice can be a rewarding challenge. The art therapist must be able to share their skills with a sceptical community or group of health professionals as well as to those who offer professional support. The main emphasis of this chapter is how to teach art therapy to colleagues, how to facilitate team-building through the use of art therapy, as well as how to work in co-therapy with other allied health professionals. The chapter answers how to integrate specialist art therapy skills into an effective clinical team, in which the art therapist is valued.

Art therapy theory

8. An overview of models of art therapy: the art therapy continuum – a useful tool for envisaging the diversity of practice in British art therapy

This chapter will assist in providing some clarity to a situation that, at first sight, particularly to training therapists, seems extremely confusing. Art therapy today is rather complex and 'the art therapy continuum' is an attempt to give an at-a-glance picture, or 'snap-shot', of this diversity. Like any snap-shot, it does not reveal the entire landscape, but the chapter gives an overview of the main models of contemporary art therapy practice. As the chapter illustrates, British art therapy today is fundamentally eclectic with a number of different theoretical models in practice. In brief, these are a gestalt psychology approach; an analytic transference-focused model; a group-interactive model which draws from existential philosophy and symbolic-interactionism (which will be explained) as well as psychodynamic theory; an art therapy support-group model which is often 'person-centred' in orientation; and finally studio-based approaches, which are favoured by some art therapists in Britain today, in which engagement with the art process is seen as fundamentally curative. These main approaches are outlined in detail.

9. The role of the image in art therapy and intercultural reflections: working as an art therapist with diverse groups

What is the fundamental difference between art therapy and psychotherapy or counselling? How does the image function in art therapy? What is the triangular relationship? This chapter will discuss the role of the image in the art therapy process and will survey different ideas about this from different theoretical perspectives. The role of the art making differs in different modes of art therapy. Some of the tensions between visual and verbal elements will be elucidated. A discussion of the pros and cons of directive and non-directive art therapy work is touched upon.

This chapter brings post-modernist theory to bear on the subject of art therapy; it challenges the reductive use of theory and the over-interpretation of clients' art, giving examples. A sketch of the main work on cultural difference within art therapy is also presented. The chapter also interrogates the importance of maintaining a critical awareness of gender norms in clinical work, whilst focusing on cultural differences and their acknowledgement within the art therapy process.

Art therapy populations and methods

10. Working as an art therapist with children

The particular skills needed to work with a wide range of different young clients is presented and discussed. Recommendations for training are made. The contribution of art therapy to working with children and adolescents is increasingly appreciated by the general population of art therapist practitioners. This chapter describes establishing an art therapy service in both mental health and community welfare settings. The chapter includes consideration of individual and group work contexts, as well the role of parents, siblings and the extended family. Reflections on the importance of non-verbal and not-knowing processes on both the part of the therapist and the child are included. Links are made to other symbolic and metaphoric uses of the creative processes such as sand play, free play, drama, music and dance. The non-verbal aspect of creative thinking and the processing of emotional issues from a neuroscience perspective are included.

11. Working as an art therapist with offenders

This chapter will outline the use of art therapy in prisons and other secure settings. It will also provide a broad context for the use of art therapy in prisons providing an overview of literature in the field on this subject, and a detailed critique of key texts.

What are the particular dilemmas faced by art therapists working in secure settings? Drawing on clinical experience, the particular implications of working with offenders are addressed. Examples from art therapy clinical practice in the form of short case studies and vignettes are presented to illuminate and illustrate this work.

12. Art therapy with couples and families

This chapter describes how art therapy is used in couple counselling and family therapy. This includes examining different theoretical approaches with an emphasis on systemic family and couple art therapy, but also includes more recent models, particularly narrative and brief solution-focused family and couple art therapy. There is an integration of psychodynamic and more cognitive approaches that acknowledges complexity. The use of art in family and couples work introduces an alternative way to communicate that provides a visual starting-point or intervention. For some family members, it is easier to say through an art task how they are affected by current relationships. It is important for art therapists to be able to adapt their skills to suit all members of the family, or to accommodate different thinking within a couples consultation. This is a highly specialised field within art therapy that needs to include couple and family art therapy assessment techniques as well as knowledge of effective strategic interventions and other therapeutic considerations. Another way to consider work with families and couples is as intensive group work where dynamics are rich, entrenched and challenging. It is easy for the therapist to become caught up in the dynamic system that is operating – art therapy offers a way to examine and reflect on the system and its operating dynamics.

13. Group work with adults and the group-interactive art therapy model

The basic principles of group art therapy will be articulated. The group-interactive method will be elucidated. The basic idea behind the group-interactive approach is that during interactions with others in the group, individuals reveal their 'characteristic patterns of interaction'; these are seen as constraining people in their everyday lives (Waller 1993: 23). These 'patterns of interaction' are acknowledged and reflected upon and provide a focus for group analysis. Therefore, the method employed involves an analysis of clients' here-and-now behaviour in the group. This is not a simple discussion of clients' issues so much as a *revelation* of their present constraints. Such constraints, or habitual ways of being and thinking, can be *revealed* through interactions with other members of the group or depicted in art works. 'Feedback' from participants is an important part of this method: 'feedback from members of the group illuminates aspects of self which have become obvious to others but which are not recognised by oneself' (Waller 1991: 23).

14. Art therapy and co-therapy

An aspect of art therapy practice that is rarely addressed is the issue of art therapists working in co-therapy. This chapter explores the advantages and importance of having a co-therapist in group-work practice to enhance service delivery to both clients and students of art therapy services. There is a focus on co-therapy in the art therapy training groups, particularly a training group that has run each year for almost twenty years. Statements and feedback from various art therapists/co-therapists will also be included as commentary in this chapter, which has been written in consultation with other co-therapists.

Supervisory issues

15. Starting supervision – vulnerability in supervision: aspects of hopelessness, inadequacy and anxiety in the supervisory relationship

This chapter provides an excellent resource for would-be art therapy supervisors. It also gives the trainee art therapist a useful insight into what they are likely to encounter at the outset of their clinical work placement, which forms an important part of their art therapy training. The chapter explores the anxiety inherent in the opening stages of the supervision groups in order that trainee art therapists will gain confidence and prospective supervisors will have a better idea of what to expect.

16. Models of supervision and personal therapy

This chapter concerns ways in which art therapy can be used within the context of clinical supervision. This is not only for art therapist practitioners, who by the completion of their training are familiar with the use of art therapy in the context of clinical supervision, but also explores the use of art therapy in the context of the art therapist supervising other allied health professionals. This chapter also includes ways art-making processes can be used in self-supervision for a daily debriefing; this is of particular benefit to those in isolated practitioner situations. Examples of client record-keeping, chart-writing and case note-keeping are presented.

Professional issues

17. International perspectives

The main differences between the North American and British systems of mental health care have been neatly summarised by Gilroy, Tipple and Brown (2012). They point out that Britain has free healthcare at the point of access, regardless of income. In sharp contrast, in North America, private health insurance is ubiquitous (and may become mandatory). Health insurance companies in North America are referred to as 'managed care'. They point out that other health-care providers are adopting this 'target-driven' culture.

As Coulter's chapter notes, North American trained art therapists are more likely than their British counterparts to be directly involved in applying standardised assessment instruments and formulating diagnoses. In any case, there is a great diversity of institutions, which leads to differences in emphasis as art therapists attempt to work within a variety of contexts and teams. Hagood (1994) has noted that in North America systematic, cognitive and humanist models are more likely to be integrated into art therapy and that there is a greater use of theme-based approaches. However, it is a misconception that British art therapy is, and has always been, utterly dominated by psychoanalytic theory (Waller 1991; Hogan 2001) and British art therapy offers a plurality of approaches which are outlined in early chapters in this volume.

Originally, the vision for the International Networking Group of Art Therapists (INGAT) was to provide a forum for an international dialogue. Many countries are faced with theoretical and ethical dilemmas as they attempt to establish the profession outside Britain and North America. There is also the need for sensitivity to cultural context. This chapter addresses how the profession copes with the problems that arise and considers what provisions are required for training standards to adapt to cultural contexts. This is illustrated by a discussion about establishing art therapy in countries where the profession was largely unknown. Part of the international field of art therapy that has barely been addressed, despite a number of articles and chapters about multi-cultural aspects of art therapy, is the fact that applying an essentially Western form of therapy into other cultural contexts has ethical, moral and theoretical complexities attached to it. The chapter also looks at the introduction of art therapy into an Eastern cultural context. How may Eastern medical practices be accommodated? Is it possible for very different cultural, spiritual and ethical beliefs to be incorporated into a Western profession?

18. A critical glossary of key terms informing art therapy

Though most technical terms will be defined in the text, some of these terms are expanded upon in this critical glossary. A definition is provided and also a critical interrogation of key concepts.

Bibliography

Gilroy, A., Tipple, R. and Brown, C. (eds) 2012. *Assessment in Art Therapy*. London: Routledge.

Hagood, M.M. 1994. Diagnosis or Dilemma: Drawings of Sexually Abused Children. *Art Therapy: Journal of the American Art Therapy Association* 11(1), 37–42.

Hogan, S. 2001. *Healing Arts: The History of Art Therapy*. London: Jessica Kingsley Publishers.

Waller, D. 1991. *Becoming a Profession: The History of Art Therapy in Britain 1940–1982*. London: Routledge.

Waller, D. 1993. *Group Interactive Art Therapy*. London: Routledge.

Chapter 2

What is art therapy?

The art therapy environment: managing and using the space

Susan Hogan

The most common misconception held about art therapy is that it involves the therapist interpreting the art work, and deciphering and unravelling the meanings hidden within; on the contrary, it is the *creator* of the image, not the therapist, who has this pleasure. The role of the therapist is primarily an insightfully enabling one. However, there are different models of art therapy and these will be explained. In the 'interactive model', for example, the therapist's role does encompass articulating group themes and dynamics.

Definitions of art therapy

Definitions of art therapy are in flux, and it would be an interesting exercise in itself to look at the ebb and flow of these over time. This chapter shall begin with some analysis of the recent American and British definitions. Here is the current definition from the British Association of Art Therapists' (BAAT) website at the time of writing:

> Art Therapy is a form of psychotherapy that uses art media as its primary mode of communication.... The overall aim of its practitioners is to enable a client to effect change and growth on a personal level through the use of art materials in a safe and facilitating environment.

The BAAT definition also clarifies that 'previous experience or skill in art' is not a prerequisite for engaging in art therapy, and that the art therapist 'is not primarily concerned with making an aesthetic or diagnostic assessment of the client's image'. 'Primarily' is curious here, for it suggests, perhaps unwittingly, that art therapists do indulge in aesthetic assessments of their client's work (though what that might entail is left for conjecture); certainly, in a British context, art therapists are seldom involved in the act of diagnosis, which is in the medical domain. On the other hand, some information about the progress of art therapy is conveyed to medical staff and often contributes significantly to the team case assessment and treatment planning decisions.

The emphasis in the above quotation is on a psychotherapy which uses art as its primary mode; thoughts and feelings are expressed pictorially and symbolically using art materials, with personal change and the amelioration of mental suffering as the goal. The use of the arts is emphasised as useful 'to people who find it hard to express their thoughts and feelings verbally', but in practice, it is often the case that discussion of images follows their making and that this in itself is enlightening. Indeed, some models of art therapy can become very verbal, but art therapy is still fundamentally different to verbal psychotherapy, because of the triangular configuration of participant, facilitator and art object.

The use of the word 'growth' is interesting, and it suggests an expansion of personal awareness in the art therapy participant, which will help him or her to deal better with problems and difficulties as they arise. There is the opportunity to externalise thoughts and feelings, to visualise them and explore them. As will be discussed in more detail later on, some of the communication which takes place in art therapy is by the participant to himself via the image: it is a dialogue with oneself. Not everything is necessarily revealed to the therapist immediately (or ever), as it may not necessarily be pictorially explicit or obvious. Certain thoughts and feelings may be revealed in the participant's own time to the art therapist and other group members; thus art therapy participants have some control over how emotionally exposed they are willing to be, which is arguably a distinct advantage over purely verbal approaches (though internal monologue and silence are potentially creative options in verbal psychotherapy).

The use of the word 'psychotherapy' rather than 'counselling' is significant, as counselling is also interested in effecting 'change and growth on a personal level'; however, counselling still retains historical connotations of giving 'guidance' in the resolution of emotional problems, whereas 'psychotherapy', though varied in its approaches, aims at the communication of conflicts and difficulties with the development of insight into problems at its core. Arguably the line between some forms of psychotherapy and counselling has dissolved.

The front page of the American Art Therapy Association's (AATA) website describes art therapy thus:

> Art therapy is a mental health profession that uses the creative process of art making to improve and enhance the physical, mental and emotional well-being of individuals of all ages. It is based on the belief that the creative process involved in artistic self-expression helps people to resolve conflicts and problems, develop interpersonal skills, manage behaviour, reduce stress, increase self-esteem and self-awareness, and achieve insight.

In this definition the resolution of problems features strongly, but also a potentially broader approach is evident with an emphasis on engaging in art for increased well-being. Much 'well-being' discourse in the UK is used by the arts in health movement, and art psychotherapy has become split off from some of these exciting developments (often community arts and participatory arts) – a split that some art therapists are trying to repair. The aim of art therapy in the American definition is also potentially more wide-ranging, with behaviour management and increased self-esteem being explicitly stated as treatment goals. We should not overlook the emphasis on artistic self-expression as pivotal.

In a section entitled 'Defining Art Therapy', the AATA website elaborates further:

> Art therapy integrates the fields of human development, visual art (drawing, painting, sculpture, and other art forms), and the creative process with models of counselling and psychotherapy. Art therapy is used with children, adolescents, adults, older adults, groups, and families to assess and treat the following: anxiety, depression, and other mental and emotional problems and disorders; substance abuse and other addictions; family and relationship issues; abuse and domestic violence; social and emotional difficulties related to disability and illness; trauma and loss; physical, cognitive, and neurological problems; and psychosocial difficulties related to medical illness.

It is interesting to note that art therapy is seen as art integrated with both 'models of counselling and psychotherapy' in this definition.

The Australian and New Zealand Arts Therapy Association (ANZATA) offers this definition in its 'What is arts therapy?' section:

> Arts therapy uses creative processes, including art making, drama, and movement to improve and enhance physical, mental and emotional well-being. It is suitable for all ages and many life situations, and can be done with individuals or groups. Arts therapy works by accessing imagination and creativity, which can generate new models of living, and contribute towards the development of a more integrated sense of self, with increased self awareness and acceptance.

Arts therapy is being used as a generic term in the above quotation to include drama and other disciplines, but art therapists in Australia and New Zealand do specialise, rather than undertaking a generic arts therapies training. Thus, art therapists specialise in using fine art materials.

Again, we can note the emphasis on enhancing well-being, including 'physical' well-being, and although 'well-being' may encompass physical well-being in the AATA definition, this explicit reference seems to point to greater emphasis in this area. In common with both the BAAT definition and that of AATA is an emphasis on increased self-awareness; however, the next section on how art therapy works would seem to remain firmly located in the well-being arena, with its emphasis on 'accessing imagination and creativity' and developing 'new models of living'. This seems quite broad and open, and oriented to enhancing quality of life.

However, the view appears to narrow slightly in the 'About arts therapy' section, which describes it as 'an interdisciplinary form of psychotherapy' that is 'generally based on psychoanalytic or psychodynamic principles'. The range of work undertaken may be broader than that of UK art therapists: 'Some art therapists also offer phototherapy, play and sand tray work', as well as diagnosis. It continues thus:

> Art therapy is a therapeutic and diagnostic tool where therapist and client/s develop a dynamic interpersonal relationship, with clear boundaries and goals. It differs from traditional art in that the emphasis is on the process of creating rather than on the end product.
> Art therapy is a creative process, suitable for all ages, and particularly for those who may be experiencing life changes, trauma, illness or disabilities causing distress for the individual and for their family.
> Art therapy works by contributing to changes in the client's inner world...

In a further section entitled 'How does art therapy help?', the ANZATA site is explicit about potential benefits of art therapy: it can enable the expression of feelings which are 'difficult to discuss'; it 'stimulates imagination and creativity'; it can contribute to the development of 'healthy coping skills and focus'; it 'increases self-esteem and confidence'; it can help to clarify 'issues and concerns'; it can enhance communication skills; and it provides 'a safe nurturing environment' in which to share feelings. In relation to physical well-being, it 'assists with development of motor skills and physical co-ordination' and aids the 'ability to identify feelings and blocks to emotional expression and personal growth'. 'Coping skills' are rather ambiguous, but most of the above is clear enough.

Art as therapy

Small differences of emphasis between countries aside, in all forms of art therapy participants are encouraged to explore their feelings using art materials, often paper and paint, but a variety of materials may be employed, such as collage, clay and sculpture (wood, wire, metal mesh, plasticine, found materials, including natural materials such as leaves or stones). As noted above, this can be done individually or in groups. The role of metaphor and symbols in depicting mood states, which are hard to articulate, is important. How participants use the art materials can also contribute to the meaning of the art produced. The art materials (their very substance) can evoke feelings in the person using them. It is possible that 'magical' powers can be invested in the image or object and that art works can take on great symbolic significance for the maker of the image or object. Therefore, how the image is changed, stored, displayed or destroyed can become relevant (Hogan 2001). A series of images viewed together might be particularly enlightening, as patterns or a 'narrative' may be discerned.

Conversely, the process of making the image or object may be more important than the end result – it may be a pictorial struggle, perhaps an inability to resolve an image which is revealing, or the actual process of constructing it or destroying it (Hogan and Pink 2010). The end result may seem irrelevant.

In group work there may be an emphasis on the individual in the group, with each participant getting an allotted time to talk to the group as a whole about their art work. Other approaches may be more interested in exploring interactions between group participants, as part of a process aimed at illuminating habitual ways of being, and opening these out for scrutiny and contemplation: this is the 'interactive model' (Waller 1991).

The art therapy environment: managing and using the space

Owning the space

Many art therapists have a preference for an art therapy room to look like an art therapy room: it has a studio-like ambience. When conducting experiential work, art therapists seek to permit their groups to develop a sense of ownership of the room by putting up art works on the walls. A number of therapists endorse the view that this is therapeutically useful; it is possible to leave the work in progress, or the group work just made, and to have absolute confidence that it will still be there on the wall the following day or week. The work then functions as a greeting, or a welcome to the space, to participants. The art object, waiting where it was left, creates a sense of security and continuity.

The ideal art therapy room is therefore that over which the art therapist has total control. To leave works out and then to have them moved by another room-user would be counter-productive and could engender feelings of insecurity and disruption, or indeed violation, in participants. Obviously, this is a potentially serious issue, especially if works could become damaged or lost.

A compromise is to have a large walk-in cupboard which can be locked, where art works can be left to dry, or pinned up, but many art therapists prefer an art studio to look like an art studio.

Conversely, some art works may feel too personal to be left on display, and so private storage must be on offer. Nevertheless, art therapy participants will sometimes wish to display their work, and having this option can feel liberating for both individuals and groups. The 'white walls' approach feels barren and constraining; however, it may be the only option if the art therapy room is used by other professionals for multiple uses. It is a worry that some art therapists may conflate sterility with professionalism.

Interruptions to sessions can usually be dealt with by liaising with other professionals, so that they understand that the space must feel contained and safe, and that interruptions impinge on the participants' feelings of safety and privacy and disrupt the therapeutic process. Informing and educating other professionals about how art therapy works is an essential part of an art therapist's role. Secondly, a 'session in progress, do not disturb sign' is often remarkably effective. Institutional dynamics can be played out in relation to rooms, especially where there are space shortages or there is hostile competition between professionals; this is when interruptions can feel quite persecutory.

Figure 2.1 The London Art Therapy Centre (© The London Art Therapy Centre/ Peter Lurie, lightworkerarts.com)

Confidential locked storage for art therapy work

Lockable storage for art works is an essential requirement for confidential art therapy work. Ideally, this is a spacious walk-in cupboard to which only the art therapist has usual access. It is, preferably, sufficiently large that work need not be folded to be stored. A plan-chest may be included, or participants may be issued with portfolios in which to keep their work safe. Shelving, or a cupboard with shelves, is necessary for the storage of sculptural works.

Art works embodied with strong emotions can become highly significant for the maker of the image. Joy Schaverien's work highlights how the storage and disposal of art works can be of great symbolic significance within the art therapy process. Schaverien (1987: 96) writes:

> Frequently the therapist is active in keeping the work. One of the first things I do with new clients is to provide a folder, on which they write their names. This sets up an expectation that their work will be kept together, safe and private, in the art room. It is common practice for art therapists *to assert the value of pictures* in this way...
>
> (my emphasis)

Another example Schaverien gives is the therapist who keeps 'a child's work on the blackboard during breaks, and the importance to that child of finding it still there on returning. In this way, even in absence a *part of them remains* ensuring that they are not forgotten' (my emphasis). This is no less important with adults. People readmitted to psychiatric hospital are reassured to find that the art therapist still has the folder containing their art, even when the previous admission was many years ago. In this way, she asserts 'the art therapist *actively places a value on the work, the person and the relationship*' (Schaverien 1987: 96; my emphasis).

There are different 'styles' of art therapy room. Some art therapists allow participants to decide if they want to take their work with them, put it away in a storage area, hide it (knowing it will be left) or simply leave it where they had been working, knowing that it will be safe until their return.

Figure 2.2 Art therapy rooms need not be sterile white boxes (© Susan Hogan 2013)

Practical aspects

A room that opens out onto an outdoor space is useful so that work that needs to be sprayed with fixative can be sprayed outside, or next to an open door if the outside space feels too overlooked to take the work outside. This is because there may be group members who have respiratory difficulties and fixative spray can precipitate an attack or discomfort (or it can just be irritating).

A sink is a pre-requisite for a permanent art therapy facility, but for workshops a line of buckets for swilling out and lots of large plastic bottles full of water will suffice.

It is obvious that a certain amount of natural light is also useful in an art therapy room. Having to use overhead fluorescent lighting can become very oppressive.

A washable floor surface is highly recommended, as carpets can be very inhibiting. Ideally, a room would contain a range of working environments: an area where participants can work on the floor; an area with tables; and another area with some artists' easels and donkeys. (Donkeys are a type of seat, which is straddled so that one sits facing an easel.)

Rubin (1984) makes the point that it is less the layout of the room that is crucial, so much as how the space is used, though she does warn about a space that is too cluttered, which can be distracting. Even an ideal space can be badly used. Rubin tells this cautionary story:

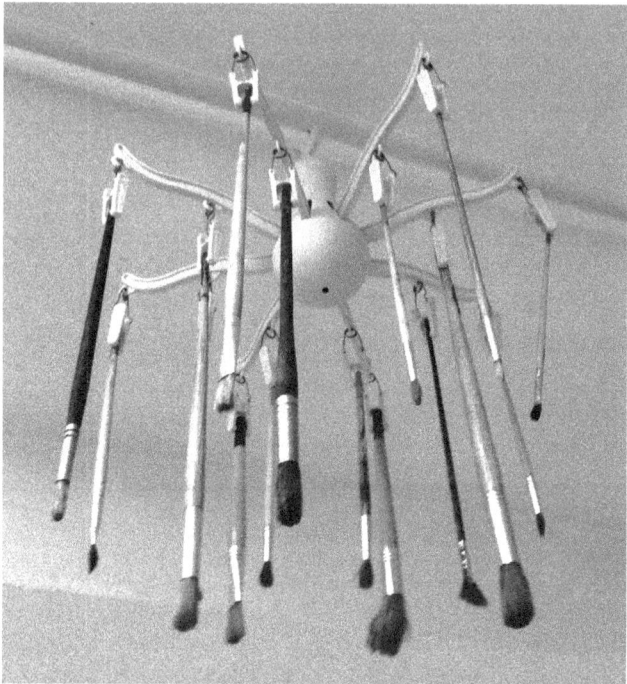

Figure 2.3 Paintbrush mobile, The London Art Therapy Centre (© The London Art Therapy Centre/Peter Lurie, lightworkerarts.com)

... the art therapist, highly skilled in relating to her elderly psychiatric patients, had pushed four small tables together – creating a nice, large working surface about eight feet square, where each group member could easily see and relate to the others. However, she selected the largest size of paper to give each of the eight patients around the table, despite the fact that there simply wasn't enough space available for everyone to use such a big sheet (19" x 24"). For these disturbed older people, this represented a serious problem, solved by a few who folded the paper, but for the others, frustrating their efforts to paint throughout the session.

Although this dilemma sounds minor, the art therapist was so involved with her presentation to the group, which was meant to motivate them to paint, that she was quite unaware of the frustration she had unwittingly stimulated.

(Rubin 1984: 81)

How the space is set up depends on the task in hand as much as the innate physical characteristics of the room: 'If one wants to observe subgroups and alliances within a family, it is helpful to have things set up to allow movement in space, so that customary interaction patterns can be easily manifest in a natural way' (Rubin 1984: 82). In the interactive model, which will be described in further detail, enabling movement in the space is of crucial importance. However, other models may be used. Here is an example:

> … each patient worked at a small easel on his individual painting, the physical setup facilitating individual involvement in the work with minimal interaction. When finished, the patients bought their paintings to another section of the large room, tacked them up on the bulletin board wall, and sat in a semicircle of comfortable chairs, where discussion took place when they were all assembled. This setup made it possible to view all of the products at once, as well as to focus on individual pictures in the course of the discussion led by the therapist.
>
> (Rubin 1984: 83)

If using a studio approach, participants could work at easels, or on donkeys, with minimal interaction with each other, and with the art therapist visiting each in turn in their working space. Group dynamics do not form part of the analysis in this studio model of working.

If art work in progress is to be left out, then liaison with cleaning staff and janitors is essential to prevent work being moved when the room is being cleaned; if the room is always cleaned on a specific day, it may be advisable to ensure that no work is left out on this day, to minimise the possibility of accidental damage.

Having a wide range of art materials on display and easily accessible is very exciting for participants; having to hunt around in little cupboards and drawers to find things is, again, potentially inhibiting, and can interrupt the flow of the activity.

Art materials

Sometimes, using simple cheap materials, perhaps materials familiar from childhood such as crayons or plasticine, can be liberating. Rubin (1984: 7–8) suggests that it is the time-boundedness of the art therapy session that leads many art therapists to be drawn to offering relatively simple materials:

> There is much to be said for media which permit the creation of satisfying products within the space of an art therapy session.

It is recommended to offer a range of materials from the most basic to the best artists' quality (excepting cheap coloured pencils, which tend to be frustrating to work with). Basic materials include water-based paints in blocks or tubes; palates of different types (some with wells for containment of fluid paints or glue, and others flat for mixing colours); a good variety of brushes, from refined thin sable to large wall painters' brushes (brushes are available in a variety of shapes, which make different marks, so a range from square-ended to long bristled is ideal); water pots; and a mixing medium such as PVA.

Other materials consist of pencils (again, cheap pencils are worth avoiding); crayons (from children's type to artists' fine quality); chalks; oil pastels; chunky graphite sticks; and charcoal. Pens, from fine-line to felt-tips and plump markers, can be included, and so too erasers, including putty rubbers.

A range of paper should be provided in different colours and qualities. Sugar paper, foil, fluorescent, tissue and textured papers may be included. The basic staples are cartridge paper in a variety of sizes, and large rolls of paper, so that there is scope to do something big. Masking tape, or a double-sided fixative tape of some kind, is a necessity (for joining sheets together). Many pairs of scissors are needed, as it is frustrating if there are not enough for group exercises. Stanley knives or pencil sharpeners, depending on who is being worked with, may be needed. Handing a person a knife is a strong symbolic gesture showing trust, which perhaps marks me out as an older practitioner, as many organisations now may have policies preventing the use of open blades or even scissors, requiring paper to instead be torn (the latter in some secure settings). Stanley knives are not appropriate with potentially volatile clients or with children. A simple printmaking kit of some sort, with boards which can be etched into, enabling relief work, may also be made available.

A good range of sculptural materials should be on offer, including air-drying clay of some sort. It is recommended that a junk box be established, and it is possible to ask group members to bring in miscellaneous items they don't want such as old Christmas decorations (but nothing of sentimental value). Staple guns (which need instruction to use, and must be clearly demonstrated), wire, wire-mesh and glue of various sorts are also needed. String and yarn are also useful.

Giving a range of materials is important, as, if only cheap materials are on offer, clients may feel devalued (Schaverien 1992). An assortment of art materials also gives increased scope to participants to find materials they want to work with. As Rubin (1984: 11) points out, 'a thick long-handled brush can seem powerful to one person and unwieldy to another', and whilst reactions to materials are to a certain extent to do with what the maker brings to them, art materials *do* have different capacities to yield different results, and some materials are much easier to contain and control than others. Discovering the aesthetic sensibility of the substances is part of the art therapy process. Certainly, art therapy facilitators need to have a sophisticated understanding of what the materials can do (Moon 2010).

Sharing space

In a shared room, even if it is only used by other art therapy or art-based groups, consideration will always need to be given to other room-users. If conducting an introductory workshop series that will include making large sculptural works, issues of storage, display and disposal come immediately to the fore, and can precipitate a useful discussion.

It should go without saying that mess should be cleared up after sessions, sinks should be left clean rather than with paint residue in them and surfaces wiped down, otherwise relations between room-users will quickly deteriorate.

Leaving art works out or displayed on walls can provoke reactions from other room-users. Sometimes, groups compete with each other to hang the largest group painting, or to hog the best exhibition areas; a sculptural work left in the room may precipitate an even larger one from another group. If these group dynamics can be acknowledged and discussed, then this shouldn't prevent some exhibition of work from occurring in a shared room (psychodynamic work is about acknowledgement, rather than misguided ideas about 'neutrality').

Art therapists may also exhibit non-clinical drawings or paintings to act as an inspiration. Other facilitators prefer to work with white walls and to have all art works always put away at the end of sessions; for rooms with multiple uses, this may be the only viable option.

The space as a form of contract

Art therapy is contained within clear boundaries. It takes place at a consistent time in the same place, and each session is of the same duration. Some group work may adopt a constant 'shape' with a certain amount of time allotted to thinking about the previous session, a specified time for art making and a further allocated slot for analysis of the images. Some therapists sit in the same place in the opening circle each week (assuming that a circle is part of the ritualistic opening of the group work), which enables participants to position themselves in relation to the facilitator or other participants. There could be a lot said here about this, but to give one example to start, a particular person may decide to work in front of the facilitator, facing towards her in a performative way. The facilitator's view is necessarily dominated by the actions of one individual. Why is this? Is this person a group monopoliser (Yalom 1995) who needs to be seen? Does this person want to communicate something *in particular* to the facilitator? Or is this person sticking close to the facilitator for comfort? So many interesting questions may be raised by the physical position in the group of an individual (but more on this later).

For clients who have experienced a great deal of instability and inconsistency in relationships, this regular, predictable space is important. The art therapy room offers, as far as possible, the same range of materials each week. It is a secure space into which other professionals will not wander – they do not disturb sessions in progress. These important boundaries combine to create a safe space. An experienced art therapist will make therapeutic use of disasters, nevertheless. For example, a very large printing press was deposited – 'dumped' is perhaps a more apt word – in the art room I was working in, as part of a 'turf' competition between factions within the institution (a more powerful bit of the institution wanted the room in question). The press was a massive and immovable object, and it had been left in the area in which we'd usually put our chairs for group discussion. The group members were upset by the intrusion; some were outraged by what they felt as a defilement of their space. This led to group themes of violation of space, and abuse, emerging in response to the incident. What the press represented for different participants was explored, with difficult emotional material being shared in the group; the incident, though disconcerting, precipitated a deepening of the group work. Once a group is established, it can withstand shocks, though the therapist endeavours to protect groups from intrusions of any sort.

This space set apart from normal life offers an opportunity for self-reflection and self-observation. The art object itself provides further containment, holding aspects of the maker's inner life, as will be explored in further detail.

The history and development of art therapy

Art therapy is a discipline which has emerged out of several tributaries. The eighteenth-century asylum reform movement arose out of a convergence between non-conformist religion and utilitarian philosophy. Utilitarian philosophy worked with ideas of causes and effects, and treatments developed which employed the idea of 'management' of the insane; 'moral treatment' assumed that even the insane possessed a common core of reason towards which treatment could be directed. The discipline required for artistic endeavour was stressed. Instilling self-control in the patient was a key characteristic of 'moral therapy' and the arts were seen as appealing to the more refined sensibilities of patients. A number of eighteenth-century physicians were happy to proclaim the therapeutic benefits of the arts (Hogan 2001).

A rather different set of discourses developed in the nineteenth century about heredity; these were reflected in early psychological and anthropological writings. Theories of degeneration alongside assumptions about the hierarchy of the races (and sexes) evident in theories of biological determinism were reflected in ideas about the cultural significance of symbols. Writers such as Lombroso (sometimes called the founder of criminology) equated symbolism in art and language with primitive mentality (as primitive or atavistic expression); other theorists saw artistic symbolism as a form of degeneration, and thus were sown some of the seeds which were to emerge later into a psychoanalytic theory of symbolism. The latter has sometimes been proclaimed as the 'roots' of art therapy, but this assertion is overly simplistic and fundamentally incorrect.

Both (competing and contradictory) sets of discourses are evident towards the end of the nineteenth century. Florence Nightingale noted in 1860 the effects of form, colour and light upon a recuperating person. She believed that both mind and body were influenced (her work was a direct inspiration for art therapy pioneer Adrian Hill's later work with tuberculosis patients during World War II).

Ideas about psychology permeated various modern artistic movements. Symbolism (c.1885–1900) laid great emphasis on the importance of imagination and fantasy, with an emphasis in art on feelings and sensations, and with an aim to evoke subjective states of mind in visual forms (Chipp 1968: 49). Hauser (1951) argues that symbolism was an irrational and spiritualistic approach that arose out of romanticism, signalling 'a sharp reaction against naturalistic and materialistic impressionism'; this was largely in response to the conventionality of the metaphoric language employed by impressionists and in realist painting in general (1951: 183).

Expressionism was to emerge as an artistic practice interested in the 'embodiment of spirit', and moved away from concrete representation towards abstractionism (Chipp 1968: 126). It was an artistic form oriented towards states of mind and subjective outlooks. Though varied, many works employed bold line and use of colour, exploring grotesque, emotional and dramatic themes, sometimes employing crude, rapid brushwork, pictorial distortions and bold jarring colours held in nervous unstable compositions, or simply explored nature with a vivid intensity particularly associated with the work of Vincent van Gogh. The artist Emil Nolde wrote in 1909:

> I rubbed and scratched the paper until I tore holes in it, trying to reach something else, something more profound, to grasp the very essence of things.
>
> (cited in Chipp 1968: 146)

Expressionism as an artistic genre was actively suppressed by the Nazis in Germany and beyond in the 1930s and 1940s as degenerate (Hogan 2001). However, in its broader sense, expressionism became the predominant form of new artistic movements of the twentieth century: its emphasis on a highly subjective, spontaneous form of self-expression is typical of a range of modern art movements.

Many artists were also to become interested in notions of the degenerate, atavistic or primitive, and went on to explore these ideas in their work. The Surrealists were to have a great impact on the development of modern art therapy in Britain, with their preoccupation on 'though freed from logic and reason' (Breton 1924, cited in Hogan 2001: 94). Surrealists such as Roland Penrose were directly involved with the early British Association of Art Therapists (Hogan 2001).

Another strand of thought that was of particular importance to the development of modern art therapy was that of analytic psychology, and a quasi-religious philosophy arose in the work of Carl Jung, which saw symbols as important aspects of the unconscious mind. This unconscious could be self-regulating, and 'messages' from the unconscious could be manifest in art and be assimilated without interpretation. There are different schools of Jungian thought based on different phases and readings of his work; however, all of them have some spiritual accent. These ideas led to a primarily 'non-directive' method being developed in therapeutic communities such as Withymead, at which a number of the founders of the British Association of Art Therapists worked (Hogan 2001: 220–89).

Radical education was another important influence on the development of modern art therapy (Waller 1991; Hogan 2001). Sometimes the arts played a central part in experimental forms of education. Attitudes varied from those who were more interested in the arts to develop self-control and concentration in their charges, to others who were more interested in 'free expression' with a more anarchist, libertarian or idealist orientation.

Art therapy today: where art therapists work

Art therapy is used in a wide variety of contexts today, from the rehabilitation of child soldiers (Kalmanowitz and Lloyde 2005); war veterans (Coulter 2008); or in former war zones and other areas of deprivation (Levine and Levine 2011); to work in hospices with people about to die (Pratt and Wood 1998; Waller and Sibbett 2005). Some art therapists work in the area of medical rehabilitation (Weston 2008); with people who are recovering from major surgery (Malchiodi 1997, 1999; Waller and Sibbett 2005; Brosh and Ogden 2008); with women who have been traumatised by their birth experience; with new mothers who are having adjustment problems; or with women have been diagnosed as suffering from post-natal depression (Hogan 1997, 2003, 2007, 2008, 2011). Art therapists also work in prisons and in the probation services (Laing and Carrell 1982; Laing 1984; Liebmann 1994; Tamminen 1998; Hastilow and Coyle 2008; Godfrey 2008; Rothwell 2008; Pittam 2008). This is sometimes referred to as 'forensic' art therapy. They work in specialist drug or alcohol rehabilitation settings (Luzzatto 1989; Waller and Mahoney 1998) or can specialise in certain disorders such as anorexia nervosa (Rehavia-Hanauer 2003, 2012). Art therapists also work in the areas of couple counselling and family therapy (Kerr *et al.* 2007).

Some art therapists work in statutory services, such as education (Welsby 1998); with children with special educational needs (Stack 1998; Evans and Dubowski 2001); or the Child and Adolescent Mental Health Services (called CAMHS in Britain). This can be quite varied and might entail working with children who are self-harming; have a wide range of behavioural problems; are suffering from family breakdown, or bereavement; or who have mental health problems and may be suicidal (Ambridge 2008). Other art therapists work in the broader arts and health arenas and attempt to use art to give voice to different 'communities' (Bird 2010; Hogan 2011), or to use art therapy as a research technique. The majority of art therapists still specialise in mental health work with adults.

Terminology

All disciplines develop a particular vocabulary, and a brief glossary of key terms is included at the end of this volume; however, the book is written in such a way that difficult terms are generally defined and explained as encountered, especially in the early chapters. I am making one distinction which is quite tricky, and that is between *'analytic'* art therapy, which is an approach drawn from psychoanalysis which privileges the relationship between the client and the therapist as the main focus, or most important aspect of the work (in a 'transference relationship', which will be explained), strictly speaking this is psychoanalytical and group-interactive approaches which nevertheless are *'analytical'* in the sense that group processes are analysed, and patterns of behaviour and inconsistencies identified as part of the therapeutic process.

Bibliography

Ambridge, M. 2008. The Anger of Abused Children, in M. Liebmann (ed.) *Art Therapy and Anger*. London: Jessica Kingsley Publishers, pp. 27–41.

Bennett, A. 1932. *The Journals of Arnold Bennett* (entry for March 18, 1897). London: Penguin.

Bird, J. 2010. Gender, Knowledge and Art: Feminist Standpoint Theory Synthesised with Arts-Based Research in the Study of Domestic Violence. Unpublished paper supplied by author (available at http://www.academia.edu/812535/Gender_Knowledge_and_Art_Feminist_Standpoint_Theory_synthesised_with_Arts-Based_research_in_the_study_of_domestic_violence).

Brosh, H. and Ogden, R. 2008. Not Being Calm: Art Therapy and Cancer, in M. Liebmann (ed.) *Art Therapy and Anger*. London and Philadelphia: Jessica Kingsley Publishers, pp. 226–37.

Chipp, H.B. 1968. *Theories of Modern Art: a Source Book by Artists and Critics*. Berkeley: University of California Press.

Coulter, A. 2008. 'Came Back – Didn't Come Home': Returning from a War Zone, in M. Liebmann (ed.) *Art Therapy and Anger*. London: Jessica Kingsley Publishers, pp. 238–56.

Evans, K. and Dubowski, J. 2001. *Beyond Words: Art Therapy with Children on the Autistic Spectrum*. London: Jessica Kingsley Publishers.

Godfrey, H. 2008. Androcles and the Lion: Prolific Offenders on Probation, in M. Liebmann (ed.) *Art Therapy and Anger*. London and Philadelphia: Jessica Kingsley Publishers, pp. 102–16.

Hastilow, S. and Coyle, T. 2008. Avoided Anger: Art and Music Therapy in a Medium Secure Setting, in M. Liebmann (ed.) *Art Therapy and Anger*. London and Philadelphia: Jessica Kingsley Publishers, pp. 134–50.

Hauser, A. 1951. *The Social History of Art Volume IV*. London: Routledge.

Hill, A. 1945. *Art Versus Illness*. London: George Allen and Unwin Ltd.

Hogan, S. 1997. A Tasty Drop of Dragon's Blood: Self-identity, Sexuality and Motherhood, in S. Hogan (ed.) *Feminist Approaches to Art Therapy*. London: Routledge, pp. 237–70.

Hogan, S. 2001. *Healing Arts: The History of Art Therapy*. London: Jessica Kingsley Publishers.

Hogan, S. (ed.) 2003. *Gender Issues in Art Therapy*. London: Jessica Kingsley Publishers.

Hogan, S. 2007. Rage and Motherhood Interrogated and Expressed Through Art Therapy. *Journal of the Australian and New Zealand Arts Therapy Association* 2(1): 58–66.

Hogan, S. 2008. Angry Mothers, in M. Liebmann (ed.) *Art Therapy and Anger*. London and Philadelphia: Jessica Kingsley Publishers, pp. 197–210.

Hogan, S. 2011. Postmodernist but Not Postfeminist! A Feminist Postmodernist Approach to Working with New Mothers, in H. Burt (ed.) *Art Therapy and Postmodernism: Creative Healing Through a Prism*. London: Jessica Kingsley Publishers, pp. 70–82.

Hogan, S. and Pink, S. 2010. Routes to Interiorities: Art Therapy, Anthropology and Knowing in Anthropology. *Visual Anthropology* 23(2), 1–16.

Kalmanowitz, D. and Lloyd, B. 2005. *Art Therapy and Political Violence: With Art, Without Illusion*. London: Routledge.

Kerr, C., Hoshino, J., Sutherland, J., Thode Parashak, S. and McCarley, L.L. 2007. *Family Art Therapy: Foundations of Theory and Practice*. London: Routledge.

Laing, J. 1984. Art Therapy in Prisons, in T. Dalley (ed.) *Art as Therapy*. London: Tavistock, pp. 115–28.

Laing, J. and Carrell, C. 1982. *The Special Unit, Barlinnie Prison: its Evolution through its Art*. Glasgow: Third Eye Centre.

Levine, E.G. and Levine, S.K. 2011. *Art in Action: Expressive Arts Therapy and Social Change*. London: Jessica Kingsley Publishers.

Liebmann, M. (ed.) 1994. *Art Therapy with Offenders*. London: Jessica Kingsley Publishers.

Luzzatto, P. 1989. Drinking Problems and Short-term Art Therapy: Working with Images of Withdrawal and Clinging, in A. Gilroy and T. Dalley (eds) *Pictures at an Exhibition*. London: Tavistock/Routledge, pp. 207–19.

Malchiodi, C. 1997. Invasive Art: Art as Empowerment for Women with Breast Cancer, in Hogan S. (ed.) *Feminist Approaches to Art Therapy*. London: Routledge, pp. 49–64.

Malchiodi, C. 1999. *Medical Art Therapy with Adults*. London: Jessica Kingsley Publishers.

Moon, C.H. 2010. *Materials and Media in Art Therapy: Critical Understandings of Diverse Artistic Vocabularies*. London: Routledge.

Nightingale, F. 1860. *Notes on Nursing: What It Is, and What It Is Not*. London: Harrison and Sons.

Pittam, S. 2008. Inside-Out/Outside-In: Art Therapy with Young Male Offenders in Prison, in M. Liebmann (ed.) *Art Therapy and Anger*. London: Jessica Kingsley Publishers, pp. 87–101.

Pratt, M. and Wood, J.M. 1998. *Art Therapy in Palliative Care: The Creative Response*. London: Routledge.

Rehavia-Hanauer, D. 2003. Identifying Conflicts of Anorexia Nervosa as Manifested in the Art Therapy Process. *The Arts in Psychotherapy* 30, 137–49.

Rehavia-Hanauer, D. 2012. Habitus and Social Control: Feminist Art Therapy and the Critical Analysis of Visual Representations, in S. Hogan (ed.) *Revisiting Feminist Approaches to Art Therapy*. London: Berg-Hahn, pp. 91–9.

Rothwell, K. 2008. What Anger? Working with Acting-out Behaviour in a Secure Setting, in M. Liebmann (ed.) *Art Therapy and Anger*. London: Jessica Kingsley Publishers, pp. 117–33.

Rubin, J.A. 1984. *The Art of Art Therapy*. New York: Brunner/Mazel.

Schaverien, J. 1987. The Scapegoat and the Talisman: Transference in Art Therapy, in T. Dalley, C. Case, J. Schaverien, F. Weir, D. Halliday, P.N. Hall and D. Waller (eds) *Images of Art Therapy: New Developments in Theory and Practice*. London: Tavistock, pp. 74–108.

Schaverien, J. 1989. The Picture Within the Frame, in A. Gilroy and T. Dalley (eds) *Pictures at an Exhibition*. London: Routledge, pp. 147–55.

Schaverien, J. 1992. *The Revealing Image: Analytical Art Psychotherapy in Theory and Practice*. London: Routledge.

Stack, M. 1998. Humpty Dumpty's Shell: Working with Autistic Defence Mechanisms, in M. Rees (ed.) *Drawing on Difference: Art Therapy with People who have Learning Difficulties*. London: Routledge, pp. 97–116.

Tamminen, K. 1998. Exploring the Landscape Within: Art Therapy in a Forensic Unit, in D. Sandle (ed.) *Development and Diversity: New Applications in Art Therapy*. London: Free Association Books, pp. 92–103.

Waller, D. 1991. *Becoming a Profession: The History of Art Therapy in Britain 1940–1982*. London: Routledge.

Waller, D. and Mahoney, J. (eds) 1998. *Treatment of Addiction: Current Issues for Art Therapists*. London: Routledge.

Waller, D. and Sibbett, C. (eds) 2005. *Art Therapy and Cancer Care*. London: Open University Press.

Welsby, C. 1998. A Part of the Whole: Art Therapy in a Comprehensive School. *Inscape* 3(1), 37–40.

Weston, S. 2008. Art Therapy and Anger after Brain Injury, in M. Liebmann (ed.) *Art Therapy and Anger*. London and Philadelphia: Jessica Kingsley Publishers, pp. 211–25.

Yalom, I.D. 1995. *The Theory and Practice of Group Psychotherapy*. New York: Basic Books.

Websites

American Arts Therapy Association: http://www.americanarttherapyassociation.org
Australian and New Zealand Arts Therapy Association: http://www.anzata.org/
British Association of Art Therapists: http://www.baat.org/

Chapter 3

Reflections on experiential learning

Susan Hogan

Experiential learning

This chapter will elaborate on the idea of experiential learning and will then proceed to explore the content of an introductory art therapy course, which is taught experientially. Experiential learning is something that many artists who have explored their thoughts and feelings through experimentation with art media take for granted as straightforward, even self-evident. But it's easy to forget that this is quite an alien way of being for many of our clients and students and sometimes we are bewildered as to why they 'don't get it'. This chapter will explore some of the problems involved in attempting to do experiential teaching.

The Macquarie Dictionary describes 'experiential' as 'pertaining to or derived from experience'. This is straightforward, we might think: learning by doing.

The word 'experience' is defined as 'a particular instance of personally encountering or undergoing something' or 'the process or fact of personally observing, encountering, or undergoing something'. I'd like to latch on here to the importance of seeing it as a 'personal' and 'particular' encounter. In teaching art therapy, it is important for students to realise the uniqueness of their own perception and the advantages and disadvantages of this. Our personal awareness distorts our perception of the here and now (the jargon for this is 'parataxic distortion'). Students can be asked to begin to think about this. Perhaps it is not something they are used to doing?

Of course every act of understanding, and every formulated question, has an interpretive element. Why do I ask my client about the red mark rather than the black streak? Perhaps one feels more insistent to me, and I have indulged in an act of interpretation in getting to that point of formulating the question.

When I started doing experiential workshops over twenty years ago, I thought that this simple understanding of what experiential learning is would be enough. 'Imagine you are a house and paint what you'd look like', I'd instruct, for example. However, not everyone could make the leap of imagination: 'Yes, I've painted a house, but what's it got to do with me though?' someone would retort. 'No, I don't know why the front door is open, but I found it relaxing to do...' There was a disjunction, a gap between their self-expression and their self-understanding.

Experience is not enough: there must also be a process of active critical reflection and self-analysis. Indeed, this is the absolute key.

Stimulating a process of critical self-perception and laying the foundations of reflective practice is not so straightforward. Perhaps this is because we have all been brought up with the concept of objectivity, which needs de-bunking. As Thomas Kuhn made clear in his tremendously influential book, *The Structure of Scientific Revolutions* (1962), there is no such thing as 'value-free observation'. Nevertheless, it's an entrenched idea: that we see what is going on and can report on it in an objective fashion. I'll elaborate on this further.

So already we have realised that the definition of 'experiential' doesn't give us enough, in terms of definition, to adequately describe what we hope will happen in an experiential art therapy workshop.

What is a student learning in the workshop? Well, at the outset:

- They are learning to be in a group that has particular boundaries and rules.
- They are participating in establishing these boundaries and rules.
- They are learning to express themselves in this environment (sitting in a circle and talking about oneself isn't something everyone is used to).
- Initially, they are forced to make statements about themselves, which means making a decision for some people; for others it may be more reflexive: 'My name is Susan Hogan and I'm blah blah blah...' Perhaps I've trotted the same thing off before. However, making a definite statement about oneself is difficult for some people, let's not forget that.
- They will have to tolerate being the focus of the group's attention.
- Initially, there may be anxiety to overcome about manipulating materials and anxiety about one's performance.

So we see that even at the outset of the group, before we've actually got started, in our terms, we are into quite complex emotional terrain. I am sometimes frustrated that groups can be so frightened and defensive. However, there are potentially profound existential aspects of personality engaged and already at stake:

- How do I feel about rules? Can I cope with the rules? Do I want to challenge or flout the rules?
- Can I assert myself? Will I be heard? Why wasn't I heard? Some people complain at the outset that they'd rather be sitting at a table and feel uncomfortable having their entire body visible to a group of people.
- Who am I? How do I wish to be seen? Is there something happening for me which will influence how I present myself in the group?
- Why do I hate being the centre of attention? Why do I have to be the centre of attention? Why am I complaisant about articulating something about myself?
- I can't paint. I must paint well.

As art therapists we are aware of these aspects of group work. There are reams and reams of articles on group dynamics and the initial fear that participants can experience when they join a new group, so this chapter won't dwell on this here further except to say that it doesn't hurt to remind oneself of this. I have often rushed this bit of group work because I was keen to 'get on with it'! I have learnt that it is useful to give participants time to settle in to the situation and to modify my expectation about how much to fit in to the session, if necessary.

Reflective practice

When students are asked to perform an art therapy task, such as the aforementioned draw yourself as a house task, they learn from other group members. Participants do realise, by listening to other people describe their house, the rich metaphorical potential of the exercise. Cellars, attics, turrets are described and explored. The terrain on which the house stands may be relevant, or perhaps there is a relationship between the house and other houses, trees, cars, etc., that enables significant relationships to be explored. Seeing how an exercise can be tackled and viewing the immensely rich and diverse pictorial material produced by different people is educational for group members who have had difficulty in grasping it. Conceivably they even become self-conscious and embellish future drawings with ostentatious symbolism – there might be competitiveness between certain group members about dramatic use of metaphors.

So, even people who find expressing themselves using pictorial symbols, analogies and metaphors difficult get the idea from listening to others and seeing what they have done. However, I want students to start to think about the totality of the experience, not just their image and what it means for them although, admittedly, this is an important aspect of the workshops.

The workshop series I run is aimed at presenting a variety of group formats to students. I want students to start to think about the shape of the sessions. I want them to think about the structure of the workshops, to compare and contrast different formats, and then to think about how different formats influenced the dynamics of the group and to start to reflect upon this.

This essay completed after the experiential component of the course I'm currently running asks students to compare and contrast two different modes of art therapy, so students are obliged to think about structure. My experience is that without the reflective diary, which I'm about to discuss, students often don't reflect deeply on the workshops and, indeed, cannot even clearly remember what they did by the time it comes to submitting the essay.

How to push them on to a deeper level of analysis? I want students to start to think about the overall dynamics of the group without losing sight of their personal material and to develop a deeper analysis of that too. Latterly, I have been asking students to keep a reflective diary. But how are they to know what to record? I give them an aid, which breaks down the group experience into different segments, asking for reflection on each segment, which some students find immensely useful and others may find overly simplistic.

At an introductory level, part of the problem for the facilitator is that they are dealing with people with markedly different levels of self-awareness and analytic skills. Some people naturally notice the body language of others, for example, or group dynamics, or the particular symbolism employed by an individual, and can recall precisely what that person did three weeks ago. We bring an impressive range of different skills into the group. Part of the reason I like group work so much is because it combines all our skills in the group's facilitation.

Using the 'how to analyse a group' handout out as a starting point, students begin to think about all the aspects of group work, they notice how different group members are sitting, responding, talking and participating, and they then reflect on and begin to share their feelings about this. They are noticing how different structural considerations affect the group. Participants have the experience of making images as a group, in pairs, in small groups and individually. They perform a variety of exercises, including a guided fantasy. They receive a description of each workshop in advance that outlines the aim of each session to help them understand it.

Participants practise analysing their own imagery while other group members sit quietly and respectfully hear what they have to say. Then group members can respond to the image in two different ways: they can share what the image stimulated in them personally or, with sensitivity, they can practise being in the facilitator role and ask questions about the image. Perhaps they can highlight an aspect of the image (or sculpture) which was not commented on. For example, they can practise asking open-ended questions such as, 'If you feel comfortable doing so, could you say more about the red area at the bottom of the picture?', or more informally, 'If you feel okay about it, would you like to tell us more about...?'

In the 'client' role, students may be preoccupied with their own emotional material, the meaning of their art work and perhaps unable to focus on other people's work. In the 'client' role, they may respond to other people's art work very much from a personal point of view: 'I feel very bleak when I look at that washed-up looking debris'. This is perfectly acceptable, as trainee therapists must become aware of their emotional reactions and practise continually monitoring and containing them (and using them constructively to help facilitation). We learn to simultaneously acknowledge our emotional responses whilst not allowing them to engulf our attention, which remains focused on our clients. At an introductory level, students develop empathy with their future clients by allowing themselves to feel emotionally vulnerable in the group.

In terms of group work, the emotional reaction I've given above could lead to a number of scenarios. Perhaps it acts as a facilitative remark to the person who made the image, who might respond by saying, 'Yes, it feels really bleak', and then elaborate on why. Or conversely, they might explain that it's not bleak, or simply refute the remark: 'That's not how I feel about it'. The group's attention might turn to the person who made the remark or someone in the group might interject and say how they feel about it. Using the 'Group Interactive Model', described by Diane Waller, analysing these interactions becomes the central focus of group work. Trainee art therapists learn to work in this way. However, at this introductory level, I am merely hoping that students will start to notice significant interactions, be able to record them or even comment on them in the group.

Students may find themselves primarily in the role of the facilitator in relation to other participants' images or primarily in the role of 'client', or they may move back and forth between these two positions. I don't expect a ten-week, or even a twenty-week, introductory course to reach the innermost depths of the participant's psyche (this can happen at professional training level). However, a certain amount of personal disclosure is necessary in order for participants to become emotionally engaged. Sometimes an individual in a group will be very open about themselves and this can be helpful in encouraging others in the group. I find it is difficult to achieve an intimate atmosphere with a group of more than sixteen participants; twelve is a comfortable number to work with to avoid too much pressure in terms of people having time to talk, if they want to. At advanced training level, the groups are usually recommended to have around eight participants.

Reflecting on the process of making the image

The final thing I hope students will achieve during participation in an introduction to art therapy course is an awareness of how the process of making the art object, not merely analysis of the finished product, is significant. The emotions engendered whilst splashing, tearing, covering, hiding, destroying, scribbling or otherwise struggling to use the materials are highly significant. They can be considered and recorded in the reflective diary.

Here is the description of my struggle with art materials in a group (incidentally, not in an introduction to art therapy group, in which I would tend not to make any personal disclosures unless the group insisted upon it):

> At the group's invitation I did make one art work. I painted a picture of myself breast-feeding. However, I struggled with the piece. I had wanted the quality of the paint to be very watery creating an image like a reflection on a pond. Whilst painting it I became aware of the fact that I wanted to depict my baby both inside and outside of my body simultaneously. I imagined her suckling one breast whilst stroking the other with her little hand. But I was not able to achieve a satisfactory result with the materials and I spent the session working and reworking the image – struggling with the boundaries. The finished art work, unresolved though it was, embodied my experience of merger and separateness. The act of painting brought to awareness and illustrated my feelings of conflict and ambivalence about these processes – my emotional struggle. Indeed, my *inability to resolve the image pictorially* was highly revealing. I had not experienced through conversation the full force of these

conflicting emotions. Participating in the group reminded me of the power and poignancy of the art therapy process which yields the possibility for the articulation of powerful embodied feelings and responses which cannot necessarily be experienced or evoked through a verbal exchange alone.

(Hogan 2003: 168; original emphasis)

Context

Regarding institutional art therapy trainings, free-floating institutional anxiety can 'land' in a workshop series. Likewise, unresolved institutional psychic material can influence a group in ways that are unlikely to be able to be acknowledged at introductory level. The only means I can think of to minimise these risks is for staff teams of institutional art therapy trainings to have psychodynamic group staff meetings to ensure that unresolved psychic material is acknowledged and resolved; otherwise, it will pollute the group work in subtle or obvious ways. Most departments are rife with interpersonal rivalries or worse and these do have an influence. However, many art therapists offering introductory workshop series will be offering these to institutions in which they are not permanently based so these complications need not arise.

In conclusion, I have summarised some of my struggles in trying to introduce the idea of art therapy to groups of students using experiential learning. In my next chapter I'd like to elaborate further on the content of workshop sessions. Even using the same material, groups vary tremendously. Some take off immediately; others remain resentful, defensive, afraid and surly even, depending on the balance of personality types in the group. Don't be put off if your first experience of running training workshops is hard work – it might be much easier the next time.

Bibliography

Hogan, S. (ed.) 2003. *Gender Issues in Art Therapy*. London: Routledge.
Kuhn, T. 1962. *The Structure of Scientific Revolutions*. Chicago: University of Chicago Press.
Waller, D. 1993. *Group Interactive Art Therapy*. London: Routledge.

Chapter 4

An introduction to art therapy

Further reflections on teaching directive art therapy at an introductory level

Susan Hogan

The last chapter reflected on the nature of experiential learning and how this related to running introductory courses on art therapy. The chapter was written mainly for the interest of art therapists who are thinking of offering art therapy workshops and courses, as well as students coming new to the subject. In this chapter I shall talk in further detail about the content of my introductory workshops and what I hope to achieve.

Let me stress that these are not professional training workshops; they are an introduction to the subject, though they may form part of the beginning of a professional training course. The closed training group, which forms an important component of the full professional training in art therapy, is a 'non-directive' psychodynamic group using Diane Waller's Group Interactive Model. These workshops, in contrast, use a 'directive' approach in that they are highly structured and designed, quite explicitly, to give participants a feel for different group compositions. All employ a different structure, which is noted and analysed. In this chapter I shall describe a number of workshops: working in pairs, group painting, group sculpture, guided fantasy, a body image workshop and a theme workshop. I shall also discuss different ways of analysing the work.

I shall also present the basic analytic 'tool' I give to students to help them to reflect on their experience of group work and get full benefit from the experiential group work. The reason why I give the students an analytic tool or aid is because reflecting on the multi-levelled nature of group work is complex. I stress that students can use the tool as a starting point for their own detailed analysis of the group work in their reflective diaries. I hope that it won't be used as a reductive checklist.

Before I move to the subject of how to analyse introductory group work, I shall elaborate further on the content of the workshop series. My aim is to present students with a variety of quite different workshop formats so that they can see the scope of 'directive' art therapy (all the sessions are structured). It's possible that participants may discover one particular way of working they enjoy or they may go on to employ a range of group formats with clients if they go on to study further in the subject and become practitioners.

I explain to the group that the workshop series should be regarded like a toolbox full of tools. You can take out the monkey wrench or screwdriver in a big house or a little house or use it for a repair on a bicycle. The tools themselves, many of them, can be adjusted for use with different jobs. So it is with the workshops – they are 'tools' to be modified as appropriate. If participants decide to engage in full professional training in art therapy, they will experience non-directive interactive art therapy as part of their training – a rather different way of working with which most qualified therapists are familiar, in which interactions between group members, along with analysis of the art work, form the focus of attention. In these introductory workshops analysing group interactions is not the primary focus, but interactive elements of each workshop are noted.

The students

The students are a mixture of people. Some of them have decided to complete full professional training in art therapy and come to complete the introductory module as preparation; others are curious as to what art therapy is and may have no intention of attempting to employ art materials with clients – they are more interested in using art therapy techniques to explore their own creativity.

I do think it's incumbent upon the facilitator to point out that art therapy can stimulate strong emotions and deeply cathartic reactions, and that it is not something that non-qualified people should attempt to do. On the other hand, if attending the introduction to art therapy workshop series enables a schoolteacher, for example, to use more creative and varied exercises with her pupils in her art class, then I'm more than happy for these new skills to be acquired. However, if we think that participants might be considering attempting to offer art therapy to others after only attending an introductory workshop series, we have a duty of care, in my opinion, to attempt to dissuade them. I don't want to dwell on this issue which Annette M. Coulter is going to explore in further detail, but feel that in introductory material, publicity material and at interview, it is important to reiterate that the full professional training for art therapists is a rigorous two-year, full-time Master's degree-level course with substantial supervised clinical placements. The introduction is aimed to give participants an overview or 'taster' of the subject. It will enable professional health workers, for example, to work closely and constructively with art therapists, having gained an understanding of what art therapists do. It will enable potential art therapy trainees to decide whether or not art therapy is really for them. However, it is perfectly possible that an introductory course may attract individuals who have an entirely unrealistic idea about how easy it would be to set up as an art therapist, and this is problematic.

I shall now outline a number of workshops I customarily offer. Generally, I have offered these in university or college settings. The order of these workshops may vary.

Boundaries and introductions

Some form of introduction will take place prior to the first art therapy exercise. This can be quite simple – such as each person saying their name and a sentence or two about why they have come to the group. Normally, I'll start this off. I ask participants to regard personal material which will be shared in the group as confidential. I explicitly ask participants not to discuss the group in their coffee break. Analysis of the processes of the group will be kept *in the group*. Other group boundaries or 'ground rules' might be discussed. Further discussion might arise spontaneously as someone has to leave early for an appointment, or a mobile phone goes off, and then group members express feelings about that.

Working in pairs

This uses the following format, which will be explained in detail:

- Introductions and discussion about group 'ground rules'.
- Explanation of workshop.
- Participants divide into pairs, get *one* sheet of paper and select art materials to work with.
- I ask participants to tell each other something about themselves non-verbally using the art materials.
- After 15–20 minutes I divide each pair up into an A and a B.
- I explain the next section of the workshop (that person A will tell person B what they thought person B was trying to tell them, whilst person B tries not to nod or otherwise indicate agreement or disagreement; because this is hard, as it feels rude to 'blank' someone talking to you, I actually role-play someone giving clues and then someone being 'impassive' to try to reinforce this point).
- I swap them around after five minutes, reiterating the instructions.
- I give couples the opportunity to talk openly about their interpretations to 'check out what they got right and what they got wrong'.
- After 10 minutes or so we form a group circle and talk about the concepts I am about to discuss, and couples share their experience with the larger group.
- There will be a short 'comfort break' before the group painting.

I quite often start by contrasting the experience of working as a couple with a group piece. I explain at the outset that participants will be making an image with a partner and then, later, doing a group painting and will have the opportunity to compare these two contrasting experiences. Students have already received a brief description of the workshop explaining that we'll be doing 'non-verbal communication exercises' and discussing the ideas of 'projection' and 'group dynamics'. I ask students to pair up (if there's an odd number then an individual can sit as an observer to a particular couple). I instruct the couples to select a range of materials they'd like to work with and to choose one sheet of paper to work on, as they will be sharing the same piece. This has to be emphasised, otherwise people assume that they will not be sharing a sheet. The therapist must check that this instruction has been heard and check that each couple is sharing a sheet. Once participants are ready, I ask them to tell their partners something about themselves, what kind of person they are or what interests them, but to do this pictorially. I explain that they should attempt to express themselves solely through the use of the materials and not talk at all. I suggest that all negotiations about how to use the page are conducted non-verbally. I tell them that they have fifteen minutes (if there are several couples who seem to be working slowly and tentatively, then I might well let the exercise continue for twenty minutes). After they have finished, I divide each pair up into an A and a B (normally I let them nominate themselves, as the more assertive and confident often choose A, who will start).

Then I explain what we'll be doing. First, person A will tell person B what they thought person B was trying to tell them. However, person B will receive the information without responding. Indeed, person B will sit impassively without nodding, smiling, gesturing or giving any clues whatsoever as to whether person A's interpretation is correct or incorrect. I explain this will be very difficult because it feels rude not to respond. Even though the As have been told that the Bs will not respond, they still give the As imploring looks to check out how they are doing with their interpretations!

Before person A gets going, I give some pointers about what students might note during their pictorial analysis. They can note:

- the relative size of objects;
- the juxtapositions of objects;
- the manner in which things were done (tentatively, with ferocity, etc.);
- the general use of space and the manner in which the space was controlled during creation;
- how B responded to A's lines;
- their use of analogies, symbols and metaphors;
- their body language in relation to the page (learning over it, or daubing tentatively);
- actual pictorial content;
- mood conjured up by the use of the materials.

After five or six minutes, A and B swap so that B now interprets A's image while A sits impassively.

After the frustrating business of having to listen to each other's interpretations without responding, I do give participants the opportunity to check out where they were right and where wrong, and normally a very animated discussion ensues between partners. Afterwards, I point out that there's no right or wrong response to the exercise. Sometimes, couples achieve a high degree of accuracy in their interpretations through intuition and correct interpretation of body language, coupled with the use of symbols and metaphors, which the other managed to understand. Sometimes quite stylised or impoverished image-making is used by someone who is keen, above all else, to be understood in a literal way. Others find that their interpretations are way off the mark.

The point is that the 'reading' of images is complex and works on a number of levels. Abstract works may reveal a lot about mood. As noted, reductive symbolism may be employed to prioritise the conveyance of facts. Pictures vary tremendously. The participants' skills of interpretation vary. Some participants find it impossible not to nod or to otherwise indicate agreement or disagreement with the interpretation proffered, even though I have asked them not to do so – therefore, they give more clues to their partner to help their interpretation than others in the group. Consequently, I'm not anticipating some sort of standardised result.

After the couples have discussed their images, I invite everyone back into a big circle. The exercise gives me the opportunity to introduce participants to the idea that interpretation of images is problematic – indeed, fraught with difficulty. Hopefully, some woefully incorrect interpretations by couples are shared to the group as a whole and underline the point. Often this is done with humour.

It is important in art therapy that the client is allowed to explore the meaning of their work. The art therapist's role is as a facilitator. Art therapists should be wary of using language that might foreclose meanings. I point out that art therapists use open-ended questions to encourage clients talking about their work. Of course, any comment or question by the therapist is based on an act of interpretation – why draw attention to one thing rather than another? But I don't go into philosophical analysis at this point. Therapists are constantly deciding what is important and this might be more to do with their own preoccupations than with those of the client. Likewise, what we hear is also an act of construal – why do we remember O but not P? Or, perhaps more significantly, why do we think that O is significant and P trivial? Or why does P seem exciting and O mundane? Or do we hear something else entirely, something not actually said? This is analysis for a later date.

The main emphasis of the workshop is to: a) introduce students to the idea of non-verbal communication with art materials; b) get students to think about the component parts of a picture during their analysis; c) encourage the participants to be wary of furnishing interpretations of their clients' work; and d) become aware of the idea of 'projection', a useful term referring to how we project our own meanings onto others.

Generally, I don't like jargon but the notion of projection is a useful one and essential for the would-be therapist. Projection is the attribution of qualities or characteristics to a person, which they do not necessarily possess. It is the result of a distortion of perception – although we all view people through our particular lens to some extent, and so some 'projection' is therefore inevitable and total objectivity impossible. Nevertheless, would-be therapists need to think about whether they are letting their own emotional responses get in the way of their relationship with others (I shall discuss this concept in further detail elsewhere).

So, as you can see, a fairly simple introductory exercise is actually immensely complex. First, participants think about how they can portray something about themselves through the use of art materials. Students think about the notion of interpretation and how to ask open questions. They think about body language and how we convey information to each other through the use of our bodies. Students, perhaps for the first time, realise how strange it is talking to someone who is not giving off normal signals of acknowledgement; they think about how we 'read' each other's gestures. They also think about the component parts of a picture during their analysis: the relative size of objects; the juxtapositions of objects; the manner in which things were done and so forth (see the check-list above). All of the students are bringing with them different amounts of knowledge of all these things. Some may be trained counsellors already, for example, so very familiar with the idea of 'reading' body language; others may be artists well used to expressing themselves through art materials. For others, all these things will be quite new.

Group painting

The second half of the workshop is a group painting. Normally, I give the group a break. Coffee breaks can be used to allow people to relax. I have often found in private practice, and training work, that changing the length of the break can have an important effect. For example, a group that is becoming over-intense can benefit from a slightly longer break. Try changing the length of breaks and observe the effects.

When the group returns from the break, I give the group a large roll of paper and suggest they create a piece about six feet square. They will have to use masking tape to stick two or three widths of paper together, depending on the size of the roll. I let the group do this.

I ask them to get materials they would like to use. Then I instruct them that they have twenty minutes to say something about themselves. After about fifteen minutes, I give the further instruction that they should each try to made pictorial contact with each member of the group – in other words, that their image or images should link up in some way with those of each member of the group. This might already have occurred, but sometimes, especially if the paper is an oblong, rather than a square, individuals can remain quite isolated, having taken hold of an area of the sheet of paper as their own territory. This is especially true when bold dividing lines have been drawn which are difficult to cross, or a person has depicted something that others feel they cannot approach. This is when the work can become very interactive: perhaps a link cannot be made with someone because their work is perceived by an individual as fragile or, conversely, as aggressive. Or perhaps someone else might feel quite upset, or delighted, by someone else's encroachment. This is grist for the mill, if I may be permitted the use of this cliché. Students can get an inkling in their analysis of the power and potential of a group painting experience. I stop the exercise before it gets too challenging and participants get the opportunity to reflect on how working in a group felt different to working in a pair.

If I've been working with a large group and two group pieces have been produced, I suggest that the participants stay gathered around their particular painting for their analysis of it. If one group painting was produced, I suggest that we place it on the floor in the centre of the room and sit around it in a circle so that it's easy to look at while we discuss the group experience. Quite often people want to point at the image while they talk.

Ending the first session

I then introduce students to the idea of keeping an analytic journal. In the course information, this will have been mentioned already. Participants' reflection on their experience is a crucial part of experiential learning. (I discussed this topic in the last chapter.) I suggest they use the handout as a starting point for a more detailed piece of analysis, if they find it useful. I go through it point by point with them (without asking them to answer the questions) and this helps to act as a 'cool down' to the session. Figure 4.1 shows the sort of analytic tool I hand out.

I ask the last question to get students to think about the shape and form of workshops. They are structured quite differently and the different group structures produce different effects, which I want students to start to think about (remember the 'tool kit' analogy). A lot of the questions ask participants to reflect on their own emotional responses, as maintaining critical self-awareness is important for art therapists or would-be carers in general. I also want the group members to develop sensitivity towards, and empathy with, their prospective clients. Hopefully, having experienced something as challenging, threatening or emotionally exposing will help them to be less insensitively gung-ho if they go on to work with clients using art materials.

Finally, I ask everyone to bring in lots of old junk, cardboard boxes, old Christmas decorations, etc., for the following week.

Group sculpture

The second workshop in the series is a group sculpture. The workshop is designed to illustrate how working on a collective project can lead to group cohesiveness and provide scope for analysis of group dynamics. The workshop offers the opportunity for participants to work in three dimensions, which can be challenging in terms of manipulating materials. This exercise, in my experience, is often fun and can enable group members to get to know each other better. It is therefore quite a good one to have fairly early on in a workshop series.

This uses the following format, which will be explained in detail:

- I put out a range of materials that will be helpful for three-dimensional work such as string, cardboard, Stanley knives, wire, staple guns and scissors.
- Materials brought by participants are put together.

Reflecting on experiential workshops

- What initial feelings did the exercise provoke in me?
- Did I talk to others during the exercise?
- At the beginning?
- As a necessity to achieve the task?
- At the end in the group discussion?
- At any other times?
- How did each phase of relating to others feel?
- Did I express myself verbally in the way that I wanted? How did that feel?
- How did I relate to the subject matter of the workshop?
- Did any group themes emerge?
- How did my position in the room and/or my use of space contribute to my experience?
- How did I express myself pictorially?
- Through the use of analogy?
- Metaphor?
- Symbols?
- Expressive use of materials (scratching, tearing, splashing, scraping, sticking, overlaying, subtle or brutal brush strokes, etc.).
- What compositional elements were employed (think about the relative scale of objects and how things are juxtaposed)?
- Did I express myself pictorially in the way that I wanted? How do I feel about that?
- How did I feel about comments made by others about my contribution?
- What was the ending of the workshop like?
- Can you imagine in what ways this workshop might be useful with people who have special needs?
- How was this workshop different from the last workshop?

Figure 4.1 Student handout: reflecting on experiential workshops

- Participants sit in a circle and are invited to say a few words about how they are feeling or whether they had any thoughts or feelings about the previous workshop they'd like to share with the group.
- I explain the workshop.
- I pass round the bag of pieces of paper on which are written different parts of the body.
- I pass round the bag of pieces of paper on which are written different positive emotions.
- I pass round the bag of pieces of paper on which are written different challenging or negative emotions.
- I give a safety warning to participants about the staple guns and stanley knives and indicate how they are used. In particular, I point out that you cannot put your hand behind a staple gun to hold materials in place; otherwise the staple may fire into your hand. Probably, participants are not yet using fixative spray, but just in case I ask that this be used outside the room, as some people are allergic to the spray.
- I ask participants to commence the task.
- After the 'person' has been constructed, I ask participants to sit around her/ him and to say a few words about how they found the experience.
- I close by making sure that everyone has had the opportunity to say what they wanted to say.
- I introduce the topic of 'disposal'.
- Finally, I discuss the next week's workshop.

I tend to approach this is in a quite light-hearted manner. It starts off rather like a party game. I ask participants to sit in a circle and, after explaining more about the workshop, I send round a bag full of bits of paper. Each student must pick a piece of paper, 'without peeking at it first'. It's a lucky dip. I've already explained that on each piece is written a body part: 'heart', 'lungs', etc. There are sometimes strong reactions, groans or shrieks of excitement as the bag goes round (usually at least twice so that everyone has at least two body parts to work on). I put 'sex organs' rather than specifying which sort, so that there is scope for choice. Then I send round two further bags – one full of uplifting and positive emotions: 'love', 'joy' and so forth and another full of negative emotions. I put a lot in the bags, as I want participants to have three or more emotions from each bag. This might seem slightly laborious, but having the positive and negative emotions separate saves some poor person getting 'chagrin', 'sorrow', 'hatred', 'abhorrence' and 'disgust', for example, as their set of emotions…

I then tell the group that they are going to construct a person and ask them to think about how to depict, and where to place, the emotions in the body. It's important to spell out that the particular body parts picked by a person don't have to embody the emotions picked by that person. So if someone has 'feet' and 'happy', they don't have to make happy feet, for example. I always hope that the materials will be used in an interesting way – my heart sinks when the person with 'love' produces a flat, red love heart... What could 'anger' look like? It's an opportunity to experiment.

Primarily, the workshop functions to force group members to interact with each other, as they have to co-operate to produce one large figure. So, at its most simple level, this is a workshop format that can be used with people who could do with interacting more with each other for whatever reason.

Analysis can include how people responded. Did they sit in a corner making their emotions without interacting, or did they organise others? How did they feel about this? Was the actual process of depicting emotions challenging? How did it feel manipulating the art materials? Was thinking about where different emotions are located in the body illuminating? Emotions are embodied, but the exercise also gives scope for an examination of how we feel about different parts of our bodies. Body-image issues may arise. I have had, over the years, disclosures of childhood sexual abuse, domestic violence, self-harm, anorexia and rape disclosed in such workshops. However, if placed early on in a workshop series, serious disclosures may not arise and the workshop may function primarily as a 'feel-good' and group-bonding exercise.

I have started to tell students at the outset, 'if you get the word "love", don't just draw a big pink heart; instead try to think about what the embodied feeling is like and try somehow to depict that'. The metaphors used in exploring the emotions can sometimes be very multi-levelled and sophisticated. Students often tell me that they found the exercise very challenging in terms of how to depict complex emotions with the materials.

Even though these group sculptures often look like a peculiar version of Frankenstein's monster, groups tend to like what they have produced. Finally, the concept of 'disposal' can be introduced to the group. The group has made a large piece of work and must think what they would like to do with it – how to dispose of it. There has been emotion invested in this piece of sculpture, so its 'demise' must be handled with sensitivity. Participants may have strong feelings either about the piece as a whole or their particular components of it. Often groups would like to photograph the piece before it's dismantled. So, if there is no storage, the facilitator can bring in a camera for this session (although mobile phones can suffice). Unless the group say they would like to dismantle the sculpture there and then, which they sometimes do, I like to give the sculpture a home in the art therapy studio for a few weeks to help the group develop a sense of the room being their own. People like to come into the room and see their creation still there.

This is a good point to discuss the importance of the storage and disposal of art work in art therapy and this discussion can serve as the 'cool down' for the session.

Guided fantasy

There are many, many types of guided fantasy, and I like to introduce one fairly early on in the introductory series as it adds contrast. The particular fantasy I often use is one adapted from the work of Dr Janek Dubowski. It's about being on a boat, waking and rowing to a tropical island, and having various experiences (which I shall elaborate on elsewhere).

Before I begin with the fantasy, I ask participants to get a life-size piece of paper and lie down on it, making any shape they'd like to. Someone else will draw round them to record an outline on the page. Some of these look a bit like the outlines drawn by police around a dead body in the murder scene in American cop movies – however, others don't look like a human form at all.

I start off by providing cushions and dimming the lights and getting everyone to follow a simple meditation exercise. Participants can banish thoughts from their mind using one or two standard techniques. One is to observe one's breath and, if one's mind wanders, concentration is simply returned to the breath – over and over again. Group members should be asked to breathe in through their nose and exhale through their mouth. Then a further prompt can include asking participants to note the sensation of the air entering their nostrils and then passing out of their mouth. 'If a thought arises, simply let it go and return your attention to your breath', I instruct. The temperature of the air can be noted: cool entering the nostrils and slightly warmer leaving the mouth. This is a basic meditation technique taught in some Buddhist monasteries.

Another technique, which I offer too because I much prefer it myself, is to imagine a clear blue sky. When a thought arises it can be attached to a passing cloud and let go. It's possible to visualise the cloud drifting off and then the mind returns to the clear blue empty sky. The idea is to stop the train of thoughts that often dominate our minds. The effect is relaxing. The body becomes calm and one's blood pressure falls; endorphins are released. Such basic meditation is very good for the body. We should all make time to do it!

However, in this instance I use the meditation to get participants in a receptive state to visualise a story I tell them. Many of the aspects of the story are quite vague so that people can attach their own meanings to them. The story starts with someone waking from a deep sleep (or being born). I play a tape of water lapping on a beach while I tell the story.

The fantasy

You are in a foetal position. You are surrounded by darkness and warmth. Colours begin to invade the darkness and you begin to move. You realise that the space you are in is moving gently back and forth...

You feel warm and relaxed – you feel a rocking sensation...

You stretch and wake to find yourself on the top bunk of a bunk bed in a dark space.

However, when your eyes adjust to the darkness you can see a door and you climb out onto the deck of a boat and look up at a sky full of stars...

As you look around you realise that the boat is moored off a tropical island – you can see that at the far end of the island is a small volcano belching out smoke and lava.

A small rowing boat is floating next to your big boat. You decide to climb down the rope ladder and row to the island.

As you row to the island there is a spectacular sunrise and mist rolls off the water.

You tether your rowing boat and wade into what looks like a cave; the tunnel becomes quite narrow and dark.

You persevere as you can see some light ahead.

You hear the sound of water; the noise intensifies as you progress through the tunnel.

You end up stepping into a magnificent underground cavern with a spectacular vast thundering waterfall.

You have the impulse to walk into the waterfall.

After some time, you continue to walk towards the light source. You emerge into a dense jungle.

You make your way through the jungle and then find yourself in a clearing. The sunlight warms you.

You see some rubble and decide to take a closer look. Two large statues lay overgrown, broken, bits jumbled in an indecipherable mass.

Then in the distance you see a tree house and walk towards it.

When you reach it there is someone friendly-looking beckoning you to come up.

You climb the suspended vine-ladder and you have an immediate rapport with the person inside.

After spending some time with this person, you take a last appreciative look at the panorama and climb down the ladder.

You explore the island.

You make your way to the beach and then, walking along the beach, you eventually come to where you moored your boat.

You reflect on your experiences as you row away from the island…

Painting the fantasy

After I've finished the fantasy, I ask people to open their eyes and to move very gently: to shake their hands, to move their heads gently and slowly to the left and right. I tell participants that they will now paint their story as they imagined it on the island (they have already created the island – their body outline). This gives extra scope for certain things from the story to be placed in certain areas of the body: the volcano might be placed in the head, stomach or crotch area. It's for participants to decide whether the placement of things in their body is relevant or not. Most participants see the outline as the island and forget it is also their body shape when they are painting so are not placing items on the body in a self-conscious manner; nevertheless, such placements, though not preconceived in a conscious way, might be revealing.

I ask the group if they'd like to keep the music on while they work. My long experience of conducting workshops has informed me that someone will be irritated by the music… However, this soundtrack of waves and birds is sufficiently innocuous that it has yet to receive complaint!

Pairs or group discussion

This is an opportunity for participants to experience using analogies, symbols and metaphors in exciting ways. (I tell or give participants a definition of each of these terms.) Every aspect of the story can be revealing – some people breeze through the jungle, others find it hard-going with their machetes; some people want to be engulfed by the waterfall, others avoid it. There is a possibility of the statues representing a significant figure, such as a person in authority or a parent, or that the person in the tree house is a would-be mate, the sort of person they'd like to meet if not in a relationship. Sometimes a deceased person is in the tree house. This gives scope for a discourse with the lost person. The interpretation of the picture is done by the person who made it. I only ask facilitative, 'how did you feel'-type questions.

Depending on the size of the group, I divide participants up into pairs to discuss their work or, if the group is eight or under (and therefore able to feel intimate), ask participants to put their picture in the middle of the group and talk about it for up to ten minutes. I never nominate someone to start.

At this early stage of the workshop series, I don't worry too much if someone doesn't get the chance to put their image in the centre. However, as compensation, I offer the opportunity for those who haven't 'shared their work with the group' (do I really talk like this?) to have the last word. Those who simply don't want to reveal much about themselves at that particular moment or those who are lacking in confidence or assertiveness are given the opportunity to say how they are feeling. They might say something along the lines of 'I'm not very good at being the centre of attention', indicating an ongoing problem with assertiveness, or 'I felt that other people might have more important things to share', indicating a self-depreciating tendency. Their small contribution can still be significant. Indeed, a person left slightly frustrated in this session often comes forward in the next (and I help to facilitate this by saying 'we've got twenty minutes left', or whatever, 'and I wonder if there is anyone who didn't speak last week who would like to discuss their work in the group'. Some people are not good at being the centre of attention, so it is helpful to provide this opportunity). I've already said that it's fine for those who feel they don't want to share their work not to (if the group was divided into pairs these issues don't arise). As noted, I give those who don't speak the opportunity to say a few words at the end – I say something along the lines of 'don't feel obliged to comment, but I'm wondering how people who didn't get to talk about their work in the group feel about that'. Helping people to air their feelings is normal practice for art therapy facilitators. Some people confirm that they were happy not to have spoken, that they learnt a lot from listening to others or declare that they intend to speak the following week. Listening to those who speak at length is illuminating for those who don't. In a different model of art therapy, the group interactive model (best described by Diane Waller), the amount of disclosure by each participant becomes absolutely crucial (non-disclosure by one or two participants can really arrest a group), but that is discussion for another time. In this very early phase of the workshop series, I don't think it matters if some people don't speak at length.

I end by thanking those who talked about their work to the group and I remind the group, having articulated this is the first session, that if anyone is left feeling emotionally churned-up then I am happy to spend time with them after the session. It's important to end the session on time and to release participants at the agreed hour, but to offer this extra support to anyone who needs it. Having run introductory workshops since 1990 (that's twenty-three years at the time of writing) up to three times a year, I can say that on only six or so occasions has this offer been taken up, always following serious revelations, such as childhood sexual abuse and so forth. Some facilitators may feel afraid to make this offer for fear of being swamped – but this is not my experience. It's comforting for participants to know that I'll stay and chat with them after the group, if necessary, so I reiterate this throughout the course.

Adding some theory

Depending on the context in which I'm teaching, I may or may not offer a theory session. If there's a half-term break, a 'reading week' or another interruption early on in the course, I'll give group members the following homework: please go to an art gallery and find two images – one you think is disturbed or 'mad' and the other you think is 'healthy'. Please bring reproductions of these images to the next session (or a sketch of the images). This ensures that participants continue to think about the course during the break. Of course there isn't a right response to this request. When participants share their 'healthy' image, some members of the group will find it sinister, disturbing or repugnant in some way. When others share their 'mad' or 'disturbing' image, others will like it or find it comforting. The point is to realise that images are open to varied interpretation. We can talk about composition and the use of materials and how these contribute to generating certain moods. The artist does not have monopoly in establishing meanings that can be attached to their painting. A lot of art history has been written about the 'artist's intention', how their psychological make-up has shaped their work, and so forth, but the work is actually up-for-grabs conceptually. If you know about nineteenth-century ideas on phrenology (a theory which saw the shape of the head and indentations of the scull indicating personality) and theories of degeneration, then you cannot view Degas' ballet dancers in quite the same way, for example, as someone just viewing them as pleasing aesthetic objects. The actual subject matter of the art work might indicate preferred meanings, but the viewer of the work always brings their unique perception to bear in their emotional reaction to the work: so, the art works might not be seen as the artist intended.

Body image workshop

This is the most substantial exercise participants will undertake in the introductory series. In this workshop, participants explore conflicting perceptions of themselves. The instruction is simple: make two images – one of how you perceive yourself to be (your 'real' or interior 'authentic' self) and another image of how you feel other people see you. If you have difficulty recognising how other people perceive you, you could pick four of five significant people in your life and think, quite explicitly, about the way you feel they view you (e.g. your mum, your lover, your boss, etc. – whoever is most significant). The images should be life-sized.

I go on to clarify that the images don't have to be figurative, that abstract work is fine. Normally, I write down the instructions on a white board, as it saves being asked to repeat them several times.

The workshop allows participants, possibly for the first time in their lives, to explore the tensions between how we feel inside and the conflicts that arise between this self-perception, or self-image, and how other people see us. This is very challenging emotionally. It is challenging in terms of representing these complex states; it may be challenging conceptually, as some people have a fluid self-identity and others a more fixed and constant one. Some people will have thought about what effect the perceptions of significant others has on their sense of self and well-being. However, for some people in the group it will be the first time they have ever analysed their feelings about these things. Some people are pleased to think about the question in a generalised way and others will want to plot out in a very careful manner the different way that selected others impact on them. What do other people's perceptions of us do to us emotionally? It's a powerful question. The exercise can help participants to analyse their relationships and also the way different perceptions of us shape our experience and, in turn, create internal conflicts.

I want participants to be challenged at this point in the course, emotionally, conceptually and in their use of art materials. I ask them to use life-sized sheets of paper for each of the images. This may be the biggest individual work they have ever completed. The workshop runs over two weeks. The first session is spent painting. The first fifteen minutes of the second session is spent finishing off. This is partly to give group members the opportunity to reconnect emotionally with their work. Then a full two hours is spent analysing the work. I prefer, at this point, to invite participants to put their work into the middle of the circle and to receive group support to talk about their image. Occasionally, I am in a position where this is untenable because of the size of the group, so the analysis can be conducted in pairs with some sort of group sharing at the end.

Because of the power and potency of the exercise, strong emotions can be expressed. It is particularly important to have some wind down or 'cool down' time for this session. This could be a discussion about the disposal of the group sculpture, if not yet dealt with, or I might ask if anyone has any questions about the theory and practice of art therapy and/or if anyone wants further reading suggestions. I might talk about the essay at this point, if it's the kind of introductory course that has an assessed written component.

Theme workshop

By about the seventh session I will offer a theme workshop. This is to offer a contrast to some of the tightly structured work already completed. Also, because the body image workshops, already described, are frequently quite intense, the groups often appreciate having a fairly open session the following week. Why are themes useful? At this stage of the group, using a theme can help to unify the group; it is helpful for group-improving cohesiveness because it is stressing commonalities between people. On the other hand, the imagery produced can be remarkably varied. Some students articulate that they feel some relief that they were given more 'freedom' at this time.

At this point in the course, I highlight how symbols, metaphors, analogies and compositional elements function in art work. What is an analogy? What is a symbol? What is a metaphor? I go over this ground again. This is when I'll give students a handout defining key terms, if I have not already done so.

The session also illustrates how symbols and metaphors can be used to bypass conscious intension to make statements about oneself. Students are often surprised by their images at this point. This is when the 'penny dropped', as one student put it to me recently. The tremendous expressive power of art-making may already have become evident but some students can get to this point in the introductory course making images in a very controlled, consciously-intentioned manner. But as participants relax and enjoy the themes, they often surprise themselves.

There are a lot of themes I really like and I imagine you have your favourites too. There are two I particularly like and have used repeatedly. One is 'my life on a plate'. This always gives a good overview of the person's life and also illustrates very vividly how they compartmentalise their life. Some people depict their life as food (so the sausages are their job and the tomatoes are their parents, etc. and you can see at a glance how they divide up significant aspects of their lives), others will produce a more metaphorical plate. Or there can be a mixture of literal and symbolic aspects: 'I've got a big mound of cabbage here and I don't really know why because I don't like cabbage...' Indeed, food for thought! Others can't contain their life on a plate at all – perhaps they'd like to be able to but can't (this can be explored); others use the total environment anyway (perhaps they are the table and other elements of the composition). There is scope for a multi-levelled exploration of one's life with this exercise.

Possibly my favourite theme is 'myself as a house'. If you were a house, what would it look like? This gives even more scope for self-exploration, as the house may be flamboyant or ordinary looking. It may have cellars, secret rooms, lifts, lofts or turrets. Different parts of the house might have quite different atmospheres. It may have open doors and windows or be fortified. The interior may be obscured by undergrowth or hidden by thick drawn curtains or behind large formidable bolted doors. It may be welcoming or not. Perhaps the curtains are gossamer thin; the viewer may get a glimpse of something, but what is it? The interior tantalises the viewer. There may be fences and paths, or not. Perhaps the house is loved despite its flaws, or disliked. Perhaps particular bits of it are disliked. 'It wasn't supposed to be black', said a black women of her house. 'This bit is a bit claustrophobic', said another women, whose sibling, it transpired, used to lock her in a cupboard as a small child as part of a regime on ongoing abuse. Quite accidentally, the emotional terrain can become very serious.

The environment, which the house inhabits, is important. Perhaps the house has a relationship with other pictorial elements such as nearby trees, for example. Perhaps the floodwaters are rising and threaten to engulf the house? Perhaps the house is big and strong or rickety and precarious? Maybe it is weather-beaten? The elements may be harsh or benign. It might be a houseboat on a rising body of water, able to slip out of trouble.

There may be trap-doors, look-out towers or guard dogs. Perhaps there is no way in to the house at all. 'I forgot to draw a front door, but actually you can get in but you have to walk round to the back and climb over the fence and then there's a key hidden…' 'Actually, perhaps I do make it rather difficult for people to get to know me…' And the 'penny drops'. The revealing image makes sense. The idea of art as therapy makes sense. And in a way, my job is now largely done in terms of providing an introduction to the subject, though I'd like participants to think more about the nuances of different structures.

Analysis and role play

Most discussion of art work takes place with participants sitting a circle and taking turns to put their work in the middle of the circle. The person who made the art work gets to talk about it, without interruption, and then I ask that person if they are happy to answer questions from other members of the group or to receive comments, and usually they are. However, at some point during an introductory workshop series I divide the group up into groups of three, after they have produced individual art works, and ask each to take turns being:

- the 'therapist'
- the 'client'
- the observer who will comment on the therapist's technique.

In terms of the therapist's role, I ask them to ask open questions: 'what's happening here?' or 'how does this part of the painting feel?' rather than foreclosing meanings by offering interpretations. Students in the therapist's role also practise using speculative questions, such as, 'where do you feel the bird is going?' or, 'if you situated yourself in this part of the picture [pointing], how would it feel?' or, 'if there was a storm, how do you think the tree house would fare?' Sometimes it can be appropriate to offer a feeling response, if handled sensitively and tentatively: 'this bit feels sad to me'. However, it is better to use open questions whenever possible. I also ask the 'therapists' to practise reiterating what a client has said at appropriate moments to illustrate that it has been heard and understood, or to underline something that sounds significant. They can repeat a significant phrase: 'it wasn't supposed to be black...' and then wait for their 'client' to digest what they have said. So, reiterating something in the latter example can serve to hold the client's attention on a point when they might have moved on. Therapists can also summarise, when a number of points have been made, and check out whether they have heard things correctly when several points have been made in quick succession, or in quite a jumbled or incoherent manner.

So they may spend fifteen or more minutes in each role. I ask the observers to note:

- Whether the therapist asked leading questions or open questions.
- To comment on whether they responded to everything said by the client or whether they missed opportunities to respond.
- Whether they were able to summarise or reiterate things said by the client in a natural-seeming way.
- To comment on the therapist's body language and tone of voice.
- To note whether there were compositional elements passed over by the therapist.
- To give any other constructive feedback they can think of. Perhaps questions are asked in quick succession, giving the client no pause for thought or conversely perhaps the 'therapist' is too tentative. Perhaps they mumble or prod the picture in a way that feels intrusive. Perhaps there were more open ways of formulating questions, which might have been employed, and this can be pointed out.

The feedback I get from participants is that they find the opportunity to be observer and then therapist very useful. I move around the room and act as an observer too. It's important to say at the outset that those in the client role must say so when they've had enough!

Student-led workshops

Still the course hasn't finished yet and, depending on whether it's a ten-, sixteen- or eighteen-week introduction, has many or few weeks to run. If it's a ten-week course then the end must be mentioned. Everyone knows that there are only three weeks left but nevertheless this fact needs to be underlined. The emotional reality of the forthcoming ending must be assimilated. Themes of loss often arise towards the end of a group. If the group is running longer, further themes can be explored and some non-directive work undertaken for contrast. In a ten-week course I often dedicate a couple of weeks to student-led workshops. These can be co-facilitated by a couple or led by an individual. I give the students who have volunteered to run a workshop a pro-forma which asks them to write their workshop title, aims, method and to state potential client groups for which the workshop might be used and why. The form ends with a participant feedback section. I make photocopies of the workshop leader's completed form and circulate it to students before the workshop starts so that everyone is clear about the aims and objectives of the workshop. At the end of the workshop participants write down what they thought of the workshop in the participant feedback section of the form. These are then returned to the workshop leader. I prefer to use a manual method for immediacy.

I ask workshop leaders if they would like me to join in or to sit on the edge and make notes to contribute constructive criticism. If asked to sit out, I produce a detailed constructive appraisal of their performance. If asked to join in, I do so and fill in the form at the end with everyone else.

Common problems noted are that insufficient time was given for an exercise, or that too many different elements were packed in, giving insufficient time for participants to reflect on their work. Sometimes instructions were not sufficiently clear, so participants ended up not doing what the facilitator had in mind. Sometimes the workshop leader sat with a closed body posture or failed to make eye contact with participants. This is a valuable opportunity for the workshop leader to get detailed feedback on how well they did. Doing too much with insufficient time for reflection on the art work produced is definitely the main fault of these novice workshop leaders. I have often felt exhausted after joining in a too densely-packed session, or frustrated that there was not enough time at the end to say what I wanted to say.

Towards the end of an experiential group, especially a group that has become cohesive and enjoyable, there can be a collective sense of loss. The ending of the group can be evocative of other endings in participants' lives and therefore generate emotions. Depending on the length of the group I will work with the theme of endings and new beginnings.

Structured ending exercise

I end the group in a highly structured way. The last workshop I run is a gifts workshop. This is always enjoyable, though it may also be serious; it is often celebratory in tone. I ask participants to make a gift for everyone in the group but not flowers or boxes of chocolate – I ask them to think about that person and to make something apt: this can be a resource like inner strength or a quality that they feel the person needs. Everyone in the group has disclosed something about their personal situation at some point. It is an opportunity to make a really personal statement and because the gifts are so personal they are often deeply appreciated.

To give an example, a fairly light-hearted gift was given to me recently. I'd talked in the group about feeling almost claustrophobic about the cumulative demands being placed upon me by caring for young children, doing a long commute, working more than full-time and having a challenging partner. I'd talked about not having enough personal space or feeling like a fairground plate-spinner with rather too many plates up on sticks, or like a little caged hamster (I'd depicted myself as a little hamster entrapped running pointlessly and wildly in a wheel, during a student-led exercise which required us to depict ourselves as an animal). One of the gifts given to me was a little plasticine bear juggling balls as a helper for me to juggle some of my balls. Although it was a light-hearted statement, it was apposite and motivated me to hire a cleaner, an au-pair and reduce my hours! Yes, I *did* need much more help! Sometimes the gifts support a resolve previously articulated in the group by the participant. Someone else in the same group gave me a little empty box containing my longed-for space. On the one hand, she was giving me what she knew I wanted, but on the other hand, she was suggesting that I should attain this, so it was a little nudge – a *do it*! Or an affirmative – *you can do it!*

The gifts might be 3D works, drawings or cards. I ask each person to give out their gifts in turn, to actually give the gift to the person it's intended for and to say a few words about why they have made what they have made. It's an ending ceremony of sorts.

After each member of the group has received their gifts, I end the group by reminding everyone about the importance of confidentiality, and ask if participants have any last words they would like to say. I think it's important to give this last opportunity for something to be said so that no one leaves frustrated.

Chapter 5

Becoming an art therapy practitioner

Annette M. Coulter

Graduating art therapists are beginning a new phase of their career, aiming to build on ideas and gain clinical experience by working with a range of clients. However, there may be challenges, such as pioneering art therapy in professional isolation, for example, when overseas graduates return home or choose to work in a remote location. Seeking work where art therapy services are not established requires acquiring an additional set of skills. This chapter offers advice and ideas for becoming an art therapist practitioner, particularly when working without the professional support systems recommended for best practice.

Success for the overseas graduate relies on the art therapist's core sense of identity, a belief in the unique service they offer and their ability to self-market and to educate professional communities as well as the general public. They need to be able to reframe a lack of understanding and support into a challenge to educate and promote their specialist skills and competencies. Rehabilitative communities are often sceptical about the benefits of art. Published art therapy resources are available, although the current dominant discourse is mostly British (UK) or North American (US) and there is little provision to equip graduates to sell their credibility, validate their clinical effectiveness or adapt art therapy to other cultural contexts.

Establishing a training programme

Overseas graduates returning home may have a choice of either securing employment or establishing a professional training programme. Once local art therapists have earned professional credibility, educational authorities are more likely to approve a training programme. Course instigators have to translate art therapy course content to a new cultural context, and foreign art therapists may have limited knowledge of local issues and systems, though some have supported the establishment of new training courses (Hagood 1993; Gilroy and Hanna 1998; Campanelli and Kaplan 1996; Slater 1999; Coulter 2006a, 2006b). However, in most parts of the world, there is an initial UK or US influence on training programmes (Potash, Bardot and Ho 2012).

Finding employment

Finding art therapy employment may not always be possible. The following suggestions are various ways newly-qualified art therapists might achieve employment or enhance better workplace terms and conditions.

Offering a 'taster'

Some potential employers may prefer to be offered a session or short series of sessions that are designed specifically for that agency. A specific package can be negotiated and a short-term group or a professional development presentation offered (see pp. 64–5). Information about an art therapy initiative can therefore be passed on through interagency networks and may lead to further work.

A trainee internship/placement

Art therapy can be introduced through offering a clinical placement or internship, which may be useful for agencies with limited funding, and can lead to employment possibilities in cautious clinical environments.

Extended clinical placement/practicum

Newly-qualified art therapists may often be employed where they did their clinical placement. When establishing a training programme, matching the student to the agency often determines the short-term future of art therapy in that facility. The workplace can see the effectiveness of the work and becomes convinced that providing this service will benefit clients, though funding issues sometimes mean initiating a compromised art therapy position, such as a part-time or a time-limited contract. The art therapist needs to avoid slipping into their previous traineeship role and has to place remunerative value on the service they offer. They need to negotiate responsibilities and make recommendations to the job description in line with professional requirements, aware that, for example, their on-site clinical supervisor is now their line manager.

Generating funding

After a short block of 'taster' sessions have been delivered, a decision can be negotiated with the agency to find short-term limited funding from a charity or service industry. The funds available may not be commensurate with industry standards fees but the art therapist may agree to be publically profiled by local media in response to the funding gesture. Pioneering a new profession often means financial compromise in order to negotiate future employment possibilities.

Promoting a previous qualification

Sometimes it is more useful for art therapists to play down their specialist skills and to promote a previous professional qualification. Where art therapy is not known or understood, a previous professional qualification might be more readily acceptable. Other therapists who complete art therapy training may find work more easily under their previous job title, and can then build up a designated 'art therapist' position.

Negotiating a job description

Most art therapists do not find themselves working in art therapy departments, and may have other job titles such as 'counsellor', 'case worker', 'child' or 'family' therapist, 'project' or 'clinical' coordinator. Whilst art therapy skills may influence successful employment, there is often no provision for demonstrating these attributes within the existing job description. When negotiating terms of employment, it pays to delineate between administrative and clinical responsibilities; the art therapist carries direct clinical responsibility even though their administrative accountability is to other staff.

Establishing an art therapy service

The newly-qualified art therapist is vulnerable to the terms and conditions that dictate their employment, especially if they are working in professional isolation. A new art therapy service must earn respect, particularly in a system that values medication, cognitive interventions and diagnostic statistics. Art therapists themselves need to respect and understand other traditional interventions. Mutual acceptance assists such things as the designation of an 'art therapist' position, salary improvement, better work facilities, the purchasing of art equipment and establishing an art therapy referral system.

Referral

The best treatment conditions are where the art therapist has direct contact with the referral source. Establishing a direct referral system builds professional respect. In medical settings, the specialist is the direct referrer but it might also be a unit director or another service. The referrer is directly informed through an assessment process about case suitability for art therapy treatment, taking into account not only the treatment offered, but also the therapist's scope of clinical experience.

The advantage of direct referral is that a relationship is established between the referrer and the art therapy service provider, so that the referrer finds out more about art therapy treatment, case discussion can become increasingly complex and skills and expertise within the working relationship expand. The referrer gains a better understanding about how art therapy might assist their clients' psychopathology and when the art therapist's skills are appreciated, there are further referrals and recommendations to other networks. Gradually, the art therapy service becomes indispensable as a treatment modality.

Art therapy assessment

An assessment phase provides an opportunity for not only the therapist to assess the client's therapeutic needs, but also for the client to assess whether the therapist can help them.

An assessment is instigated primarily to determine the appropriateness for art therapy treatment, and so is more for the benefit of therapist and the referrer than the client. Referrers more easily accept case unsuitability if an assessment process has taken place. An assessment also assists case management where legal documentation is required.

There is often a misunderstanding that through providing an assessment, the art therapist diagnoses pathology. Art therapists are not trained to diagnose and assessments should never take the place of therapy. Through image content, the assessment determines self-perception, psychomotor activity and unconscious expression through images. Art tasks tap directly into how the maker perceives their visual world; often clients may not be able to say in words what can be described through image production.

The therapist explains the limits of confidentiality before the assessment is administered. The client needs to understand that this is not therapy but is an alternate way to find out their personal perceptions. Interpretation is substantiated only by what is said by the client. In order to avoid litigation, it is important when documenting client statements to quote directly what is said. Recording the image assists ease of review – for example, an unnoticed theme becomes evident when the art work is regarded as one completed body of work. Assessment requires a distinction between what is observed during the art procedures and what is projected by the client and/or hypothesised by the therapist. Expressive components such as sequence, size, pressure, stroke, detailing, symmetry, placement and motion show *how* art work is executed and content components describe *what* is drawn.

Some art therapists are able to administer specific art therapy assessment procedures, whereas others focus on the level of initial engagement and the monitoring of conscious and unconscious processes within the therapeutic relationship (Case and Dalley 2006; Gilroy, Tipple and Brown 2012). The following assessment procedures can help work colleagues understand art therapy; they are easy to explain, administer and are effective.

The Kramer Art Evaluation

Edith Kramer developed one of the earliest art therapy assessment procedures that is still widely used (Kramer and Schehr 1983). In this procedure, the client is given three non-directive art tasks: painting, drawing and clay-work, and is instructed: 'I am going to ask you to make three pieces of art today with the materials provided for you. You are to draw, paint, and use clay in whatever order you choose, and you may choose the subject matter. I will ask you a few questions when you are finished with all three tasks.' (Kramer and Schehr 1983).

Ulman Assessment

The Ulman Assessment procedure includes an optional scoring system for the quality of marks made. Art materials include grey paper and a new set of chalk pastels, a drawing board, masking tape and a stop-watch. Instructions include:

i   You will be making four drawings. Please use these materials to make your first picture.
ii Follow me in these exercises (physical warm-up); now make these same movements with chalk on paper.
iii With your eyes closed, make a rhythmic scribble on this piece of paper. Look for images in the scribble. You may see one, you may see several. Select the images you wish to develop into a picture. You may use the lines already on the paper, colour over them, ignore them, change them, or add lines.
iv This will be your last picture. You have the choice of making a picture from a scribble or of making a picture as you did originally – directly on the paper.

(Ulman 1975: 362–5)

The Diagnostic Drawing Series (DDS)

The DDS is a systemic approach to art therapy evaluation and research, originally designed as a format for the study of drawings in relation to diagnosis (Cohen, Hammer and Singer 1988).

Three pictures are produced that reflect how an individual responds to structure and directives, allowing for a range of psychological and graphic responses. Art materials are a set of drawing pastels and a piece of 18″ × 24″ paper. There are three tasks, after each of which the client is asked a series of questions.

TASK 1: MAKE A PICTURE USING THESE MATERIALS (UNSTRUCTURED)

Can you describe this picture? Can you tell me what the colours mean? Can you tell me what these images mean or represent? What else would you like to say about the picture? What would you title the picture?

TASK 2: MAKE A PICTURE OF A TREE (STRUCTURED)

Can you describe this tree? Is this a tree you know or is it imaginary? Where would it be located? Are there special meanings to the colours? What part of the tree do you like best? What part of the tree do you like least? What else would you like to say about the picture?

TASK 3: MAKE A PICTURE OF HOW YOU ARE FEELING USING LINES, SHAPES
AND COLOURS (STRUCTURED)

Can you describe this picture? Can you tell me what these colours mean? Can you tell me what these images represent? What would you title this picture? (Cohen, Hammer and Singer 1988).

Designing an art therapy assessment

There is a real skill in being able to design an assessment to specifically suit client needs. The following ideas can be used.

- *A 'free' picture:* The client is invited to 'draw whatever comes to mind'. A free picture is the first task of a number of assessment procedures (Kwiatkowska 1978; Ulman 1975; Cohen, Hammer and Singer 1988). This open-ended task provides a choice of content and art media to determine the client at the outset of therapy. Artistic merit is not the primary interest (see p. 69).
- *A family picture:* This task can begin with an instruction such as 'draw your family, including yourself, as animals', or a more complex task such as 'draw an abstract family portrait' (Kwiatkowska 1978). Alternatively, a family art task can be designed that is relevant to a specific family event. This could be an action-oriented task, for example, 'draw everyone in the family, including yourself, doing something' (Burns and Kaufman 1970: 5). The family can do more than one art task together (see p. 69). Media tends to favour oil pastels, but three-dimensional media such as clay can also be used (see Figure 5.1).
- *The problem:* The purpose of this task is to determine the client's ability to visually conceptualise the problem. The task might be, 'draw a picture of the problem, as you understand it'. However, a more specific instruction might

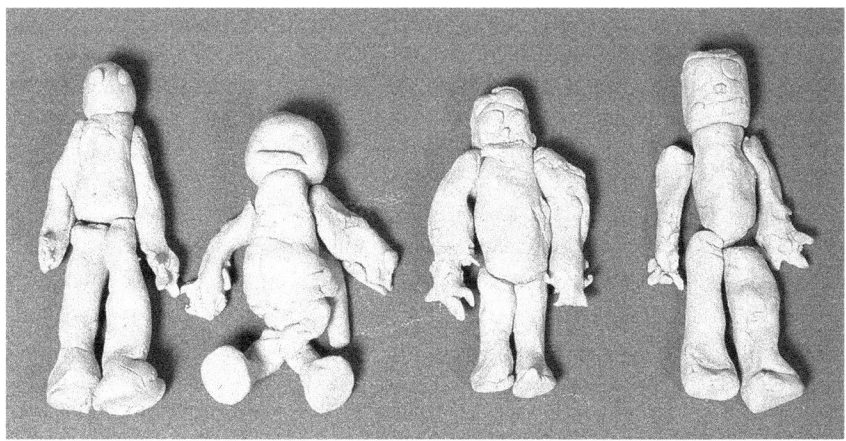

Figure 5.1 My family, by Elizabeth, age 8

be required, such as 'draw this recurring dream', or 'draw how this person makes you feel'. This task is not always suitable because the client may have no concept of why they feel the way they do, or may not believe there is a problem. Therefore an image about feelings might be more appropriate; for example, if they feel depressed, 'in some way can you put those feelings onto the paper?'

- *Self-image:* Self-concept tasks are nearly always relevant where issues of self-esteem are affecting mood and especially in the assessment of young people. A task might simply be 'draw a picture of yourself', or could be more complex, such as 'draw how others see you.' It could be symbolic: 'draw yourself as a tree/animal/object, with any qualities, any colour'; or abstract: 'describe yourself in shape and colour only', or extended to '… so that when you look at the picture, it conveys a sense of who you are at this point in time'. The task can also be contextual or diagrammatic, such as 'draw your life as a map, up until now'. A mirror can be used for realistic self-portraiture (Ault 1999).
- *Future focus:* The inclusion of a future-focused task helps determine goals of treatment, contributing to the therapist's contract with the client. Formulating clear goals might be an agreed condition of treatment. The art task might be, 'draw how you would like to be in one/five/ten years time'. It could also be something like, 'draw how your life/you would be, if you no longer needed to come to therapy'. The task can incorporate the 'Miracle Question' where the client is invited to imagine their life problem-free: 'if a miracle happened, how would your life be different?' (de Shazer 1994: 95). The art therapist then adds, 'can you draw that?' (Coulter 2011: 88). This task requires the ability to positively reframe a current difficulty.
- A *'free'picture:* The invitation to complete a final 'free' picture helps indicate how the assessment procedure has affected the client's sense of well-being. Comparing the first and last 'free' picture is informative (Kwiatkowska 1978; Ulman 1975).

Generally, client suitability is determined and rapport and safety can be reasonably established after three sessions. The art therapist might choose to extend the assessment to six sessions to consolidate their initial impressions or restrict it to two or three sessions if there are only six to twelve sessions available because of funding, health insurance or agency in-take policy. Some therapists have longer initial sessions, so that the assessment is completed in one or two two-hour sessions. An assessment report determining appropriateness for art therapy is sent to the referrer after the initial contact sessions are completed.

Writing reports

Anything written about a client is a legal document. It is therefore important to only document facts, not unsubstantiated subjective comments. A written report to the referrer is usually required on completion of an art therapy assessment, particularly in medical settings. It assists the professional profile of the art therapist to have a pro-forma for report-writing that includes client information provided at the time of referral; the number of sessions to date; a brief history; initial impressions; in the case of a family, who was seen and the frequency; nature of the assessment or treatment; and anything significant worth noting such as client statements, thoughts and comments; recommendations; further treatment; and concluding remarks.

Client self-evaluation can be a spontaneous gesture drawing in a visual diary at the beginning and end of each therapy session (see p. 84). Alternatively, client feedback can be the completion of a brief form at the termination of therapy, designed to indicate whether or not the client has found art therapy beneficial, including a question about using art materials in this context.

Designing forms and policies

Delivering an art therapy service requires forms to support efficient clinical practice, especially in a sole worker service. For best practice, the following should be included: referral; client evaluation/feedback; exchange of information; consent to be recorded; consent that art work can be shared or used for educational purposes, or permission to exhibit or photograph client art work.

Referral forms

Collaborative team work

An advantage of finding employment in a clinical team is that the art therapist is part of the joint case management, and the possibility of working with others affected by an individual's difficulties. For example, a referral might be to work with extended family members such as parents, grandparents or siblings of the client or another family sub-system.

Ownership and ethical responsibility

Consent forms are always required to share art work in clinical or educational settings, although it is often questionable whether the client can refuse such requests. It is not always in the client's best interests for art work to be shared with other team members, parents or the doctor, particularly in the case of child art therapy. Because signed permission is given, the art therapist meets their ethical obligation, although the client's motivation to sign a release form is often to please their therapist rather than in their own best interest. However, art work display can demonstrate art therapy's effectiveness as well as provide therapeutic gain (Coulter 2008). There are limitations to confidentiality. The art therapist is ethically responsible to report imagery that might indicate destructive intent to self or others, and it is mandatory to report disclosures of abuse or intention to harm self or others.

Professional indemnity insurance

When employed within an agency, professional indemnity is usually part of the employment package, whilst in contract work the art therapist must have personal indemnity insurance for session work. Some professional membership is conditional on the therapist maintaining up-to-date indemnity insurance cover. This protects the art therapist from personal liability regarding a client complaint.

Private practice

It is better to consolidate training through successful agency employment before establishing private practice. Training courses recommend supervised post-training clinical practice to gain experience because there is no back-up in private practice. Where there are limited employment opportunities, however, private practice can become a necessity.

Remuneration as a private practitioner is likely to be greater than agency work but there is greater clinical responsibility and larger overhead costs, such as indemnity and third party liability insurance, and hiring private rooms which can be costly particularly if an art studio is required. It is sometimes easier to invest in purpose-built rooms or to establish practice rooms from home. Working from a counselling room located at a private residence may present boundary issues and for some is not viable. Where counselling rooms are rented or shared, there may be constraints on art media usage and the degree of mess that is manageable.

In some countries, counselling, including art therapy, is subsidised through a rebate scheme or health insurance. In other countries, private health funds support alternative programmes including art therapy and sometimes these apply internationally. It is often only those who are financially secure who can afford art therapy services, although there are special circumstances where government services fund client art therapy treatment.

Personal dress code

In health settings an 'arty' look does not earn the same respect as that of someone who is easily identified as a fellow professional. Art therapists are greatly advantaged if they consider their professional persona, including how they dress. A professional dress code also affects clients' perceptions of the art therapist. For example, no visible cleavage assists the management of sexual transference onto female therapists, and filled-in shoes the management of a client who may have an undiagnosed foot or toe fetish. Imposing personal beliefs onto the therapeutic relationship through attire is problematic. For example, wearing religious symbols can disturb or offend someone with conflicting spiritual or delusional beliefs. In some cultures there are demands of dress such as the burka, the yarmulke or a turban. The potential impact of personal dress on the therapeutic relationship can be managed through clinical supervision.

Owning the name 'art therapy'

When delivering short training workshops to workers who already claim to 'do a bit of art therapy', it's helpful to mention that art therapy is a post-graduate specialist training and that everything cannot be taught in a one-day workshop. Where other professionals are using art techniques, confusion is avoided by encouraging that they call this 'creative art', 'art and self-expression', 'creative expression' or 'art and personal growth'. When establishing a national association, the term of 'art therapy' can be claimed through government legislation.

Forming partnerships: other professional groups

The art therapist is sometimes eligible to join an association that has a more generic membership such as family therapists or counsellors and psychotherapists. Where registration for art therapy is not established, belonging to another organisation can assist in becoming a local registered practitioner, providing opportunity for professional development and skills-promotion. Conferences and training presentations can help educate others about art therapy practice (see pp. 62–4). Finding ways to profile one's work, such as collaborative presentations with other professionals, helps generate referrals and promote an art therapy service.

Establishing a national association

Professional respect, public education and opportunities for art therapy promotion are greatly enhanced through the establishment of a national organisation. An information centre can be set up that recommends the growth of art therapy in a particular country. Knowledge can be made accessible by translating into the local language. Founding members can promote a national understanding of art therapy through workshops and conferences, as well as short training courses.

The first step is to form a small local working party of art therapists. This founding group or steering committee consider: (i) a terms of reference; (ii) a purpose of intent; and (iii) formulate membership criteria. Policy documents need to be drafted: (i) a constitution; (ii) a code of ethics; (iii) a standards of practice; and eventually, (iv) training guidelines. Sometimes differences in overseas training programmes require debate to assist the adaptation of educational influences to local contexts. When founding members come from varied overseas training backgrounds, supporting conflicting codes of practice and contradictory theoretical frameworks, the need for a more global appreciation of art therapy is required; difference requires integration and respectful compromise (see Chapter 17). An international perspective better supports the sole worker practitioner who is pioneering the profession in isolation.

Conclusion

Pioneering art therapy internationally involves integrating aspects of the profession that have infiltrated the local culture, and which may be challenging to the art therapist's core beliefs and understandings. Global variances of the profession need to be resolved from a perspective that is respectful of differences in practice. Although there are many aspects of becoming an art therapist, increasingly the challenge is to establish the profession in a resistive environment with few professional supports.

Bibliography

Ault, R.E. 1999. Drawing on the Contours of the Mind–Contour Drawing as a Psychotherapeutic Process. Keynote address, the Sixth International Annual Conference of the Korean Art Therapy Association, Seoul, Korea, October.

Burns, R.C. and Kaufman, S.F. 1970. *Kinetic Family Drawings*. New York: Brunner/Mazel.

Campanelli, M. and Kaplan, F.F. 1996. Art Therapy in Oz: Report from Australia. *The Arts in Psychotherapy* 23(1), 61–7.

Case, C. and Dalley, T. 2006. *The Handbook of Art Therapy*. Second edition. London: Routledge.

Cohen, B.M., Hammer, J.S. and Singer, S, 1988. The Diagnostic Drawing Series: a Systematic Approach to Art Therapy Evaluation and Research. *Arts in Psychotherapy* 15(1): 11–21.

Coulter, A. 2006a. Art Therapy in Australia: The Extended Family. *Australian and New Zealand Journal of Art Therapy* 1(1), 8–18.

Coulter, A. 2006b. Art Therapy Education: No More Lip-Service to Cultural Diversity! Panel presentation, International Networking Group of Art Therapists: Education Development, Current Practice and Research, American Art Therapy Association Conference, 16 November.

Coulter, A. 2008. 'Came Back – Didn't Come Home': Returning from a War Zone, in M. Liebmann (ed.) *Art Therapy and Anger.* London: Jessica Kingsley Publishers, pp. 238–56.

Coulter, A. 2011. Contemporary Art Therapy: Working with Transient Youth, in H. Burt (ed.) *Art Therapy and Postmodernism: Creative Healing Through a Prism.* London: Jessica Kingsley Publishers, pp. 83–93.

Gilroy, A. and Hanna, M. 1998. Conflict and Culture in Art Therapy, in A.R. Hiscox and A.C. Calisch (eds) *Tapestry of Cultural Issues in Art Therapy*. London: Jessica Kingsley Publishers, pp. 249–75.

Gilroy, A., Tipple, R. and Brown, C. (eds) 2012. *Assessment in Art Therapy*. London: Routledge.

Hagood, M.M. 1993. Letter to the Editor. *The Arts in Psychotherapy* 20(4), 279–81.

Kramer, E. & Schehr, J. 1983. An Art Therapy Evaluation Session for Children. *American Journal of Art Therapy* 23, 3–12.

Kwiatkowska, H.Y. 1978. *Family Therapy and Evaluation Through Art.* Springfield, IL: C.C. Thomas.

Potash, J.S., Bardot, H. and Ho, R.T.H. 2012. Conceptualizing International Art Therapy Education Standards. *The Arts in Psychotherapy* 39, 143–50.

de Shazer, S. 1994. *Words Were Originally Magic*. New York: W.W. Norton and Company.

Slater, N. 1999. Keynote Address (unpublished). Tenth Annual Conference of the Australian National Art Therapy Association, Coming Full Circle: An Unfolding Journey, Brisbane, Queensland, Australia.

Ulman, E. 1975. The New Use of Art in Psychiatric Analysis, in E. Ulman and P. Dachinger (eds) *Art Therapy in Theory and Practice*. New York: Schocken Books, pp. 361–86.

Chapter 6

Teaching art therapy to other allied health professionals

Annette M. Coulter

When pioneering the profession, the art therapist is often required to run educative training. This might be a guest lecture, an experiential workshop or a brief overview that introduces the use of art therapy in a specific setting. Participants may include interested allied health professionals, community workers and employees from other institutional departments such as education, corrective services or private health agencies and systems. This delivery might also include the corporate sector, where art therapy can benefit team building, mediate conflict or contribute to human resourcing within business.

These professionals do not want a qualification in art therapy, but there is a wish for skills enhancement, and frequently an expectation that staff will be able to use art more effectively in their workplace. Some allied health professionals may already use art in their clients' treatment and attend training to enhance their repertoire of skills, often motivated by awareness that art therapy is a profession in which they have not completed formal training. When delivering professional development training, art therapists need to be sensitive to what is already known or experienced.

Delivering professional development is an opportunity to promote art therapy as a credible profession and to educate and inform the wider community. Finding out the audience's understanding of art therapy is a useful first step. Art therapists wish to protect the profession from misrepresentation and also to promote awareness about the specialist nature of their work. When educating allied health professionals, the following questions should be of concern to art therapists: how effective is the therapeutic application of art from someone who is untrained? Who is responsible for the effective misuse of art in therapeutic settings? What role do art therapists have in providing information about effective clinical practice?

By making the profession accessible, the concern is that art therapists run the risk of prostituting their specialist expertise and experience. But protecting the profession from malpractice doesn't necessarily mean remaining mysterious, providing oblique information and aiming not to give away 'trade secrets'. Allied health professionals and others may not be skilled in art therapy, but their expertise and professionalism can challenge an inexperienced, newly qualified art therapist. However, they can also enhance the quality of the presentation, if the art therapist can deliver from a position of respect that is open to the knowledge or experience the audience offers.

Running introductory training

The art therapist must have a clear training brief. Organisations use their professional development budgets to send staff to training, which might be professional development either requested by staff members or that a manager or supervisor believes will enhance best practice. Personal enthusiasm for using art may be the motivation or participants may be there begrudgingly, having been instructed to attend. A manager or employer may wish them to improve their skills or may have concerns about irregularities or complaints about their use of art in the workplace. When an art therapist runs professional development training for community agencies, they cater for a broad audience. It is important to see these as one-off opportunities to educate the public about the profession. For the duration of the professional development training, there is a captive audience of interested professionals.

There are differences in approach, depending on the type of presentation and the length of time available. The art therapist might be called upon to present in a variety of different ways and contexts, for example, for a government department that is considering funding some contracted art therapy work; a small agency interested in professional development for their staff; an organisation that is considering employing an art therapist; an indigenous group of workers who consider art therapy might complement the work within their culture; or as a service for a specific client group where it is thought art therapy may have something new to offer.

Presenting a one-off lecture or talk

It's useful to begin by defining art therapy from several perspectives, using both UK and US official definitions as well as the local definition if that country has developed a statement. The belief that art therapists interpret art work, or that the end product is used in diagnosis, needs to be clarified or dispelled, depending on the art therapist's model of understanding. What art therapy is and is not needs to be explained (The Hong Kong Association of Art Therapists 2002), followed by theoretical content that suits the orientation of the therapist and relates to the audience to whom the presentation is directed. Generally, definition is followed by something on the creative process (see pp. 81–2), psychological factors contributing to creative thinking, theoretical approaches to art therapy, clinical application which may or may not include case material and then a conclusion on the values of art therapy. Case examples can enhance a presentation but client information is used minimally and only to illustrate a particular point.

An experiential workshop

Provide time for the group to introduce themselves to you and to each other, finding out what skills, experience and knowledge they have, as well as what their exposure to art therapy has been, in particular, and whether this has been from a UK or US perspective (see pp. 81–2). This will dictate participants' training expectations. Although an experiential workshop has a practical, skills-enhancement focus, a theoretical component provides an academic baseline that helps engage the sceptic who may be present.

The agenda for a two-day introductory training could include: art kits, group guidelines, processing guidelines, an introductory DVD (Rubin 2004) and visual diaries. The theoretical components might include: definition and creativity, the Expressive Therapies Continuum (ETC) (Lusebrink 1990), designing an ETC intervention, values of art therapy, documentation of art work, ownership and storage, a book-list and other resources. Experiential content could include: communication through art, an exploration of art media, introducing yourself through art, group art therapy, art and self-image and visual diary entries. At the end of each day, it's useful to have time for questions and seminar discussion, as well as an evaluation at the end of the course.

Introductory tasks

These might include a line conversation, an image found within a scribble (see pp. 79, 157, 159) or a 'free' picture (see pp. 57–8, 79). Although these *Communication Through Art* tasks are usually experienced as fun and engaging, they begin to demonstrate the effectiveness of art therapy, reflecting an assessment phase of treatment. Once group trust is established, in-depth, self-disclosure-type tasks, such as *Art and Self-Image*, are reflective of the treatment phase. Resources for art therapy tasks can be recommended to workshop participants (Liebmann 2004; Makin 1999; Malchiodi 1998; Buchalter 2009; Ross 1997). The art therapist also needs to deliver educative instruction on group guidelines and on processing art work.

Group guidelines

These are a basic set of parameters for the duration of the training and should be delivered prior to producing any art work. This helps establish safety, particularly if a participant is resistant, suspicious about art therapy or is there under duress. As a training tool, these guidelines instil ethical considerations from the outset and allow time to clarify understandings and stimulate discussion relevant to the participant's frame of reference. This prepares for the processing of art work in a training context, desensitises participant's expectations and introduces strategies for the non-art therapist practitioner. If there is limited time to teach about art therapy, the inclusion of group and processing guidelines are likely to enhance the safe use of art in therapy. This is a summary of training group guidelines:

Be responsible for yourself

This is training, not therapy. If unexpected personal insights surface, these can be discussed elsewhere, outside the workshop. Where possible, work in a private space – avoid looking at others' art work, which can influence or intimidate the art-making process. You do not have to share your art work. It is the art therapist's responsibility to provide personal boundaries for participants, and the participants' responsibility to self-monitor within these boundaries.

Allow 'internal dialogue'

This may take place while making an art work, so do not talk or make distracting noises. Try and relax and let the art materials do the thinking. Allow spontaneous, unconscious processes to be mobilised.

Maintain therapeutic boundaries

Do not talk about art work outside the room (this can disrupt the 'holding' space of the room). The room, the art work, the length of time and the art therapist's presence should also act as the boundary that helps contain content. The workshop is confidential, and the walls of the room are the 'frame' – hence the notion of the 'frame within the frame' (Schaverien 1989). Participants should remain in the room for the duration of the session.

Maintain confidentiality

What is shared remains confidential. You might discuss your own art work with a partner or close friend, but do not discuss anyone else's. During breaks, art work is not discussed. Seek permission to photograph any art work and document everything on the reverse. Point out that participants are not art therapists and so not bound by the same professional code of ethics; however, they should be alerted to best practice within the profession.

Respect art work

Art work is an extension of the person. Do not overlap your work with anyone else's and respect their working spaces. The therapist does not touch a participant's art work without their permission. Maintain confidentiality.

Document all art work

When art work is completed, contemplate and reflect on your personal process, making notes and debriefing in your visual diary. Document work on reverse side with name, date, title, time of day and number of art work in a sequence of completion.

The importance of process

Artistic skills are not important, but the process is. Think about what has taken place for you during the 'internal dialogue'. The art work is not an end in itself, but a statement of where the process is up to. It does not matter how 'good' or 'bad' the work is aesthetically.

Keep art materials tidy

The art materials are your clinical tools and you have been provided with a basic 'tool kit' to use during and after the workshop. 'Contaminated' art materials should be avoided. It is up to each participant to look after and maintain their art materials, and this is more effective when ownership is involved, as opposed to supplying communal art materials. Art materials should meet the criteria of the Expressive Therapies Continuum (Lusebrink 1990) and can be used later in clinical settings.

Use visual diaries

Use these for spontaneous gesture drawing (p. 84). Document all entries, which are private and only to be shared if you choose to. Throughout the workshop, the visual diary is used to support and reflect on the training process.

Training group processing of art work

Workshop participants can process in pairs, small groups or in the larger group. If it is workplace training, working with the larger group is more effective because relationships are already established – the workshop can strengthen team-building. However, if the team is dysfunctional, sharing in the larger group may not be as effective because participants want privacy from their colleagues. Decisions on how work is to be processed are made as the facilitator gains an understanding of the training group and observes relationships within the group.

More often, participants do not know each other. In this situation, group cohesiveness or trust needs to be established if art work is to be processed safely. Therefore, starting interactions in pairs and/or small groups is more effective. There are definite limitations to what can be achieved from a short-term training workshop. There are basic points to get across regarding the processing of art work. It is easier for participants to understand these points with explanation and example. Processing guidelines (see pp. 69–70) can be combined with group guidelines (see pp. 66–8) where there are time constraints. However, for information absorption, it is easier if there is a break, some art work produced and then the processing guidelines delivered.

Working in pairs

People can join up with someone they know, someone they intuitively feel comfortable with or with someone they know the least. Try to create a pair situation that reflects a client–therapist situation, so initial workshop tasks reflect the therapist trying to establish rapport or engage with the client. In this scenario, it is likely that the therapist and client do not know each other, so asking participants to pair with someone they know the least will reflect this new relationship. When doing more in-depth sharing, encouraging participants to pair with someone they feel more comfortable with, or someone they know well, is better suited to a client–therapist scenario once rapport is established. Encourage participants to give each other feedback on processing style, so that they learn from the training experience what worked well and what aspects need further consideration.

Processing guidelines

The following processing guidelines are small and larger group situations. The advantage of processing art work with the whole group is that it is easier to demonstrate these points by example.

You don't have to share your work

The art work has only just become conscious and the maker needs time to contemplate it before verbalising can take place. The making of art work is therapeutic in itself and words are not always relevant or necessary. Sometimes the maker may never fully understand the work.

Always own your comments

Don't make assumptions about other people's art work. Own your own comments; for example: 'When *I* look at this *I* feel…' It's fine to share your gut response to someone else's work, but acknowledge this is about your own experience; for example: 'When I look at *your* family, I get a feeling of…'

Be non-judgemental about artistic merit

Avoid comments on artistic merit (for example, 'What a lovely picture'), even though we are socially conditioned to congratulate artistic skill. Judgements are value-laden and subjective, and not useful in the context of art therapy, which is different from the outside world.

Only one person speaks at a time

This can be overlooked if participants get excited about the art-making process. Each person has their own unique visual language based on cultural background, belief system and personal life experience – listen to their language of 'word-symbols'. Be respectful.

You can stop sharing at any time

A personal insight can break through at any moment – this can be confronting. You can stop sharing at any time without further explanation, or simply say, 'I'd like to leave it there', for example. The art work is a permanent record and can be returned to later. Important material will be repeated until it is understood and processed.

You do not have to respond

You do not have to reply to questions or comments – there are no polite social norms within the workshop. You can simply nod, say 'uh huh' or just contemplate the art work.

Phrase a question into a statement

Questions about art work come from a thought – share the thought as an open-ended statement or comment. The maker does not always want to be bombarded with questions about their work.

Listen to the language used

When sharing your art work, you are describing your visual world to others – this can be a surprisingly emotional experience. If you are the receiver, listen to the language used and do not assume your thoughts are right until they are confirmed. When responding, use the terms the maker uses.

Let go of a therapist's agenda

Wait until the person is ready to share their work; don't get carried away by what you think the work is about. Remember that making art work is therapeutic in itself.

The Expressive Therapies Continuum

Lusebrink's Expressive Therapies Continuum, or ETC (Lusebrink 1990), packages a clear theory that is easy for the allied health worker to grasp in a time-limited workshop. Two publications (Lusebrink 1990; Hinz 2009) refer the participant to further information on the impact of art materials in relation to the ETC and on the therapeutic process, and their contribution to the process of change. When providing training for allied health professionals, allocating time for participants to consider the importance of art materials as an intervention in their own right is highly recommended. Allied health professionals have often not considered the significance of providing an incomplete spectrum of colours or the impact of 'contaminated' art materials (see group guidelines above) on client

Table 6.1 Art 'tool' kit

ETC level	Art media	Purpose/notes
Cognitive/Symbolic (C/S)	1 × graphite stick (4B/6B)	Although controlled, allows flexibility if wanting to move from C/S Level
	1 × box coloured pencils	12 colours, minimum
	1 × pencil sharpener	Pencil shavings can be used to move from C/S Level
	1 × visual diary	A4 size, white cartridge
Perceptual/Affective (P/A)	1 × box oil pastels	16 colours, water-soluble for media flexibility – frequently used as are quick, clean and vibrant – a main requirement
	1 × box chalk pastels	12 colours, minimum
	1 × packet plasticine (also known as 'coloured clay')	Full colour spectrum that includes black and white
	1 pair scissors	Rounded ends – for client safety. Where scissors cannot be used, paper can be torn
	1 × glue stick	Mainly for collage work
	1 × 300ml liquid PVA glue	A stronger glue and can be watered down for varnished effects or to seal something
Kinaesthetic/Sensory (K/S)	5 tubes × 300ml acrylic paint	Primary colours, i.e. red, blue, yellow, plus black and white. Mixing of secondary colours is part of the art media training
	500gm block of air-dry clay	Can be painted – no firing required
	3 × paint brushes	Hog-hair effective. Sizes are small, medium and large

engagement. The art materials the client gravitates towards, or that the therapist chooses to provide, are significant. A focus on art media ensures that allied health workers are informed about the effective use of art materials in their clinical practice. The ETC provides a framework that celebrates the constructive use of art materials, and can be summarised as follows.

Lusebrink divides art media into three levels of involvement: the Cognitive/ Symbolic, the Perceptual/Affective and the Kinesthetic/Sensory (Lusebrink 1990), which are shown in Table 6.1.

Cognitive/Symbolic Level

This level uses refined media (coloured pencils, graphite sticks, compressed charcoal) involving fine-motor precision and thinking processes that involve conceptual formulation, abstraction, verbal self-instructions, intuitive, self-oriented concept formation and synthetical thinking.

- It requires the development of abstract thought.
- Information processing is complex and deals with what is not present.
- It provides a release from the present.
- It engages cognitive, analytical and logical thought processes.
- Problem solving through the use of media properties is at the cognitive end.

Provide some case studies – for example, an academic who experiences a 'nervous breakdown' will probably be more at ease on this level because the art media relates to what is more familiar. Helping clients to gradually experience more flexible art media with which they are less comfortable will have a therapeutic aspect because a degree of unfamiliarity with risk-taking is successfully achieved.

Perceptual/Affective Level

There is an emphasis on form and the more formal elements of concrete images. There is a focus on the expression of feelings and moods, and the use of colour. Art materials include photo collage, felt pens, chalk pastels, oil pastels and plasticine.

- Interaction with art materials creates perceptions and arouses affect.
- Visual articulation encourages perception.
- Visual organising creates 'good gestalts' from past perceptions, assisting closure on the experience.
- Affect is activated through responses to the visual form – emotional responses to image/art work are encouraged.
- May express intimate and primitive sensations and emotions, of which there is no previous awareness.

An example here might be a reference back to an art task already completed, such as the *abstract family portrait*, or something symbolic of self, such as *a picture of yourself as a tree*, where there is a focus on colour and how something or someone is perceived. If working with a limited budget, this level provides the art materials that have the most flexibility from which to move up or down the ETC.

Kinaesthetic/Sensory Level

This level involves a physical approach to art media such as soft pastel/chalk, water-based paints and clay, using motor movements, gestures and flexible exploration of the art materials – tactile quality has significance and there is a focus on inner sensations.

- There is a focus on the release of energy through bodily action/movement.
- Either stimulates arousal or allows energy to be discharged, lowering tension.
- Sensory experience without awareness or involvement of an affective response.
- No particular goal – potential for how sensation of art materials are utilised.

There is more likelihood of accidental and more spontaneous interaction with art materials on this level because of their invitation for less control. A case example might be the child with ADHD who is likely to enjoy and be familiar with this level of art media involvement. However, this might not necessarily be therapeutic for him/her because it can stimulate chaotic feelings and heighten out-of-control behaviour.

Finally, workshop participants could consider which ETC level resonates as most familiar for them, and be asked to explore and push art media boundaries. The use of 'media dimension variables' (MDVs), 'mediators' and 'reflective distance' (RD) (Lusebrink 1990) can also be considered. There is an invitation to break rules, to move from what is known to discovering what is less known, to mix media, to take risks, to work in a less familiar way and to extend the boundaries from where participants feel comfortable in order to release a freedom in their approach.

Art therapist trainees aim to become familiar with all aspects of art media – for workshops, this is a taster of the same requirement. Ask participants: 'What happens when you mix water with coloured pencil, or push plasticine around on the page with your finger or work pastel into the acrylic paint?' Advise at the outset that there is no expectation to share this art work, apart from a brief viewing, where different techniques are appreciated and curiosity about how effects were achieved is encouraged. By allowing time for the extension of media dimension variables, participants experience an exhilaration as they consider art materials as a new frontier to their learning and work with clients. The categories above are a guide that is useful when delivering short training packages but are not absolute, as how the materials are actually used will also have an impact. Workshop evaluations often mention how much participants enjoyed the art media exploration part of their training, possibly because it gives them permission to play in a training context.

Art kits

Rather than supplying a broad range of art materials, an option is to supply art kits, which can be factored into the workshop fee and are kept by the participant, providing an immediate and comprehensive starter kit for clinical work. When demonstrating the Expressive Therapies Continuum, the art materials need to fit the ETC requirements (see Table 6.1).

Coloured paper and cartridge paper are supplied and other collage materials are also provided, such as glitter, pipe cleaners and magazine-torn images (Landgarten 1993), as well as clay tools and a clay cutter. (Fishing line wrapped around a wooden peg, split in two for handles, makes an inexpensive clay cutter.) Further materials can be added at a later date and an extensive list of essential and optional art media extensions is provided and discussed as a training resource.

Basic art materials

- pencils: graphite stick, coloured, water-based
- charcoal: compressed, sticks, pencils
- ink: coloured, calligraphy, Indian
- collage materials: threads/wools, natural and found objects, fabric, cardboard
- photo images: magazine, postcard, family
- coloured paper: crepe, cellophane, wrapping, tissue, cards, brown
- plaster: moulds, sculpture (for body image work)
- crayons: Conte, wax, water-based
- pastels: chalk, oil, wax
- clay: air-dry, terracotta, Fimo, plasticine
- paint: acrylic, finger, water, sticks, tempura, gouache.

A further component of an introduction to art media is the provision of a list of basic art principles that are also abstract art considerations. These can be briefly explained or brainstormed, and include:

- orientation of space – open/crowded/barriers/vistas
- colour – primary/secondary; contrasting/complementary; overlay of colour
- dominant movement – vertical/horizontal/diagonal
- structure – rigid/loose; uneven/balanced
- balance – symmetrical/asymmetrical
- relationships within the picture – repetition; dominance; overlaying; borders
- quality of line – thick/thin; fragile/bold; hard/soft
- shape – geometric/biomorphic
- texture – rough/smooth/patterned/coarse
- tone – light/dark/gradations of shade
- rhythm – repetition/flowing/progressive
- proportion/size – distorted/obscured/incomplete/absent.

Contemplating art work

When participants first process art work, they are invited to take a few moments to gaze at the work. This viewing of the art work gives participants a taste of Betensky's phenomenological intuiting (Betensky 1995), capitalising on the existential notion of contemplation of the work, be this the maker or the trainer, the client or the therapist, or workshop participant one or workshop participant two.

The instruction to contemplate the work is as follows: decide who is going to share their art work first. Before discussing the art work, both the maker and their partner take two minutes to contemplate the marks on the paper. Together, they contemplate the art work, and the maker moves from personal involvement to a more reflective position with the art work. The maker becomes the beholder who in turn becomes the receiver (Betensky 1995: 14–25). The workshop partner then asks the maker to consider, 'What do you see?' (Betensky 1995: 17). Encourage participants to listen to their 'gut' reaction to the art work, before the maker of the work tells them anything about it. As the beholder, the participant is allowing the art work to resonate. For the maker, this is also an extension of the group guideline about allowing opportunity to listen to the 'internal dialogue' (see pp. 67–8).

If the workshop includes instruction to use theoretical approaches, in a phenomenological approach, the art media component plus this list of basic art principles assists discussion as well as further self-reflective narratives (see p. 80). This also extends an understanding of visual language.

Workshop evaluation

At the end of a professional development course for allied health professionals, success is achieved when there is a new respect for the profession of art therapy. Evaluation forms allow constructive feedback that shapes and enhances future workshop delivery.

End of a training workshop

As in clinical work, the end of a workshop can bring up issues for some participants. Some facilitators provide their contact details so that participants can follow up with requests for clinical supervision or to refer a client for art therapy. Some may want to discuss their workshop experience in more detail. When the training is over, you need to consider the degree of unpaid availability you are prepared to offer. It is better to ask people to follow up enquiries away from the workshop setting. Spending personal time talking to participants who remain behind is not recommended. If they wish to continue their personal art therapy work, they can be referred to an art therapist practitioner. Boundaries between workshop training, delivery and clinical practice need to be clear. Some participants stay behind because they want more time with the presenter. Some participants choose to place their art work in the rubbish bin as they tidy up at the end of the workshop. If this is part of someone's personal process, facilitators must not be offended. It can be disconcerting and easily interpreted that personal processing is not valued. Remember that a training workshop is not a time for personal therapy and the therapist delivering training must leave their therapist hat off.

Conclusion

When providing an art therapy introductory workshop for allied health professionals, treat this as an opportunity to educate about common misunderstandings. Be respectful of their knowledge and expertise. Although the art therapist is an expert in their field, participants can also contribute to the presentation in terms of fitting theory to specialist clinical practice and relevant possible case scenarios with art materials. Work on the assumption that there is always something more to learn and be humbled by the privilege to impart information about the profession to an interested group of allied health professionals.

Bibliography

Betensky, M.G. 1995. *What Do You See? Phenomenology of Therapeutic Art Expression.* London: Jessica Kingsley Publishers.

Buchalter, S.I. 2009. *Art Therapy Techniques and Applications.* London: Jessica Kingsley Publishers.

Hinz, L.D. 2009. *Expressive Therapies Continuum: a Framework for Using Art in Therapy.* London: Routledge.

The Hong Kong Association of Art Therapists. 2002. Association Brochure.

Landgarten, H.B. 1993. *Magazine Photo Collage: a Multicultural Assessment and Treatment Tool.* New York: Brunner Mazel, Inc.

Liebmann, M. 2004. *Art Therapy for Groups: a Handbook of Themes and Exercises.* Second edition. London: Jessica Kingsley Publishers.

Lusebrink, V.B. 1990. *Imagery and Visual Expression in Therapy.* New York: Plenum Press.

Makin, S.R. 1999. *Therapeutic Art Directives and Resources: Activities and Initiatives for Individuals and Groups.* London: Jessica Kingsley Publishers.

Malchiodi, C.A. 1998. *The Art Therapy Sourcebook.* Los Angeles, CA: Lowell House.

Ross, C. 1997. *Something to Draw On: Activities and Interventions Using an Art Therapy Approach.* London: Jessica Kingsley Publishers.

Rubin, J.A. 2004. *Art Therapy Has Many Faces.* VHS/DVD. Pittsburgh, PA: Expressive Media, Inc.

Schaverien, J. 1989. The Picture within the Frame, in A. Gilroy and T. Dalley (eds) *Pictures at an Exhibition: Selected Essays on Art and Art Therapy.* London: Tavistock/Routledge, pp. 147–55.

Chapter 7

Innovative teaching strategies

Annette M. Coulter

Art therapists are often called upon to teach art therapy practice to therapists and counsellors who are already experienced practitioners in their own right. This chapter extends ideas introduced in Chapter 6 to provide further practical implementation of teaching strategies to a range of professional groups, incorporating current art therapy education techniques with the skills and experience other therapists bring to such training. These practitioners wish to make use of art more effectively in their work, but usually do not wish to become 'art therapists'. As argued above, art therapists cannot afford to be over-protective of their skills or unprepared to share their expertise with non-art therapists. The reality of being part of a clinical team involves introducing colleagues to effective art therapy practice. This has the potential to be a rewarding experience for both the art therapist and work colleagues. The art therapist must be able to share her skills both with a sceptical community of health professionals and with those who are enthusiastic and offer professional support.

Teaching art therapy to work colleagues

One-off opportunities

An invitation to conduct a presentation is an opportunity to share skills and educate professional colleagues, whether this is part of a regular internal staff meeting, a clinical supervision group, a professional development event, a lecture series or as part of a wider network, such as an interagency meeting, mental health forum or medical meeting. While the context is an important consideration, so is a successful presentation. The art therapist may need to clarify what is already known about art therapy and be prepared to present to a challenging and possibly diverse group.

A definition of art therapy with an overview on creative process theory is recommended, as well as relevant case material that demonstrates the diversity of clinical application. An ethical challenge, for example about ownership of art work, congratulating artistic merit or interpretation of art work can stimulate discussion.

Interpretation

There is a common expectation that art therapy is about learning how to interpret art work. Ensure you are prepared for questions about this and have a clear position on your understanding of an interpretive model, ensuring that it respects the historical dimensions of art therapy. In particular, one strand of art therapy development originates from early twentieth-century psychoanalysis where attempts to interpret images using psychoanalytic concepts informed an interpretive model (Naumburg 1950, 1966; Junge 1994). The origins of this notion of art therapy are well documented (Ulman 1975a; Kramer *et al.* 1974; Waller 1991; Hogan 2001). However, this is not common practice in contemporary art therapy, though it is important to not confuse interpretation with art therapy assessment procedures where interpretation must be substantiated by what the client says and does in terms of behaviour or relevance to personal history. Assessment should never take the place of therapy; however, the US idea of art psychology and the use of visual techniques in assessment has merit when conducted from an informed perspective (Betts 2006, 2012).

Assuming the audience is untrained in art therapy, the point to be made here is that interpretation can be destructive and damaging, and that it is often due to the therapist's need or concern to understand the work. Coming from a UK perspective, an art therapist would aim to remain curious about the client's art work, to allow a multitude of possibilities to emerge. In art therapy, we wait for the client to inform us, to explain their image, to reply to the question, 'What do you see?' (Betensky 1995).

Processing art work

The following points are discussed with examples.

- Casual interpretation or a chance remark can be insensitive, clumsy and inappropriate.
- Naming an image can cause distress and anxiety – the client may be depicting something entirely different, which may not be clear. Wait for explanation – do not assume.
- Interpreting art work disrespects the fact that the client has a mind of their own.
- If the 'all-knowing' therapist intrudes, the client feels exposed – their sense of identity or autonomy invaded or attacked.

Points to remember

- Important material will re-emerge in subsequent sessions.
- Crucial to the interaction between therapist and client is to remain in a state of 'not-knowing'.

- Therapists need to remain in a state of curiosity and allow meaning to expand and other possibilities to emerge.
- Therapy requires a continuity of respect for the client's personal, private space – a balance of intimacy and distance, of togetherness and aloneness (Dalley, Rifkind and Terry 1993).

Experiential content

Scribbles

Regardless of theoretical explanation and case material, a small experiential task is often remembered as the highlight of a presentation. For example, an audience can be invited to make a random scribble. To encourage spontaneity and a less-controlled scribble, suggest the use of the non-dominant hand or to work with partially closed eyes, to allow accidental mark-making. Participants then pass their scribble to someone else who is invited to look for an image within the random mark(s). This experience, done without special art equipment and while participants remain in their seats, is non-threatening yet engages the participants in a quick demonstration about the importance of spontaneity, taking a risk and the use of unconscious images. A simple art activity visually bypasses language and is easier to retain in the non-verbal part of the brain. This intervention is adapted from the Winnicott Scribble Technique (Winnicott 1971b), but in this accessible context is arguably an effective introduction to art therapy for a conservative, disinterested or resistive audience. Warm-ups to enhance a 'good' scribble are also well documented (Kwiatkowska 1978; Ulman 1975b; Cane 1951; Naumburg 1966).

Other experiential tasks

Provide participants with a choice of introductory tasks, such as a free picture (see pp. 57–8), drawing your name and making an art work that tells something about you.

There is no right or wrong way to do any of these tasks – they are each designed to allow the person to interpret the task as best suits their personal frame of reference. The 'free picture task' is explained as a standard part of a number of art assessment techniques (Kwiatkowska 1978; Ulman 1975b). The 'picture of your name task' appeals to all age groups from children (see p. 125) to adults to the elderly – everyone knows their name and it is a great group introductory task because it helps everyone remember each other's name, including the workshop presenter. The 'picture that tells the group something about you' can be a significant personal piece of information one wishes to share, such as a recent medical diagnosis of a family member, or it can be something minor, such as what the person had for breakfast that day. This choice will be dictated by how well-established group trust is prior to the workshop event.

Self-image

An introductory workshop could include at least one task that explores self-image, which may be dictated by art media recommendations. For example, for 'myself as a tree' (any type of tree with any qualities, including fantasy qualities; any colour, any shape – all qualities describe you, as a tree) you might encourage the use of paint, whereas for three full-bodied 'self-portraits' (how I see myself – real self; how others see me – external self; how I'd like to be seen – ideal self) one might use oil or chalk pastels because of their rich, immediate colour. Provide an explanation for media recommendation, but allow people to choose media also – they don't necessarily have to go with your recommendation. They may choose to construct themselves a tree from plasticine or clay, or they might choose to use coloured pencils or paints for their three self-portraits. Media choice can be another point to discuss in the application of theory to practise as part of the presentation.

Participants can be encouraged to practice self-reflective documentation. For example, with 'myself as a tree', a diagram might be drawn of the completed image, and the work documented in a visual diary as a self-reflective exercise and visual debriefing. This could include writing a narrative description/script in the first person that describes what you know about yourself, for example, 'This is me, I am…, I have …', 'I like it when…', 'Where I am growing…' Similarly, for 'three self-portraits', a narrative description/script for each portrait could begin, 'This is ideal me. I am…, I have…, I like it when…'

Encouraging participants to write about a symbol for themselves in the first person can be a positive training experience because the use of narrative description encourages insightful responses. People choose how much of any new insight(s) they wish to share with the larger group but feedback often describes the self-image tasks as where the most significant learning happened in the experiential component of the training.

Self-box

The self-box is a popular task that is used effectively both in clinical practice and in workshops (Keyes 1974), showing how simple materials can be effective in self-reflective work. For this task, an array of different-sized boxes are supplied. The outside of the box represents the *outside* part(s) of the person, the part that the external world sees. It involves self-perception of what is presented to the outside world as well as, to some extent, feedback one receives from others. The inside of the box represents the *inside* aspects of the person, the part(s) that are more private and hidden from external scrutiny. This basic concept is easily grasped by participants and is an enjoyable self-reflective task that involves engagement with collage materials and construction. There is a focus on how the surface of the box is worked and how the inside of one surface relates to the external part of that same surface. One workshop participant was reflecting on an abortion she had experienced. On the lid of the box, she threaded torn white strips of rag. These strips remained white on the outside, whereas, on the inside, they were painted red.

The surface of the cardboard lid became the area of transition between internal and external effect on this physiological trauma to her body. The surface can also be worked with windows, mirrors, doors, spy holes, etc.

A variation is to introduce a theme for each of the six sides of the box: family, physical, emotional, professional/work/school, spiritual, social. This is optional but appeals to those wanting a structured training experience. The six sides of the box are each allocated a surface theme and the inside and outside surfaces of that theme are then worked – for example, spiritual inside, versus spiritual outside, looking at how the external surface relates to the internal surface for 'spiritual'. What themes are chosen for the top and bottom of the box can also be explored.

Creative processes

All creative processes can be seen as examples of the person testing self against reality: their subjective internal world of imagination, personal experiences, fantasy, dreams and images tested against their external world of objective reality and fact. These ideas can be expanded to include information on right- and left-brain theory, conscious and unconscious processes, and personal internal non-verbal world versus collective/group external verbal world, and the fact that we respond to the world visually before we have language, so that emotional development based on attachment to external visuals, such as the mother's face, is linked to 'vitality of affect' (Stern 1985; Evans and Dubowski 1988).

The creative process can be simplified into four stages (Wallas 1926):

1 Preparation: conscious concern and struggle – when the task is considered, researched and examined thoroughly. At this is stage, it is often that an art task has been suggested to the client, who is considering what they might draw, paint or create.

2 Incubation: at this stage, a block is experienced that might be a fleeting moment of hesitation or it may be a protracted period of time, for several sessions or months as the client works through their creative block what this means. The client might say, 'I don't know what to draw'. The therapist's role is to support the client through this phase and to not offer suggestions but might respond, 'let the crayon/your hands do the thinking'. Such statements help the client disconnect from impasses that block creative expression.

3 Illumination: a sudden flash of inspiration, exuberance or elation is experienced when an idea bubbles in from the unconscious. The source of the idea is not known but simply appears in one's consciousness, unannounced and unexpected.

4 Verification: this is when the illuminating idea is tested out and critically examined. The idea may not work and the person returns to preparation or incubation expanding the creative process stages being experienced to more than four but, essentially, these four are a simple way to provide a basic understanding of creative process theory.

Essentially you are also trying to explain what participants might experience in the workshop, so examples of these stages being applied to common day activity is useful preparatory theory. For example, when cooking a meal a person might go through the following process: What's in the fridge? Too hard, nothing to cook! Wait a minute, I could do something with this egg. Start cooking. When completing an art task, the process might be as follows: Draw... Can't start, too hard, I'm not creative. Sudden flash of idea, pick up art materials and make a mark. Start doing art task.

Psychological processes involved in creativity

- *Perception*: we perceive the world through our senses as a 'reductive system'. If we experienced everything we sensed we would be overwhelmed but by editing things out of sensory awareness, important information can be consciously lost (Gordon 1985). Art therapy can reawaken past perceptions that have been relegated to the unconscious.
- *Imagery*: this is based on memory traces of past perceptions that are now absent. In their absence images can be embellished based upon perceptions.
- *Symbolisation*: one symbol can have many meanings. There is the intended meaning but as the symbol is explored, other less conscious meaning can surface. There is also the wider unconscious which Jung referred to as the 'collective unconscious' (Jung 1964).
- *Transitional object*: this bridges what is internal with what is external through the *experience* of the object. In art therapy our interest is in the art object as the bridge between inner and outer worlds. This notion was developed by Winnicott, who noticed that a child attached themself to an object in the absence of their mother (Winnicott 1971a). The transitional object is a found object from the child's external world, such as a sucking vest, a soft toy or even a tune, that is invested with meaning and significance from the child's internal world. The child experiences the world through this object.
- *Play*: this focuses on process rather than a valued end-product in play. Society is generally quite end-focused: for example, we work for a wage or achieve a degree after completing study. In a therapy that focuses on play processes, the end product is merely a statement of where that process is at one point in time. A client may make an aesthetically beautiful piece of art work, but if the play process is that this needs to be destroyed, that might be what needs to happen in order for therapy to take place.

Interactive drawing therapy (IDT)

This is an effective therapy tool recently developed by Russell Withers, a New Zealand architect, who noticed therapeutic processes taking place in his visual consultations with clients, and developed the IDT tool for counsellors and therapists (Withers 2006). It is increasingly popular in New Zealand and Australia and, as more IDT trainers become qualified, is expanding further afield. There are similarities and differences between IDT and art therapy that deserve separate explanation. However, IDT offers an innovative, structured framework for the effective use of 'a unique page-based way of working with words, images and feelings to access different parts of the psyche' (Withers 2009: 1). The basic technique involves the client providing the content and the counsellor managing the process. The client's primary relationship is with 'the page', not the counsellor, and the counsellor assists this relationship by holding the page up, inviting the client to contemplate and add words, images or feelings to the page. It is a respectful way to work because it allows the client to dictate content and the counsellor to facilitate the process. When running introductory training, the IDT tool can be recommended to counsellors and therapists as an effective way to build on their skills in incorporating images into therapy. The IDT method teaches the therapist ways to use drawing processes therapeutically: 'The page becomes a mirror for your client, helping them see themselves more objectively from new perspectives, and facilitating insight, inner resourcefulness and profound change' (Withers 2009: 1). Therapists are taught to follow the client's lead in terms of content, regardless of what agenda the therapist might think is appropriate. As in some schools of art therapy, trusting the process is part of the mantra for the IDT method, where participants are taught not to impose themselves onto the client's material, but to work with whatever the client brings to the counselling session.

Visual diaries

Part of an ongoing personal process in art therapy training or personal therapy is the use of the visual diary (Coulter 2008). This is like a normal written diary, except that it has a visual starting point. It is therefore private and is only shown to others if the author chooses to share an entry with their therapist, clinical supervisor, or a training/tutorial or peer supervision group (see Chapter 16). However, there is no expectation that the diary must be shared – it is a safe place to process feelings freely. This agreement forms part of a contract with a workshop participant at the outset of training, as with a client in therapy (Coulter 2008). The greater the use of the visual diary as part of the workshop experience, the richer the training experience is likely to be. Entries are invited at commencement and ending of a training segment, as well as before and after specific tasks. Entries can also be made away from the workshop venue.

Any art media can be used; articles, images, poems, thoughts, quotes, jokes or any other found item that is significant to the ongoing daily diary process can be included. All entries benefit from some form of documentation because it is easy to forget thoughts pertaining to an entry, as visual work is so often a relationship with less conscious processes. As well as the date, time of day and title, documentation might include relevant thoughts and feelings, an account of some event that has happened in relationship to the entry or that triggered the entry in the first place. When reflecting back through the diary, further personal insights may be revealed and these can also be documented.

The potential use of visual diaries in clinical work is demonstrated through the workshop experience, where allied health professionals can be taught the general use of visual diaries, summarised in the six points below (see pp. 65–6, 67–8, 146 and 211–12 for further information on the use of visual diaries):

1 *Dream diary*: to record dreams visually and in writing.
2 *General visual diary*: for general use during training workshops, personal therapy or course work. This could include spontaneous diary pictures, visual journaling and group processing.
3 *Group work diary*: this is used specifically on art therapy training for art psychotherapy training groups.
4 *Supervision diary*: this is used to record responses to issues that arise in clinical supervision and also to focus specifically on transference and counter-transference material as it arises.
5 *Self-supervision*: this can help maintain the art therapist between sessions, self-monitoring and recording responses to clients and their issues.
6 *Client support*: this is used to maintain clients between sessions.

Use of visual diaries in training workshops

Participants are encouraged to use the visual diary as frequently as possible during a short training workshop to demonstrate that visual journaling is a backbone to art therapy training and best practice. A visual diary entry is often the first mark on paper a workshop participant makes.

Spontaneous diary pictures: these are quick gesture drawings that are reflective of a feeling state. Participants are encouraged to make marks without thinking too deeply, in whatever media they are inclined towards, and to work quickly, taking only two or three minutes to complete their diary entry. The instruction includes reassurance that visual diary work is private and will not be discussed. The notion of relaxing conscious concern and struggle, being willing to take risks and even to let the art materials do the thinking can all be prompts. The less conscious thinking on the participant's part, the better. It is not necessary to understand or to try to make sense of these drawings; however, spontaneous gesture drawings can be a doorway to less conscious information and accidental marks are encouraged. There is time to think and to understand content and meaning later.

Visual journaling: these entries are used later in the workshop training, usually in relation to processing and reflecting on a particular piece of work or workshop experience. There is an intention of purpose before a diary entry is drawn, and time is taken to think and plan it. This is in direct contrast to spontaneous gesture drawing entries, that rely on accidental marks and promote that less thinking is better. In the planning and execution of a journaling entry, images are visualised and words formulated. After completion of the entry, participants are encouraged to reflect on the image. They may be inspired to complete another drawing in their diary as part of this reflective journaling process. Visual journaling is also used to further process art tasks completed in the workshop content; for example, a diagram of a larger image might be recorded and documented in the diary with explanatory notes.

Group processing: These visual diary entries are focused on group reflections in relationship to art therapy training with a focus on what is difficult to verbalise in the larger group context. The visual diary provides a place of escape from difficult group processing and allows some private time in relation to the group-training context. Reflecting in the visual diary about the group experience also allows less conscious images to enter the experience of the particular group, which can also be related to other groups of which the therapist is a part.

Facilitating team building through art therapy

Corporate art therapy

Art therapy has much to offer the corporate sector, where trainers, life coaches and business mentors, often from a psychology and helping profession background, are already utilising art therapy techniques in personal training, team development and small business strategic planning. Art therapy offers the sector innovative ways to look at its operations, for example, in team-building enhancement or organisational management, and can also provide a point of referral for troubled executives who might not otherwise access therapeutic services.

Giving a presentation to the business sector: promotional packaging

In order to win a contract in the corporate sector, the art therapist needs to make a presentation portfolio. Preparing something that the therapist thinks is best for the organisation may not necessarily work; rather, being able to hear the request and design something specific to meeting that need is how a contract is negotiated and won. Sometimes, it is better to not title yourself as an 'art therapist', even though these are the skills you are utilising for the consultation. The business sector does not know what an 'art therapist' does, but they might relate to a 'creativity consultant' who delivers a creative team-building day, or a 'media motivator' who knows about symbolic use of digital and visual media, or a 'communication consultant' who has skills in exploring and improving team communication networks, and facilitating ways to self-reflect on these and to build on team knowledge.

Consider key words to use in promotional material: language becomes part of the symbolic system in which a corporate art package is approached, with therapeutic intent. Organisations will seek a trainer who is competent and insightful, who displays positive communication skills, an ability to problem solve and sensitivity in relation to specific organisational needs and requests.

Team-building

The use of art therapy in team-building is focused on delivering a positive perception of the team, who are motivated to work together. Art tasks are designed to heighten staff awareness of their assets, skills, knowledge and values as a team and to promote individual and team validation. Team-building tasks are designed to examine participants' ability to work collaboratively on joint projects and to co-operate through the communication of 'balanced messages', and working towards common goals, once these are agreed and established. A team-building task can simply offer improvement because it has a positive future focus.

Team-building has both a personal and social focus. Part of a team-building task has an individual focus, showing the creative and spontaneous assets of the individual. This builds confidence and a sense of self-validation in the context of the individual's potential contribution to the team. There can be an opportunity to develop as an individual within the team, and for increased personal autonomy and motivation in the team's best interests. Often team members have not had the freedom to make decisions, to think creatively, to experiment and to test ideas. Team-building can also assist with the expression of feelings, emotions and conflicts that may be hindering healthy team function. Art therapy, in corporate team-building, allows an opportunity to work with fantasy, and to develop a better understanding of less conscious processes that might be impacting on team productivity. Art tasks are designed to promote insight, self-awareness and reflection as participants order their visual and verbal experience.

The social focus of team-building promotes an awareness and recognition of self, as this is appreciated by others and acknowledged in the team group forum. This understanding of self in relation to others promotes communication, and the notion of a cohesive team is stimulated through art tasks that promote co-operation and provide a safe place to share. There is an experience of universality, being part of a team where co-operation with others offers social support as issues of trust are addressed and opportunities are created to work towards improving negative dynamics between staff. The use of art offers an opportunity for initial non-verbal expression, bringing great relief about issues that might be difficult to verbalise. Teams learn more about how they interact with others, which promotes interpersonal learning as old patterns are examined and reworked, and staff members are encouraged to behave more assertively and to manage issues independently.

There is joint processing as the participants' perceptions are dealt with in the context of working together to find patterns and systems, to create formulations for change, to explain and to be heard. Joint collaborative exercises focus on combining team strengths and skills, creating co-operation and something tangible to draw on with such concepts as 'wish fulfilment' in the context of the team. Working with colour, metaphor, symbol, myth and journaling in visual diaries can all contribute.

Value of art therapy

When concluding art therapy short-course training workshops, it is recommended that the art therapist provide a list of values that summarise what has been demonstrated and experienced.

The following list builds on some theoretical concepts and concretises some of the learning experiences. Art therapy:

- is an expressive outlet that utilises symbolic and metaphoric language and is therefore less threatening than more verbal forms of therapy for some clients;
- provides direct expression of inner experiences, such as dreams and fantasies, that occur as pictures rather than words;
- is usually a new experience for the individual, evoking ideas, feelings and thoughts that were previously unexpressed;
- can be task focused, thus providing a directed stimulus that helps reduce anxiety and confusion;
- provides an integrative experience, where thinking is organised around an activity that has a beginning, a working-through and an end as part of the private individual non-verbal process;
- draws on cognitive, affective and kinesthetic capacities simultaneously;
- requires active problem-solving within the limits of the various art materials;
- provides a cathartic release that is directed to and contained within a piece of art work, promoting integration and synthesis of psychopathology;
- provides an opportunity to create something that is uniquely individual;
- provides a permanent record whose content cannot be erased and whose authorship is hard to deny; the work can be reviewed at a later date and is therefore an important link to past thoughts and feelings;
- allows projections of unconscious material that escape censorship more easily than verbal expression;
- encourages individual autonomy – the maker experiences freedom and control over mark-making and learns to understand and find meaning in their art work;
- helps the therapist gain access to intra-psychic functioning otherwise inaccessible;
- heralds growth and integration before language can communicate it.

Bibliography

Betensky, M.G. 1995. *What Do You See? Phenomenology of Therapeutic Art Expression.* London: Jessica Kingsley Publishers.

Betts, D. 2006. Art Therapy Assessments and Rating Instruments: Do They Measure Up? *Arts in Psychotherapy* 33(5), 371–472.

Betts, D. 2012. Positive Art Therapy Assessment: Looking Towards Positive Psychology for New Directions in the Art Therapy Evaluation Process, in A. Gilroy, R. Tipple and C. Brown (eds) *Assessment in Art Therapy.* London: Routledge, pp. 203–18.

Cane, F. 1951. *The Artist in Each of Us.* Craftsbury Common, VT: Art Therapy.

Coulter, A. 2008. 'Came Back – Didn't Come Home': Returning from a War Zone, in M. Liebmann (ed.) *Art Therapy and Anger.* London: Jessica Kingsley Publishers, pp. 238–56.

Dalley, T., Rifkind, G. and Terry, K. 1993. *Three Voices of Art Therapy: Image, Client, Therapist.* London: Routledge

Evans, K. and Dubowski, J. 1988. *Art Therapy with Children on the Autistic Spectrum: Beyond Words.* London: Jessica Kingsley Publishers.

Gordon, R. 1985. Imagination as Mediator Between Inner and Outer Reality. *The Arts in Psychotherapy* 12, 11–15.

Hogan, S. 2001. *Healing Arts: the History of Art Therapy.* London: Jessica Kingsley Publishers.

Jung, C.G. 1964. Approaching the Unconscious, in C.G. Jung (ed.) *Man and his Symbols.* London: Aldus Books, pp. 1–94.

Junge, M.B. 1994. *A History of Art Therapy in the United States.* Alexandria, VA: American Art Therapy Association.

Keyes, M.F. 1974. *The Inward Journey: Art As Psychotherapy for You.* Millbrae, CA: Celestial Arts.

Kramer, E., Kwiatkowska, H.Y., Lachman, M., Levy, B.I., Rhyne, J. and Ulman, E. 1974. Symposium: Integration of Divergent Points of View in Art Therapy. *American Journal of Art Therapy* 14(1), 13–17.

Kwiatkowska, H.Y. 1978. *Family Therapy and Evaluation Through Art.* Springfield, IL: C.C. Thomas.

Naumburg, M. 1950. *An Introduction to Art Therapy: Studies in the 'Free' Art Expression of Behavior Problem Children and Adolescents as a Means of Diagnosis and Therapy.* New York: Columbia University, Teachers College Press.

Naumburg, M. 1966. *Dynamically-Oriented Art Therapy: Its Principles and Practice.* Chicago, IL: Magnolia Street Publishers.

Stern, D. 1985. *The Interpersonal World of the Infant.* New York: Basic Books.

Ulman, E. 1975a. Art Therapy: Problems of Definition, in E. Ulman and P. Dachinger (eds) *Art Therapy in Theory and Practice.* New York: Schocken Books, pp. 3–13.

Ulman, E. 1975b. The New Use of Art in Psychiatric Analysis, in E. Ulman and P. Dachinger (eds) *Art Therapy in Theory and Practice.* New York: Schocken Books, pp. 361–86.

Wallas, J. 1926. *The Art of Thought.* New York: Harcourt, Brace.

Waller, D. 1991. *Becoming a Profession: The History of Art Therapy in Britain 1940–82.* London: Routledge.

Winnicott, D.W. 1971a. *Playing and Reality.* London: Tavistock Publications.

Winnicott, D.W. 1971b. *Therapeutic Consultations in Child Psychiatry.* New York: Basic Books.

Withers, R. 2006. *Interactive Drawing Therapy: Working with Therapeutic Imagery.* New Zealand Journal of Counselling 26(4), 1–14.

Withers, R.W. 2009. *IDT Information Brochure.* Auckland, NZ: IDT Ltd.

Chapter 8

An overview of models of art therapy

The art therapy continuum – a useful tool for envisaging the diversity of practice in British art therapy

Susan Hogan

Introduction

This chapter aims to provide a comprehensible and accessible overview of British art therapy practice. It is a 'snap-shot' of the main styles of art therapy. It presents an outline of theory in the form of a continuum which illustrates the range of art therapy practice that is available in Britain today. Although the focus is on British practice, the model is applicable to other settings. A longer continuum might appear in North America or Canada, for example, where attempts are made to use images for diagnostic purposes, but this chapter is an outline of the main range of art therapy practices within Britain.

I continue to be amazed at the strength of feeling that this chapter, originally a paper in *The International Journal of Art Therapy: Inscape*, continues to generate. A number of critical readers and students have remarked that they have found it helpful in helping them think about where they stand (though I have to say that was not primarily my intention).

The layout of the diagram is not intended to illustrate a hierarchy or judgements about what I considered to be superior. It could be depicted in a horse-shoe shape. The theory which informs these different practices varies. My motivation for the development of the continuum is to assist in providing some clarity to a situation which, at first sight, particularly to training therapists but also to art therapists in general, seems extremely confusing (and there are some real points of confusion, especially the diversity of ways in which the term 'analytic' is used in literature).

Art therapy today is rather complex and 'the art therapy continuum', as I shall henceforth refer to it, is an attempt to give an at-a-glance picture or 'snap-shot' of this diversity. Like any snap-shot it does not reveal the entire landscape. Of course, there may well be nude art therapy being offered somewhere in California for all I know! I have certainly come across a small minority of North American art therapists combining art therapy with other practices, such as the dubious use of so-called 'healing crystals', but my intention here is to discuss what most art therapists are doing in Britain, to help to make it more accessible, rather than looking at what might be happening on the outermost fringes with respect to practices of which most of us would prefer to utterly dissociate ourselves.

Furthermore, there may be some models of practice which don't quite fit comfortably into one of the niches described but straddle one or more, using different elements of each. The framework isn't completely 'neat'. It is, I hope, conceptually useful though.

Many of us may use more than one type of art therapy practice depending on context, time frame, client group and brief. The ability to be flexible about the model to be employed may, arguably, have advantages in the range of work we are able to undertake.

The idea of a continuum implies both a range of differences and a continuity of relationships. For instance, in a rainbow every colour is a colour of light, but the wavelength of each colour is different. In this continuum the shared characteristic is the production of art work, but precisely how this is conceptualised and managed varies throughout the continuum, as will be illustrated.

A

Art as an adjunct to verbal psychotherapy – including a 'gestalt' style of art therapy.
(The emphasis is not on the pictorial quality of the art work or analysis of its making, but more as a cue for verbal psychotherapy.)

B

Analytic art therapy – art therapy which has an emphasis on the 'transference relationship' between client and therapist.
(This is often dubbed as 'analytic' though it is psychoanalytic in origin.)

C

The group-interactive approach – art therapy which is interested in interpersonal experiential learning and works with all aspects in a group 'interactive' approach.
(Including an analysis of the manner in which it is produced, what the clients wish to say about it and what clients say to each other and how they interact. This may include cognisance of 'transference relationships', but the latter is not the main emphasis.)

D

The individual in the group – art therapy concentrated on the personal support of the individual in the group.
(This approach gives equal emphasis to the art work, including an analysis of the manner in which is produced and what the clients wish to say about it, but does not attempt to work with group psychodynamics.)

E

Art therapy which has its emphasis on the production of the art work and verbal analysis of it.

(This may include an analysis of the manner in which it is produced: the materiality of the piece, emotions generated during different phases of production, the evolution of the art work. The work may be worked on over a period of time, rather than fresh art works being produced in each session.)

F

Aesthetically orientated art therapy – art therapy which privileges the art in art therapy with minimal verbal analysis.

(The production of art works as a container for strong emotions, which are then assimilated by the client without verbal analysis. The art therapist provides a 'holding' environment, acts as a 'witness' to the process and may offer encouragement in the course of production.)

A: Art as an adjunct to verbal psychotherapy

Using images as an adjunct to verbal psychotherapy is a perfectly reasonable technique employed by a minority of practising art therapists, or art psychotherapists depending on their nomenclature of choice. I shall use 'art therapy' as the generic term, as there are not clearly defined and consistently used established differences between the terms 'art therapy' and 'art psychotherapy'.

Art therapy may be used as an adjunct or aid – what do I mean by this? Well, the image is used in the context of a primarily verbal exchange. Therapy is underway and a point may be reached in which the therapist feels the client is getting 'blocked' or inhibited. But this is not cathartic paint-splashing being advocated, but a focused use of imagery we are talking about here.

In the 'gestalt' model, a parallel can be drawn with the use of drama therapy where it is not uncommon for a technique called the 'empty chair technique' to be used, which has been attributed to Moreno and Pearls and popularised by Landy (1994), amongst others. An empty chair is placed in front of the therapist. The therapist asks the client to imagine that their mother/father/abuser/sibling is sitting in the empty chair and invites the client to tell them what they would like to say: 'I always loved you','I hate you' or 'you abused me as a child' – whatever they need to say. Then they can change chairs and imagine they are the mother/father/abuser/sibling and talk directly to themselves as the other person. Such drama therapy techniques are widely used.

Similarly, images can be used to stimulate such discourse. As John Birtchnell puts it:

> Talking to the picture, particularly in the here and now, is the most powerful devise I know...

(Birtchnell 1998: 149)

'Draw your mother/father/abuser/sibling', a therapist such as John Birtchnell might instruct. 'Now draw a phone. Now imagine you are picking up the receiver and tell them what you'd like to say to him...' That's what I mean by art as an adjunct to verbal psychotherapy. It's essentially a psychotherapy which employs drama therapy methods into which image-making is then incorporated.

The art work in the gestalt approach is usually a brief sketch rather than an involved piece aesthetically. As Birtchnell (2003) says:

> There is a useful parallel between the therapy that I do (Birtchnell, 1998) and psychodrama (Moreno, 1972). What I do has little to do with art and requires no artistic ability, just as psychodrama has little to do with drama and requires no acting ability (Birtchnell, 2002b). When I do this kind of therapy with trained artists, as I sometimes do, their visual productions are no reflection of their artistic ability and they do not look like works of art. In fact they are not works of art. The relationship between what I do and conventional art therapy is similar to the relationship between psychodrama and drama therapy....

The emphasis is on the client expressing themselves, and the image provides a supplementary text, an alternative discourse to that which is spoken. This approach is not interested in the aesthetic aspects of art making:

> ... the patient depicts, or enacts, his or her own personal reality. It is not original, imaginative, fictitious or creative. That is not the point of it. The point is to complement [via the process of making art work] what she is saying, to convey in visual terms what it is like to be herself, what her relationships to certain relevant others feel like, to clarify these things for the therapist and for herself, to get in touch with them and to help her and the therapist make sense of them. I, just like the psycho-dramatist, do not want the patient to create anything. Creativity is not what therapy is about. Intentionally, I do not give the patient time to create a work of art...
>
> (Birtchnell 2003)

As we will see later, this approach is rather different to those which are particularly interested in focusing of the aesthetic aspects on the art-making process. Birtchnell often works in a fairly intensive way with one individual in the group, with the other group members in a supportive role. He will encourage the person under focus to make a succession of images, but also to continue talking. Towards the end of a period of intensive focus on one person, the facilitator may become very directive and this can provoke an intense emotional outpouring. Birtchnell explains this approach:

> An extremely valuable Gestalt technique is to invite the person to address his or her remarks to whomever they should actually be directed at. This is much more emotional than telling the therapist.... Similarly, in art therapy,

a woman may be drawing her husband, and saying as she draws, 'He's a bully.' I say, 'Tell him.' She looks at me strangely. I explain, 'Look at the drawing and imagine it really is him and just talk to him.... Perhaps, as a way of escaping from this confrontation, she may revert to talking to me, and say, 'He used to lock me in our bedroom.' I correct her by saying, '*You* used to'. She turns back to the drawing and says to it, 'You used to lock me in our bedroom', and then continues to talk to her husband about that.... Adopting a here and now approach would involve my saying – 'Draw the bedroom from above. Put yourself inside and him outside. Imagine it is now, and tell him what you are feeling now.' She then begins to talk in the present tense. The whole scene feels horribly real. She is shaking and pleading with him to let her out.

(Birchnell 1998: 148–9)

Because other group members may have resonated with aspects of the story which has just been told, the focus then returns to the group members as a whole, who are then given an opportunity to express their feelings about the disclosure made and to explore their emotions triggered by it. The focus of attention returns to the group as a whole, before the process of working intensively with an individual may recommence.

Some art therapists might usually use a different way or 'model' of working but occasionally employ such techniques.

B: Analytic art therapy

The term 'analytic' is being used here in a generic way to indicate all approaches which are particularly concerned with working with 'transference', but which also have art on offer. I think because of the current situation being rather 'blurry' in regard to terminology (as a colleague of mine put it), it is best to assume that 'analytic' could mean informed by either psychoanalytic thought or by analytical psychology, but in either case the therapist will be working with the idea of 'transference' (historically, 'analytic' tended to be used to mean Jungian and 'psychoanalytic' Freudian, but this distinction is often no longer maintained, and many 'analytic' practitioners are psychoanalytic in orientation). What is the transference relationship? We should all know from our training that this is the displacement of feelings to do with other previous or current figures in the client's life onto their therapist, resulting in the client relating to the therapist as if they were that person; in other words, the projection of attributes of the other person onto the therapist by which the therapist is endowed with the significance of the other, which then becomes an important part of the therapy. The 'object representations' are what the client can project and are explored as a central part of the therapeutic process (Rycroft 1968: 168).

It is not my intention to examine claims about the superiority of this model of working. Joy Schaverien discussed the 'transference within the transference' in her work (that is, put simply, the client's transference to the art object contained within the transference relationship with the therapist). This is an acknowledgement of the multi-levelled nature of both one-to-one and group work in which there may be both 'projections' to the therapist *and* the art object. The projective field, if I may use this term, can become quite complex (especially in group work) and ultimately ambiguous and difficult to work with. However, it is not my intention to provide a critique here: instead, I wish to focus on distinguishing between different styles of art therapy. I will permit Joy Schaverien to describe her approach in her own words, thus:

> Analytical art psychotherapy is the term I use to distinguish the type of art therapy where analysis of the transference is parallel with the analytical differentiation which comes about through the picture. This form of art therapy is composed of two, linked strands; it is both a transference to *the person of the therapist*, and a transference to the *picture*. These threads of the transference both have their complement in separate, but linked, strands of countertransference.
>
> (Schaverien 1990: 15; my/original emphasis)

Her notion of the transference being in 'strands' or in some way split caused some argument, because most analytic therapists see transference as projected into the total therapeutic environment. Consequently, her ideas were strongly criticised:

> Transference will be made to the person of the therapist, his/her furniture, the therapist's family, their training, the room, the painting, the institution etc. That is the reason why the idea of 'transference within the transference' is so confusing suggesting as it does that there is something separate to or different from the total transference situation. The painting is indivisible from the total transference and can be fully understood only in that context. There is just one transference where the focus may shift from the person of the therapist to the painting and move back and forth from there. The transference to the painting is therefore not something within, or different to, or parallel to, or in addition to the transference to the whole analytic setting. There are not two transferences.
>
> (Mann 1990: 33–4)

Consequently, her distinction between 'art psychotherapy', in which the client–therapist axis 'is the main focus', and 'analytic art psychotherapy', in which 'the dynamic field is fully activated', is a slightly problematic distinction and potentially confusing (Schaverien 2000: 61). It is therefore not a term I shall be using.

Regarding transference, it is quite possible to use a different 'model' of art therapy but then suddenly to become aware of a client's projection of emotions to do with another person onto oneself, and to work with such feelings in a constructive way. We *feel* other people's emotions; sometimes we can even feel engulfed by them. Whitaker (1985: 221) notes of his group work that 'sometimes a person is carried into the realms of usually avoided feeling through processes of [emotional] contagion.' Interestingly, Tolstoy's definition of art also speaks of 'contagion' and if we were to accept this definition of art, then we must accept that there must be a 'transferential' aspect throughout the continuum:

> Art is a human activity consisting in this, that one man consciously, by means of external signs, hands on to others feelings he has lived through, and that others *are infected by these feelings and also experience them.*
>
> (cited Harris 1996: 2; my emphasis)

Skaife suggests that analytic art therapy groups tend to view art works as 'primarily a reflection of group processes' (2000: 116) and that there is often a tension between image making and the verbal interaction that surrounds it (2000: 115). Although, art work as a reflection of group processes can be:

> … helpful in expanding the material in the group and in holding and containing strong feelings in symbol and metaphor, it can leave other aspects of art-making unexplored for their therapeutic potential. These are essentially about the aesthetic aspects of art making…
>
> (2000: 116)

Skaife's remarks apply equally well to the next model of art therapy where a tension between verbal and visual aspects of the group's processes can also exist. It is a question of emphasis: some therapists may feel that the transference relationship is at the very heart of their art therapy practice and this is the particular distinguishing feature of what I am calling 'analytic art therapy'.

C: The group-interactive approach

The group-interactive approach (described by Waller 1991) is an example of a model of art therapy which gives emphasis to the art work (including an analysis of the manner in which is produced), what the clients wish to say about it and what clients say to each other. This may include cognisance of 'transference relationships'. Group interactive groups may be *more or less* 'analytic' and may vary in emphasis regarding their focus on the individual *in* the group. Subtle differences of emphasis notwithstanding, some art therapists will want to try to work with *all* elements and regard this as a real challenge. As Skaife and Huet have pointed out, there is simply *'too much material'* being generated in such groups, causing tensions between different elements and requiring the facilitator to make choices about what they wish to emphasise (1998: 17):

> … one person's contribution to the group process in terms of their image may spark off a substantial amount of verbal group interactive material. The

dilemma is, will the focus stay with the images, or will the images be used as a spring-board for further interactive work? There never seems to be enough time for both.

(1998: 28)

The basic idea behind the group-interactive approach is that during interactions with others in the group, individuals reveal their 'characteristic patterns of interaction'; these are seen as constraining people in their everyday lives (Waller 1993: 23). These 'patterns of interaction' are acknowledged and reflected upon and provide a focus for group analysis. Therefore, the method employed involves an analysis of clients' here-and-now behaviour in the group. This is not a simple discussion of clients' issues so much as a *revelation* of their present constraints. Such constraints, or habitual ways of being and thinking, can be *revealed* through interactions with other members of the group or depicted in art works. Furthermore, the art works can represent aspects of the client's self or other 'objects' (in other words, be used for the projection and containment of transference emotions – see above regarding 'object representations').

'Feedback' from participants is an important part of this method: 'feedback from members of the group illuminates aspects of self which have become obvious to others but which are not recognised by oneself' (Waller 1991: 23). Feedback which does not seem justified is challenged and its impetus explored. Indeed, as Waller points out, 'the members' tendency to distort their perceptions of others (parataxic distortions) provides valuable material for the group to work on' (Waller 1991: 24).

The theory underpinning this method is particularly influenced by Stack Sullivan (1953), Foulkes (1948) and Yalom (1975), who regard interactions with 'significant others' as more important to the aetiology of disease than early childhood experiences, and indeed, personality is seen in a constant state of flux, rather than laid down in early childhood (Waller 1991: 22). These ideas draw on symbolic-interactionist thought:

> People create and continually re-create themselves in contact with others; indeed, the self *is* ultimately a process.
>
> (Alvesson and Skoldberg 2000: 4)

Philosophically this method is rather different to those which see the aetiology of disease as laid down in early childhood, and it is arguably more in keeping with post-structuralist developments in psychology and the social sciences.

The group-interactive method is very mobile and multi-levelled, so the focus can move from an exchange between participants to analysis of an art work, to a reflection on feelings evoked by a disclosure by an individual, to an analysis of feelings experienced by a participant during the production of an art work, back to an analysis of an exchange between two members and so forth. Group dynamics are reflected upon as part of the therapeutic process. Individuals may also project emotions onto the group as a whole which may be experienced, momentarily, as an individual. The result is very dynamic and rich.

Some of the interactive elements of the group are evident in this trainee art therapist's analysis of his experience:

> ... following her disclosure of childhood sexual abuse.... I made an image it was hoped would represent what it felt like – as a man – to be in this group. These were anger and rage at power abused by men, generalised guilt for being a man, hopelessness and helplessness that threatened becoming overwhelming depression and fear that my desire for affection would destroy me and the group. These feelings and ideas came together in the image of the bull.... The articulation of anger seemed to give permission to others to express their own anger. It is added to the increasing level of honest interpersonal disclosure and feedback....
>
> (This quotation was reproduced with kind permission
> from the student, now a practising art therapist)

D: The individual in the group

Art support groups and art studio groups are two types of art therapy groups which include analysis of verbal disclosures and analysis of art works but don't always work in an intentional way with group psychodynamics. The individual in the group is the emphasis.

Edward Adamson's original studio, which he described in *Art as Healing,* had participants working individually on artists' donkeys or easels but not coming together at any point to talk together in a group. Adamson had a relationship with each individual and talked to each about their art work in turn (Hogan 2001).

However, some groups, which do not include an analysis of group psychodynamics as their focus, do allow participants to talk about their work as a group: typically this will involve taking turns and encouraging respectful listening by participants of other participants' disclosures (a common 'ground rule' might be not interrupting others while they are talking). One participant may be moved to remark upon another's art work or disclosure, but unlike in the group-interactive model (above), this exchange does not then become the focus of the group's prolonged attention. Perhaps the person talking about an art work will thank the other person or disagree with their remarks, but the focus quickly returns to the person whose turn it is to speak, and to the art work under discussion. (Being allowed to disagree with an interpretative remark made by another participant which 'feels wrong' might be another 'ground rule' established at the outset. See Liebmann 2004 for more on 'ground rules'.) Turn taking is not necessarily a feature of this model, but the point is that an analysis of transference reactions between members, or other interactive features, is *not* the main focus of the group, which is more interested in understanding the art works produced, the analysis of which may be extremely sophisticated. I am not depreciating this model of working.

Art therapy support groups work well, for example, with clients who all have the same presenting issue: all have had a recent bereavement, for example, or all are being treated for cancer. So although the group is not focused on an analysis of group interaction, being with people who you feel truly understand what you are experiencing can feel very powerful for participants; thus, 'empathy' is an important, probably remedial, feature. (Of course, similar presenting features can occur in other types of group so I am not suggesting it as necessarily unique to this model.)

Like in other approaches, it may be the case that sometimes a group interaction is so forceful and dominating that it *has to* become the focus of the group's attention, in order for it to be dealt with so that the group can return its focus to the images and discourse about them. For example, if one participant is rude to another the matter would simply have to be thrashed-out and resolved, which might involve an exploration of possible projection and transference (or analysis of what *pattern* of behaviour the person might be indulging in). The safety of the group being threatened in this way might also cause group members to project fears onto the group as an entity, and an exploration of these feelings could shift the focus of the group's attention temporarily away from analysis of the art works.

Those therapists who do not work with a concept of 'transference', or do not wish to work with group dynamics in an interactive manner, notably Rogerian or 'person-centred' oriented art therapists, would attempt to resolve safety issues differently, perhaps by re-stating the 'ground rules' established at the beginning of the group, rather than delving into psychological aspects of the exchange (see the work of Silverstone (1997) for an example of a 'person-centred' art therapy).

E and F: Art therapy which has its emphasis on the production of the art work and verbal analysis of it and aesthetically orientated art therapy – art therapy which privileges the art in art therapy with minimal verbal analysis

At the other end of the art therapy continuum is art therapy which has its emphasis on the production of the art work (this may include an analysis of the manner in which it is produced: the materiality of the piece, emotions generated during different phases of production and the evolution of the art work). The work may be worked on over a period of time, rather than fresh art works being produced in each session, so that the emphasis is on change generated by responses to the art object, the evolution of the art work and corresponding emotional reactions; or, new works may be produced in response to the image in an ongoing emotional process.

Working on one piece of art work for more than one session is, needless to say, also possible in other models, including in group-interactive groups. Skaife and Huet identify some of the problems identified with making brief works in a group-interactive group (described above):

The time the group allows for art making is just about enough time for the initial setting out of the visual idea, or for finding of the visual idea. At the point at which the artist needs to look at what she has done and think about it aesthetically, they stop. This means the art work is never pushed into the next stage. It appears that in response to the group process, symbols and metaphors can be released through spontaneous art-making which then come to be seen as a reflection of the group process. They can extend the group process helping to focus the group on important issues... *but clients do not have the space to fully engage in the creative process of, for example, putting the idea down, pushing it on, losing it and moving into chaos, and then finding it again in a renewed form. [This is a] creative process which is a microcosm of life itself, and so useful therapeutic material.*

(1998: 27; my emphasis)

As we can see from the above quotation, there are advantages to being able to spend more time concentrating on working with the art materials to explore emotional material: this is what Skaife refers to as the 'aesthetic aspects of art making' which can sometimes get lost in other more verbally-oriented models of working (2000: 116).

It may be that, at this end of the continuum, the time spent discussing the art works produced is relatively brief, or that no analysis of the art work takes place at all. In E there may be ongoing in-depth conversation, and in F very little.

As one of the people critiquing this paper pointed out, in art therapy there is not always an 'other', be it an interlocutor, therapist, critic, friend or fellow spectator: 'I think primarily, communication in art is with the self and with the art process and its subject matter. This is also where communication in art therapy begins' (Gunn 2007). This is a key point, as it is what *all* these different approaches have in common. Despite very different ways of working and structuring the experience, this is a feature throughout the continuum, though it may be rather limited in A. This is what makes *all* these approaches *art therapy*.

At the end of the continuum (in F) would be located approaches in which little or no verbal exchange took place about the art works. Michael Edwards, describing his early work at Withymead, a tremendously influential 'Jungian' arts-based therapeutic community, recounted that therapists there were seen as 'facilitating a process' which involved a policy of 'non-interference', a standing back and allowing emotions to surface at their own pace (cited by Hogan 200: 245). As another art therapist who had worked at Withymead explained, through painting the 'individual can experience personally the *natural* balance and autonomy of the self-regulating power of the psyche' (Godfrey, cited Hogan 2001: 245). As Godfrey put it, 'the core of meaning in healing through artistic expression lies in experiencing spiritual values'; painting was viewed as a means to achieving a *natural* healing process, hence the very concept of art *as* therapy (see Hogan 2001 for a detailed analysis of this way of working).

Of course, there may be aspects of 'witnessing' and 'holding' in other models of art therapy, and it is not my intention to suggest an absolutely clear-cut division between these ways of working, but rather a shift in emphasis, which may also be underpinned with different theoretical ideas.

Discussion

My feeling is that all of these techniques have their particular strengths and weaknesses and that flexibility on the part of the therapist is advantageous. It is possible that having a particular focus on any one aspect of art therapy may blind us to other aspects. Perhaps 'blind' is too strong: perhaps we merely maintain a focus and the expense of working with other possible elements. As Skaife puts it above, there is simply *too much material*.

When I do short-term work with women, using art therapy as a support tool to enable them to explore their changed sense of self-identity as a result of pregnancy and motherhood, I would locate the practice mainly in D.

When I am training art therapists, facilitating their in-depth closed group work, I am working mainly with C, with the group-interactive model being taught (however, there can be movement up and down the continuum – with A moments – moments in which the art work functions very much as an adjunct to verbal psychotherapy, through to F moments – moments in which the group is silent and contemplative, immersed in the mood-tone of an art work). When I teach a workshop-based introduction to art therapy I'm located mainly in D again, but I'd hope to create some time where in-depth reflection on aesthetic aspects might form part of this (taking participants into E and F). When I do in-depth clinical work I'm working in B and C (or on the cusp of B and mainly within C, if I think about it carefully). In fact, all my work normally straddles B to D and I do not work consistently at either of the ends of the continuum. This is because of personal preferences, as well as the nature of the participants. I feel slightly uncomfortable with facilitating interventionist drama therapy-style techniques used in conjunction with art-making. I have used some A methods in the past. Nowadays, I might very, very rarely use an A technique with a client who feels exceptionally stuck. As a participant, I have gained a lot from such groups so whilst I can see the benefit of this way of working, it is not a model in which I feel I can generally employ myself. We probably all have, or develop, an intuitive sense of where we feel most comfortable on the continuum (and I *do* think personal proclivity is to some extent at play here). Likewise, I can't work entirely in F because I enjoy verbal analysis and interactive group work, but that is not to depreciate the powerful work that can be achieved by those so inclined to work in this manner (and there are elements of F in the other models in which the non-verbal assimilation of a powerful image is a component). I also enjoy working *analytically* (as opposed to being situated within the analytic model).

I feel that there has been some divisive theorising in recent years, which has described different models of art therapy in an *oppositional* way. The continuum does *not* invite practitioners to locate themselves in one spot and then to defend their patch. It is not intended to set up false and erroneous divisions. Rather, movement through the continuum is possible. The continuum is a fluid way of conceptualising art therapy practice: it depicts practitioners as potentially *not* locked into a particular way of working, though some people may well only work in one way because of personal preferences and particular aptitudes.

I am very verbal, and perhaps when I am noticing and reiterating what someone has said, I am missing something else – the paint dripping down the side of a 3D piece. As I said earlier, perhaps we maintain a focus on one aspect at the expense of another. Often we see more happening in groups than we can possibly respond to: simultaneously we see the paint-dripping forming a suggestive pool on the floor; we see her gesture at him; we see someone else respond to the gesture; two people are trying to talk at once; someone else sighs; we are filled with a particular emotion generated by an art work or a previous disclosure. Which of the many possible elements occurring simultaneously we instantaneously choose to respond to will depend on our emphasis, our place in the continuum – surely? *After all, our responses cannot be infinitely multi-faceted.* Groups are, as has been noted, very complex, and are multi-dimensional; as has been discussed, movement from one focus to another can sometimes be very rapid. For those using an interactive model, there are a wealth of para-linguistic features which may be remarked upon (the eye contact, body language, etc.), as well as important prosodic features (pitch, tone, intonation, stress and so forth); working with these potentially important elements may mean that some aspect of the art work is overlooked.

Sometimes the aesthetic aspect forces itself to the fore: a woman from a former war zone says, 'I feel like I'm covered with blood', her arms outstretched, like those of Macbeth, are covered in red pastel. The art materials have a power of their own to unlock deep feelings.

To repeat, it is not my intention to suggest an absolutely clear-cut division between these ways of working, but rather a shift in emphasis, which may *also* be underpinned with different theoretical ideas.

Areas of conflict and natural tension within the continuum

The areas of natural tension are located at the 'ends' of the continuum: A and F are not best friends. Indeed, they may be anathema to each other.

The first model which uses art as an adjunct to verbal psychotherapy (A) is sometimes very directive and such intrusive directives are the very antithesis of the 'natural' and 'intuitive''healing process' of art-making promoted by many Fs. Some Fs might argue that the assimilation of aesthetic qualities through interaction with the art materials is at the very heart of art therapy (note Gunn's remark earlier) and that what As are doing is not actually art therapy at all.

I would just ask practitioners to note that both models are useful and to respect their differences, without making claims that one model is more efficacious than another (for which there is no real evidence, as yet).

Where is feminist art therapy you might ask? The answer is anywhere throughout the continuum; again, it is, I would suggest, a matter of emphasis and awareness: of privileging certain elements over others.

I have discussed areas of natural tension within the continuum. The continuum is, unfortunately, not a conflict-free way of conceptualising art therapy practice. Conceivably, there is scope for argument within A about precisely how directive to be.

There is plenty of scope in B for different analytical theories to compete with each other; for example, the Kleinians might disagree with the Freudians, and so forth. In C there might be divergence of opinion, for example, about how much work with transference should be undertaken, or whether transference is a valid concept at all. In D there could be disagreement about how to handle interactive elements. In E and F there might be disagreement about the role of the therapist and whether verbal analysis is necessary or useful. So *within* each model there is scope for disagreement.

There is also some scope for disagreement *between* models. There may be some tension between A and B, because the first is very directive and the second would tend towards being non-directive, or those in A might find some Bs' practice of furnishing interpretations of transference unacceptable, or those in B might view the role of the therapist in A as intrusive.

There might be tension between B and C in terms of oppositional explanatory schemas (the universal versus the particular) and theories of the aetiology of illness (individual pathology originating from early in infancy, versus socially-conditioned and socially-generated responses formed during social interaction in an ongoing way), as well as different ideas arising from these ideas about what is actually curative. Indeed, there may be disagreement about what the 'self' actually is, based on these different philosophical positions.

Some F-inclined art therapists might also be suspicious of some analytic (B) work and might regard psychoanalytically-inclined practitioners who employ art and subsume it into their discourse to be ignoring vital aesthetic aspects – indeed, what they regard as the very heart of art therapy: they might view such art therapists as having an insufficient understanding of art processes. Nevertheless, though potential for conflict can be found, I feel the continuum is a *less divisive* way of conceptualising the totality of practice. I have found some of the assertions made about differences between 'art therapists' and 'art psychotherapists' irksome; this emphasis on nomenclature really is a red herring, as many 'art therapists' and 'art psychotherapists' are doing the same thing at different points of the continuum.

There are aspects of art therapy practice which I would like to critique and condemn, but that is not the purpose of this particular piece of writing (see Hogan 1997 and 2011 for some trenchant criticisms of reductive theorising and discussion of problematic work with transference, especially on misinterpretations of transference caused by the therapist's dogmatic adherence to a particular theory – what I have called 'psychic abuse').

My motivation for the development of the continuum was to help to add some clarity to a situation which, at first sight, particularly to training therapists but also to many practitioners, seems extremely confusing. I hope it is useful.

Conclusion

The continuum is intended to give a relatively non-judgemental 'snap-shot' of the rich diversity of practice which constitutes art therapy today. Hopefully, we can all move about in the continuum, if we wish, depending on what seems most appropriate in terms of our particular client's needs.

Perhaps the main value of this chapter will be, as Gunn put it, to 'stimulate question, discussion and argument'!

Suggested further reading

Hogan, S. 2014. *Art Therapy Theories*. London: Routledge.

Bibliography

Adamson, E. 1990. *Art as Healing*. London: Conventure.

Alvesson, M. and Skoldberg, K. 2000. *Reflexive Methodology: New Vistas for Qualitative Research*. London: Sage.

Birtchnell, J. 1998. The Gestalt Art Therapy Approach to Family and Other Interpersonal Problems, in D. Sandle (ed.) *Development and Diversity*. London: Free Association Press, pp. 142–53.

Birtchnell, J. 2003. The Visual and the Verbal in Art Therapy. *International Arts Therapies Journal* 2 (online).

Gilroy, A. and McNeilly, G. 2000. *The Changing Shape of Art Therapy: New Developments in Theory and Practice*. London: Jessica Kingsley Publishers.

Gunn, M, 2007. Personal correspondence, 21 February.

Foulkes, S. 1948. *Introduction to Group-Analytic Psychotherapy*. London: Maresfield Reprints.

Harris, R. 1996. *Signs, Language and Communication*. London: Routledge.

Hogan, S. (ed.) 1997. *Feminist Approaches to Art Therapy*. London: Routledge.

Hogan, S. 2001. *Healing Arts: The History of Art Therapy*. London: Jessica Kingsley Publishers.

Hogan, S. (ed.) 2003. *Gender Issues in Art Therapy*. London: Jessica Kingsley Publishers.

Hogan, S. 2011. Postmodernist but Not Postfeminist! A Feminist Postmodernist Approach to Working with New Mothers, in H. Burt (ed.) *Art Therapy and Postmodernism: Creative Healing Through a Prism*. London: Jessica Kingsley Publishers, pp. 70–82.

Landy, R. 1994. *Dramatherapy: Concepts, Theories, and Practices*. Second edition. Springfield, IL: Charles C. Thomas.

Liebmann, M. 2004. *Art Therapy for Groups: a Handbook of Themes and Exercises*. Second edition. London: Jessica Kingsley Publishers.

Mann, D. 1990. Some Further Thoughts on Projective Identification in Art Therapy: a Partial Reply to Joy Schaverien. *Journal of the British Association of Art Therapists* Winter 1990, 33–4.

Rycroft, C. 1968. *A Critical Dictionary of Psychoanalysis*. London: Thomas Nelson and Sons.

Schaverien, J. 1987. The Scapegoat and the Talisman: Transference in Art Therapy, in T. Dalley, C. Case, J. Schaverien, F. Weir, D. Halliday, P.N. Hall and D. Waller (eds)

Images of Art Therapy: New Developments in Theory and Practice. London: Tavistock, pp. 74–108.

Schaverien, J. 1990. Triangular Relationship (2): Desire Alchemy and the Picture. *Inscape. The Journal of the British Association of Art Therapists* Winter 1990, 14–19.

Schaverien, J. 1992. *The Revealing Image: Analytical Art Psychotherapy in Theory and Practice*. London: Routledge.

Schaverien, J. 2000. The Triangular Relationship and the Aesthetic Countertransference in Analytical Art Psychotherapy, in A. Gilroy and G. McNeilly (eds) *The Changing Shape of Art Therapy: New Developments in Theory and Practice*. London: Jessica Kingsley Publishers, pp. 55–83.

Silverstone, L. 1997. *Art Therapy: The Person-Centred Way*. London. Jessica Kingsley Publishers.

Skaife, S. 2000. Keeping the Balance: Further Thoughts on the Dialectics of Art Therapy, in A. Gilroy and G. McNeilly (eds) *The Changing Shape of Art Therapy: New Developments in Theory and Practice*. London: Jessica Kingsley Publishers, pp. 55–83.

Skaife, S. and Huet, V. 1998. Dissonance and Harmony: Theoretical Issues in Art Psychotherapy Groups, in S. Skaife and V. Huet (eds) *Art Psychotherapy Groups: Between Pictures and Words*. London: Routledge, pp. 17–43.

Stack Sullivan, H. 1953. *The Interpersonal Theory of Psychiatry*. New York: Norton.

Waller, D. 1991. *Becoming a Profession: The History of Art Therapy in Britain 1940–1982*. London: Routledge.

Waller, D. 1993. *Group-Interactive Art Therapy*. London: Routledge.

Whitaker, D.S. 1985. *Using Groups to Help People*. London: Routledge.

Yalom, I.D. 1975. *The Theory and Practice of Group Psychotherapy*. Second edition. New York: Basic Books.

Yalom, I.D. 1983. *In-Patient Group Psychotherapy*. New York: Basic Books.

Chapter 9

The role of the image in art therapy and intercultural reflections

Working as an art therapist with diverse groups

Susan Hogan

Responding to art work in art therapy

The art produced in art therapy has already been discussed in previous chapters, the role of symbolism and metaphor elucidated, and a variety of themes and their potential discussed in detail. In the last chapter it was made evident that different models of art therapy have implications for how the art work may be approached.

This chapter will reflect in further detail on aesthetics and issues of interpretation. Art therapy trainees are asked to hold on to their interpretations and to remain as open as possible to other possible ways of understanding the therapeutic encounter to avoid premature foreclosure of meanings. On the simplest level, art therapists practise asking open rather than closed questions:

> 'That letter box is in the street', says the inexperienced trainee, to which the disgruntled client responds, 'It's a double-decker bus, not a letter box!'

Of course every act of understanding and every formulated question has an interpretive element. Why do I ask my client about the red mark rather than the black streak? Perhaps one feels more insistent to me, and I have indulged in an act of interpretation in getting to that point of formulating the question (Hogan and Pink 2010; Hogan 2011).

Art therapists will help facilitate their clients in thinking about their art work in slightly different ways (depending on which model of working they are using), largely by asking open questions, such as, 'Would you like to tell me about what's happening?' or pointing out specific elements, like 'How do you feel about the river?' or even employing speculative questions, such as, 'Where is this bird flying to?' There is also a technique called 'amplification', which developed out of Carl Jung's work, and this might include asking the bird depicted how it feels, and thus entering imaginatively into the pictorial schema. Yet another technique is a 'gestalt' one, in which a character depicted might be talked to as if present in the room, as elaborated in the previous chapter.

As will also be explored in further depth, the process of making the work may be queried, or commented on: 'I noticed that you tore up your first drawing and then cellotaped the pieces back together again – what were you feeling when you did this?' Or, with reference to a 3D piece: 'How did you feel when it collapsed?' Not all art therapists do this, and trained art therapists should not indulge in telling their clients what they think their art work means, based on a particular psychological theory. It is the art therapy participant who is active in the interpretation of the work, *not the therapist,* whose role is primarily a facilitative one. I say 'primarily', because in the group-interactive model, group dynamics may be elucidated by the art therapist (preferably not in such a dogmatic way that their perception can't be scrutinised, embellished or questioned, but with a view to enabling participants to reflect on events); furthermore, in ongoing one-to-one therapy, the art therapist may point out what she sees as patterns of behaviour or emerging themes, to help her client to perceive these. For example, a client may have said that he felt dizzy and sick on the way back from his latest visit to his father. The therapist might see a pattern and reflect on it: 'You were physically unwell following your last three visits to your father, are you aware of that?' Such observations must be handled with care, and sparingly; there will be more on the nuances of this later. However, pointing out recurring psychological patterns in an *analytical* manner is legitimate and helpful; this could even include reflections on body language: 'When you talk about your workplace, you hug yourself like this – what are you feeling when you do this?' is a question an art therapist might ask.

The role of the image in art therapy and thinking critically about interpretation

Gestalt art psychotherapy

In the gestalt model of working, which was outlined in the previous chapter, the aesthetic qualities of the art work are not to the fore, and diagrammatic images, quickly produced, may often be made. As was articulated, the therapist in this model may become directive and instruct the participant to sketch this or that. As Birtchnell (2003) points out, he does not give his participants enough time to create a 'work of art'. However, visual elements can intrude at any juncture, and a client with red paint or chalk on his hands might say, 'This feels like his blood' – arguably a very gestalt moment! The art works in this approach are seldom reworked and may be disposed of at the end of each session, rather than kept as an ongoing reference. Many brief works may be produced and tossed aside as the dialogue moves on.

(Psycho)analytic art therapy

Terminology is used in different ways by different authors, but I am using the term *psychoanalytic art therapy* to mean those approaches that are particularly focused on 'transference relationships' and are broadly psychoanalytical (as opposed to simply analytical) in orientation (and analytic psychotherapy is properly Jungian). How does this have an impact on how the art therapist sees the art? In this model of working, the therapist may offer interpretations of art work to help the client discover 'latent content'; the therapist may seek to 'verify its accuracy' by asking the client to respond; however, it is clear that the client is likely to be influenced by the therapist. Furthermore, the notion of 'premature interpretation' is also intensely problematic, and 'refers to an interpretation made to a person in therapy before they are ready to understand it' (Case and Dalley 2006: 281). I think the phrase '*before they are ready to understand it*' is an interesting one, and whilst the complexity and multi-levelled meanings within a work may take time to unfold, the meanings and understandings within it must surely be those of the client and *not those of the facilitator*?

> When latent feelings become manifest through an interpretation, meaning is generated. The thought or the word comes from either the artist/client in an attempt to make sense of the significance of her art work, *or from the therapist* who might see some important aspects emerging either in the picture or within the relationship. This can be either clarification of the transference process between therapist and client or some feelings, on a symbolic level, emerging through the image itself…. Direct interpretation might prevent or deny the client the satisfaction of discovering and finding out for herself…. The art therapist waits… until the client is ready to begin to understand and let the meaning unfold.
>
> (Case and Dalley 2006: 82; my emphasis)

The onus here appears to be on holding back to the optimal moment to interpret the art work, otherwise it is 'premature'; but this is clearly very problematic, as the interpretation may simply be wrong, or reductive. The interpretation may be the therapist's projections. It is my fundamental worry about this model of working that, in the absence of strongly felt transferential material, the therapist will fill the space with their own projections. I have highlighted fairly obvious examples of this in previous work, with examples of outrageous interpretations being proffered (for example, in Hogan 1997: 37–42 and Hogan 2012: 29–33).

Similarly, in the supervisory relationship, Schaverien and Case (2007) suggest that the supervisee's personal material may be triggered in relation to the client work, '*but it may be unconscious and picked up by the supervisor*, who then has to decide whether to discuss this in supervision…' (17; my emphasis). Again, there is scope here for the more powerful in the relationship – the supervisor – to project their own psychological material into the dynamics of the therapeutic relationship, which is being presented in the case material. Consequently, there is potential here for misinterpretation and abuse, and I have come across this in my long professional career in giving personal therapy to trainees who are also undergoing problematic supervision; some of the interventions and remarks made by supervisors were more about the supervisors than the case material. If the material is 'unconscious', it is out of view to *both* student and supervisor, except where there is a peculiar *lack* of engagement with certain aspects of the client's art work on the part of the trainee: the latter may indicate a simple lack of awareness – a 'blind spot' or something potentially more complex – but supervisors must not leap to the conclusion that the student has unresolved psychic material in this area.

On a profound level, psychoanalysis and object-relations theory are seductive explanatory fictions. When various trainees complete 'baby observations' (fortunately, not a standard part of art therapy training), for example, they imagine a 'paranoid orientation' or distinguish other developmental phenomena in the baby. Someone *with a different explanatory schema would actually see the baby's behaviour differently*, and interpret it differently. There is no such thing as theory-free observation, as Thomas Kuhn famously observed. These explanatory schemas have important implications for the conduct of therapy as I have previously noted:

> Whilst it may be quite harmless to project material onto a baby who is too young to notice, on the one hand, it is potentially psychologically damaging, on the other, to tell a seven-year-old that she thinks her mother is a witch or that she wishes to eat her father's genitals. I have called dogmatic reductive interpretations of clients' art work 'psychic abuse'.
>
> (Hogan 1997: 39)

As Dorothy Rowe has pointed out, psychotherapists, by virtue of their training, knowledge and special insights, sometimes feel that 'they have access to truths above and beyond the capacity of the patients... the psychotherapist interprets the patient's truths and tells them what they *really* mean' (Rowe 1993: 94).

Unfortunately, dogmatic interpretation takes place in art therapy through art therapists feeling that they *should* interpret the art work or the transference (Hogan 2011). This sort of performance pressure must be resisted.

In earlier writing, I questioned this phenomenon and gave several examples of reductive interpretation of a sort that I regard as constituting dangerous practice (Hogan 1997: 37–42). Here I ask the question:

> Are those art therapists working with a model of the Oedipus complex or using the notion of the Kleinian 'paranoid-schizoid position' (at which a client may supposedly be arrested), who couch their interventions in these terms, actually helping their patients at all? Worse still, is the art therapist working to an agenda and not making this evident to the client? In simple terms, are such art therapists just making confused people more confused through their use of strange interpretative schemas which do not correspond with the client's sense of reality? I am not suggesting that this confusion is merely the inability of the patient to understand the peculiar and jargon-ridden language favoured by some therapists. Are art therapists exacerbating their clients' suffering by *overlaying it with their own version of reality?* I suggest they are, and that this constitutes in extreme cases a form of psychological abuse.
>
> (Hogan 1997: 39)

McNiff (2004) also critiqued the same reductive tendency in North America:

> I was incredulous when first exposed to catalogs for the interpretations of art, which reduced images to negative character traits and various forms of psychopathology. Drawings and paintings were analysed according to narrow theoretic frameworks. The resulting interpretations were simplistic and literal, imposing a caricatured and laughably pornographic sensibility on the individualized expression of patients. With an insistence on finding hidden conflicts and motives, they dissected imagery and gave no attention to the sensibility of the artist.
>
> (p.75)

Recently, I have produced a detailed critique of the reductive application of object-relations theory (Hogan 2012). It is not just a particular theoretical orientation I am questioning here (though certain forms appear to predominate in reductive theorising): I am questioning whether art therapists should make interpretations at all.

Art therapy, which is primarily focused on interpretations of the transference relationship, is highly problematic in my view for the reasons outlined.

Interactive art therapy

To add to the general complexity and potential confusion, some art therapists refer to their work as 'analytic', when what they are doing is art therapy that is broadly psychotherapeutic. Psychotherapy is an experiential method which includes a range of techniques aimed at increasing self-awareness in those participating, often through developing experiential relationships, which lead to an enhanced capacity for self-observation, and in turn to changed thinking and behavior. Art psychotherapy can be directive or non-directive. Within this model can be seen a continuum of approaches from those that abutt the psychoanalytic, to more interactive approaches, through to group work that is more focused on the individual in the group.

In the interactive model, participants are thought to reveal their habitual ways of behaving in the group and these are then reflected upon (see Chapter 13 for a more detailed elaboration of this method). This model of art therapy can be more or less interested in transference relationships depending on the style and focus of the therapist (and what happens in the group with regard to group dynamics), but as Skaife (2007) has pointed out, there is 'too much material' and so transference may not be a particular focus (and it is theoretically possible to use the interactive model and not work with a concept of transference at all). The model of therapy is 'analytical' insofar as it is investigative and there is an interpretative element here too, in that part of the facilitator's role is to comment on group processes; however, this can be done in a way that is not dogmatic or definitive, and the facilitator may invite group members to challenge or augment her perceptions so that a collective understanding is generated. Rudimentary consensus is possible in a group, and this is useful if a member of the group has an obviously 'faulty' perception of an event in the group, where 'feedback' is a useful challenge to habitual unproductive ways of being.

The focus of the group moves back and forth between the art works and analysis of interactions and 'events'. A thematic approach can be used. However, if 'non-directive', there are two main modes of working which are as follows: that which regulates the time (creating a 'frame' in which the non-directed work occurs), so that a regular amount of each session is spent making art work and then talking; the second non-directive approach is that which does not regulate the time at all (except with respect to the start and end times of the group), so that the group determines the direction of the sessions. Sometimes there can be a strong consensus in the latter approach about how the group wishes to organise itself, but on other occasions, there may be conflict between members about how much time they want to spend talking and how much time making art work. This can be a productive conflict. The unregulated or 'group-led' approach has the advantage that the aesthetic dimensions of the art work can be explored more fully; for example, a group may decide to spend an entire session painting and then the following week talking about the works. There are pros and cons to this, as work left for a week may lose its emotional power and impact and the producer of the art may feel distanced from it. On the other hand, a more complex piece of art can be produced (so there is potentially more time for self-reflection in the process of actually doing the work involved). The latter approach can feel less contained than the former, and therefore less safe – though a facilitator who uses the non-directive structure may insist on a short 'debrief' following a session comprising only of art-making to help create a sense of closure of that session. However, the facilitator might just announce that there is five minutes to the end of the session to flag-up the end.

In both non-directive approaches participants talk about their art works (be they brief or elaborated) and how they feel about them, and reflect on the process of making them. Although these differences may sound subtle, they can make for rather different group experiences, as shall be further elaborated. These subtle shifts of emphasis do make a difference.

Art therapy support groups

As outlined in the previous chapter, this approach may be more focused on the individual in the group rather than on group processes. Art works are produced and then discussed with the art therapist either individually or as a group. There is potentially great opportunity in this model to really focus on the image, and the image-making process. This process of image-making can be highly informative and it is sometimes the *struggle* of making an image which can be revealing and can lead to reflections on, and awareness of, one's own interiority:

> At the group's invitation I did make one art work. I painted a picture of myself breast-feeding. However, I struggled with the piece. I had wanted the

quality of the paint to be very watery creating an image like a reflection on a pond. Whilst painting it I became aware of the fact that I wanted to depict my baby both inside and outside of my body simultaneously. I imagined her suckling one breast whilst stroking the other with her little hand. But I was not able to achieve a satisfactory result with the materials and I spent the session working and reworking the image – struggling with the boundaries. The finished art work, unresolved though it was, embodied my experience of merger and separateness. The act of painting brought to awareness and illustrated my feelings of conflict and ambivalence about these processes – my emotional struggle. Indeed, my *inability to resolve the image pictorially* was highly revealing. I had not experienced through conversation the full force of these conflicting emotions. Participating in the group reminded me of the power and poignancy of the art therapy process which yields the possibility for the articulation of powerful embodied feelings and responses which cannot necessarily be experienced or evoked through a verbal exchange alone.

(Hogan 2003: 168; original emphasis)

Thus the way the art work is constructed, reworked – areas obliterated and reshaped – can be deeply revealing, giving immediate access to areas of inner-conflict and ambivalence. Discussion of these aspects may come to the fore. How the work is subsequently handled or destroyed can also become relevant, as it is an object embodied with emotions. Art therapy is a powerful and immediate method; there is also the possibility of exhibition, and though much art therapy work remains confidential, for some participants the revealing image being revealed can be both cathartic and empowering – as a woman said to me fairly recently, 'I feel heard' (Hogan and Pink 2010). Working with these aesthetic dimensions is not exclusive to this model as should be evident but, if not working interactively and analysing interpersonal elements between group members, there can be more space for making and thinking about the art.

Again there can be a spectrum of activity under this heading, from work which has many interactive elements, to approaches where the main relationship is between participant and therapist (with 'ground rules' to contain the interventions of other group members), to approaches which have a studio-like atmosphere.

Art therapy studio

As outlined in the previous chapter, there are approaches that may not function as a group at all. The studio may be open or closed. If open, potential users can wander in as they choose and use the space; they can choose to come or not to, and if they don't attend that is not an issue. The pace can be set completely by the participants in deciding how much art work they wish to engage in. This suits some people better than a fixed weekly time slot, as some people may not feel they can be 'creative on demand', as a mental-health services user put it to me recently.

If the studio is 'closed' it means that a designated set of people are invited in at a particular time, for example on Monday afternoons. Thus, with the latter approach, there is potentially more consistency in attendance, and so it feels more group-like and offers a more uniform and predictable experience. Studios vary between those that use tables, easels or donkeys (a seat with an easel which is straddled) or a combination of all of these.

In most studio approaches, the art work is discussed on a one-to-one basis with the art therapist. In this model, there is time and space to work in a sustained way on art works, and time to reflect on the art-making process (note Michelle Gunn's remarks in the previous chapter).

In a recent online debate entitled 'Questions about Interpretation and Assessment in Art Therapy', Randall James (2010) provided a summary of the discussion:

> The general consensus is that:
> 1 Art therapists do not offer psychological interpretations of their clients' art work to the clients.
> 2 The art therapist engages in facilitating a mutual dialogue concerning meaning of the art work with the client and encourages the client to make his or her own interpretations.
> 3 That to offer psychological interpretations of client art work to the client can be dangerous and potentially be seen as abusing the client.
> 4 That interpretation of art work can result in 'imagecide,' or the reduction of the meaning of an image to one single thing that may or may not have anything to do with the client.
> 5 Interpretation is not necessary to help clients feel better.
> 6 There is a general hesitation about making any interpretation of client art work, whether it is shared with the client or not.
> 7 The art work has built-in meaning and by exploring the art work with the client we can help to unpack that meaning over time.

I am not utterly sure that there is always 'built-in meaning', as the actual making of the work may create the meaning: it is the active engagement with materials which can generate significance (Hogan and Pink 2010). However, for much art therapy work, this statement may hold true.

Cultural issues and interpretation

The importance of greater acknowledgement of 'issues of culture' more broadly in art therapy has been highlighted as crucially important, if we are not to inadvertently oppress others (Talwar, Iyer and Doby-Copeland 2004). Issues of interpretation are always important and some acknowledgement of cultural issues has been made in the art therapy literature to date, most notably Hogan (1997, 2003, 2012); Hiscox and Calisch (1998); Dokter (1998); Campbell *et al.* (1999).

Hogan's edited volume (1997) looked broadly at women's issues and art therapy, and especially at negative discourses surrounding definitions of femininity and claims about female instability, especially with reference to the negative positioning of women within psychiatric discourses (Hogan, Burt, Joyce). Biological determinism in psychiatry was highlighted and critiqued. Cultural misogyny and violence against women was also emphasised, as well as lesbian issues (Jones and Martin). The book also contained an exploration of blackness in the art therapeutic encounter and a ground-breaking essay on internalised racism (Campbell and Gaga). Women's bodies, especially the experience of pregnancy and childbirth, also received attention (Hogan, Lewin, Malchiodi, Skaife). This work has been reissued (2012) in a new edition called *Revisiting Feminist Approaches,* which more fully addresses the issue of domestic violence (Jones) and includes other new voices.

Further work on women's issues includes an examination of women's changed sense of self-identity and sexuality as a result of pregnancy and childbirth, and a trenchant critique of the reductive application of object-relations theory, as well as a critical appraisal of frankly misogynist theories about 'too good' mothering. Maternal guilt, depression and anger are reappraised in the light of negative theories about mothers (Hogan 2012).

Hiscox and Calisch, and Campbell's edited collections examined cultural diversity and highlighted problems of institutionalised racism, as well as the experience of being a member of a 'visible minority' and an art therapist (Annoual 1998: 14). The 'racial identity' of the therapist in relation to clinical practice was considered. The editors (Hiscock and Calisch) emphasise an acknowledgement of cultural context:

> All human behaviour is influenced by, and is a reflection of, the cultural context within which it is nurtured. Culture includes such features as attitudes, forms of emotional expression, patterns of relating to others and ways of thought. It is a patterned, organised and integrated collection of characteristics and traits like a weaving or tapestry. Members of a culture share common threads with the group as a whole while also retaining some individuality.
>
> (1998: 9)

Skaife (2007), summarising some of the concerns put forward by Blackwell (1994), suggests that issues of racism in group work can get lost when there is just one 'other' in the white group: 'The single black person will be absorbed into the group in a beneficent denial of their difference' (2007: 146). And, of course, it is important to point out, that some people of colour will collude with this. Such 'colour blindness', she suggests, can obscure the particularity of the individual. Dokter (1998) also notes a reluctance to acknowledge difference in art therapy group work, but sees this arising out of 'deep-seated fears about labels' (1998: 148).

Kalmanowitz and Lloyd (1998) discuss the interaction of traditional forms of South African healing and Western therapy. One of their case examples is very instructive:

a black woman was being seen by two therapists concurrently – one black and the other white. Shamanism was recommended by the black therapist, 'who believed that the girl's anger needed to be addressed to the ancestors, through a medium, before it could be released' (1998: 122). Only after this process did she think therapy could be effective; the white therapist was willing to consider this, and then, 'A third (black) member [of the therapeutic staff team] entered the debate resolute that she herself would stick with the therapy until the anger found expression. What had seemed a black–white issue transpired to be more subtle' (1998: 122). Kalmanowitz and Lloyd's point is that skin colour was not the dividing issue; rather, different ideas about therapeutic efficacy in a particular cultural context were to the fore, as well as underlying tensions between 'native' and 'Western' treatment models.

Lala (2011) points out her work with a white woman who identified as black, for complex reasons, and usefully reminds us that our clients 'are the experts on their own lives'. It is those we work with who 'must be seen as self-determining unique beings who are constantly composing and reconfiguring their own identity, experiences and struggles' (2011: 33).

When running a varied group myself recently, *diversity* is precisely what came to the fore, with the British Caribbean women dissimilar to each other in their experience of being black women, and others, such as a British Yemeni Muslim woman, having had a very different life experience, especially with reference to community expectations and restraints. Explication of different cultural perspectives was intrinsic to the group process.

McNiff (1984: 104) notes a tendency towards greater and obvious acknowledgement of differences in 'cross-cultural' art therapy relationships:

> The process of intersubjectivity characterizes all human relations. Cross-cultural communications simply make the perception of differences more explicit. Within cross-cultural therapeutic relationships and art therapy training groups differences tend to increase curiosity and interest.

Lala (2011) also emphasises the recognition of heterogeneity, using the term 'ethnically diverse' to describe her work with women from several different countries; she writes, 'It was important for me as a clinician to recognize that individuals who embrace the same ethnicity do not always share the same race, culture or religion' (2011: 32); furthermore, her interest is in acknowledging women's 'complex self-identification' in an attempt to avoid stereotyping (2011: 33).

Rosal, Turner-Schikler and Yurt (1998) advocate against separatism in their work with obese teenagers, arguing that the 'diversity of membership enriched the group' and also brought together young people who did not normally socialise, allowing them to 'find commonalities and gain respect for each other' (1998: 131).

Conversely, Farris-Dufrene and Garrett (with reference to work with the native North American population) go so far as to raise questions as to the efficacy of art therapy across different cultures. Farris-Dufrene and Garrett emphasise that sickness in a Shamanistic tradition is not seen as just 'located' in the individual in Native American culture, and emphasise that cultural sensitivity and insight is necessary for meaningful engagement:

> The use of the arts in healing goes beyond sickness *per se* and encompasses a multilevel concern with the well-being of the individual and the community. Healing deals with psychological, social and spiritual crises. With its emphasis on prevention, traditional healing effectively addresses a wide range of physical and social ills.
>
> (1998: 244)

Dokter's edited book considered therapeutic work with refugees and migrants across a range of disciplines, including art therapy. She emphasises complexity, and points out that ethnic groups tend to be composed of a number of different cultural groups with *varying orientations*. Her argument is that *cultural differences* between people (including people who *look* the same) are always important to self-identity.

Dokter's position is supported by Annoual, who writes, somewhat disconcertingly, about 'blacks' in the US as a collective, but then goes on to assert that:

> Black, as an identity, is highly contested and is by no means a static concept. In fact, it is to be understood as a highly individualistic process in the construction of identity. As with other elements of self-identification, one's blackness is something that may change depending on situation and context.
>
> (1998: 20)

Indeed, it is cultural affiliation that is key; Dokter warns that visible similarities can obscure heterogeneity. The situation is further complicated, she suggests, because of intermarriage between different cultural groups.

However, Dokter (1998) points out specific stresses of migration concerned with cultural transition and potential conflicts of values. Lala (2011: 35) is astute in summarising the multiple issues at play in work with immigrant and refugee women:

> While going through the immigration process, the constant reminders [of] traumatic material from the client's past, coupled with an on-going imminent threat of deportation, pose a real and damaging deterrent to recovery and healing. For example, women without immigrant status have less access to services and resources but, at the same time, are dealing with the stress of multiple settlement issues. Issues such as language, culture shock, financial constraints, housing security and isolation all impact [on] the client directly and need to be considered during the therapeutic process.

Chebaro (in Hiscox and Calisch's edited volume) also addresses immigration. She writes:

Art helped me open the door between the life I left behind and the new one I was about to adopt. This travel in time (past life and present) was part of the healing process which I needed to face in order to grieve the loss of my country of origin and accept my new foreign life.

(1998: 232)

Chebaro warns against the possibility of misinterpretation and against the over-generalisation of symbolic material. She is particularly critical of pictorial diagnostic tests, which are more widespread in the US than the UK and Australia. She is also disdainful of the cultural stereotyping of Arabs that she encountered, especially in schools.

Schaverien's (1998) chapter in Dokter explores the transmission of grief and trauma across generations through collective memory, with reference to Jewish cultural identity. In this essay she discusses how art works can allow 'previously terrifying' images to become assimilated. Also explored are the positive aspects of the 'scapegoat transference' (Schaverien 1987, 1991) in which the art work may:

... come to be experienced by its maker as the embodiment of the image it carries.... It may temporarily be experienced as 'live' and, so, if consciously handled, its disposal may have the effect of a cleansing ritual.

(1987: 167)

Case (1998) noted some cultural pressures and constraints in her work with members of the Chinese population in Hong Kong, who saw themselves as unrepressed and pragmatic, but also as very willing to engage in group work; however, this was coupled with a strong expectation that she would make authoritative interpretations (1998: 255).

My second edited collection (Hogan 2003) explored gay, lesbian and transgendered identities, and particular symbolism and cultural understandings within these communities that are potentially open to misunderstanding. McNiff (1984) asked the question whether we might 'view all therapeutic relationships as meetings between cultures' (1984: 128); the circumspect position generated by this stance is a useful one for art therapists to adopt in my opinion.

It is interesting that Dokter's comments above, about heterogeneity, echo those of Modood (2005). How to capture the complexity of cultural identities today is an interesting question, as 'non-white immigrants do not form a separate socio-economic class, nor are they distinctively located in one class' (2005: 53); it therefore seems more useful to consider more cultural information. A critique of the concept of 'ethnicity' is that, like 'race', it is:

... an externally imposed identity on a group of people who may not have thought of themselves as a group... [Consequently] the categorizations of a dominant group can create a quasi-group out of those who share similar physical appearance, so an ethnic group is a quasi-group based on what are perceived by non-members to be distinctive cultural characteristics of a given population.

(2005: 55)

Clearly, this is problematic. More palatable is the idea of 'ethnicity' as a form of *group understanding*. This is described thus: 'An ethnic group is, theoretically, one where the association with both a particular origin and specific customs is adopted by people themselves to establish a shared identity' (Platt 2007: 17).

However, Modood (2005: 58) cautions against the use of the concept, making this interesting analogy:

Racial categories may be like the artificial boundaries of some postcolonial independent states, reflecting colonial administrative divisions and great powers' geopolitics, forcing together those who do not belong together and separating those who do.

Even those who feel that the term 'ethnicity' has promise are cautious about its use. Platt (2007), for example, drawing on the work of Geertz (1993), stresses the 'contingent and fluid' nature of ethnicity. She suggests that 'ethnicity' is potentially useful in suggesting 'flexible cultural bonds', but worries that the term can be abused to suggest fixed hereditary differences which can lead to a rigid and fixed essentialist view of culture, where 'culture' becomes the preserve of 'the other' and viewed as an 'additional characteristic' of the ethnic groups, rather than the terrain 'through and in which all people live, which is inherently relational and which gives meaning to the world and all social relations' (Platt 2007: 18). Clearly, the very concept of 'ethnicity' must be called into question, or at least used with great caution.

An art therapy writer from North America, Denise Lofgren (1981) has highlighted how some of her assumptions were unhelpful to her understanding of images made by a Navajo Indian client in the United States. In the first image, Navajo symbolism is used to represent a guardian enclosing three sides of the paper with the fourth side containing an opening to allow for the movement of the spirits (see Figure 9.1); Lofgren was 'dismayed' by the image and thought it was pathological and impoverished, because she was unacquainted with such symbolism.

A further example of her cultural assumptions, in direct response to the art work, is described by Lofgren as the introduction of a personal history timeline, which the therapist assumed would start on the left and work towards the right, illustrating a chronological sequence of events; however, a more global and less linear approach was taken, with the image divided into four quarters (see Figure 9.2). This approach concords with a Native American outlook about time, but could easily be misconstrued. Lofgren concluded that without more training towards cultural sensitivity in the analysis of behaviour and symbolism, art therapists could unwittingly abuse their clients:

Figure 9.1 Navajo symbolism

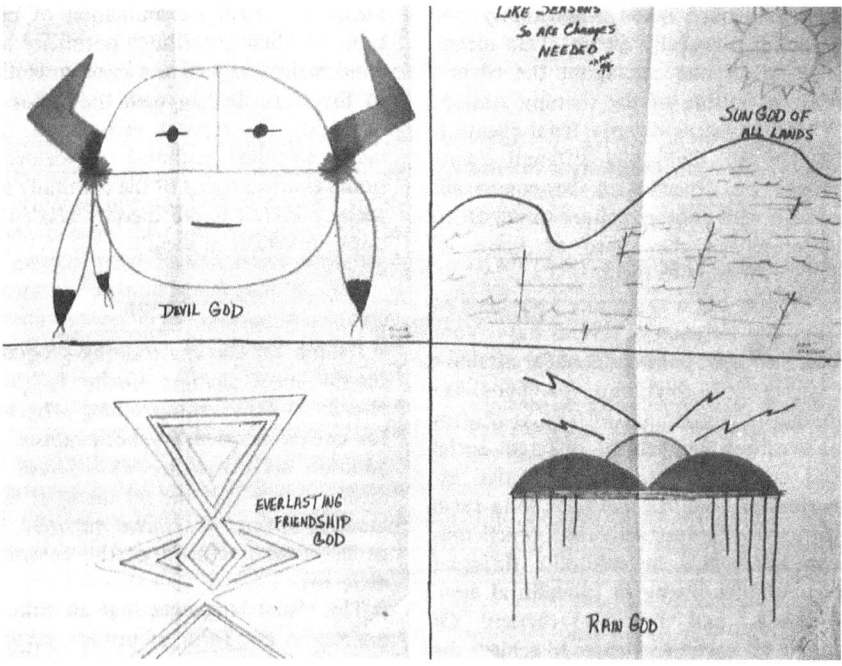

Figure 9.2 Life history

Everyone can cite examples of individual incompetence or insensitivity within the mental health field. What I wish to emphasise is that *institutionalized* forms of cultural bias affect the practice of even the most conscientious therapist.

(1982: 29; original emphasis)

It is imperative that art therapists avoid interpreting art and work in a facilitative manner, especially so with those using unfamiliar symbolic schemas. To have an in-depth understanding of diverse literary and cultural perspectives is probably beyond the scope of basic art therapy training; but a conceptual understanding and sensitivity towards cultural diversity is imperative. 'How can a white Australian art therapist work effectively in a plural society without first having confronted the prejudices so seamlessly inherent in her upbringing and history?' demands Holloway rhetorically (2009). Certainly, creating some space in art therapy training to reflect on this feels imperative. As stated earlier, the safest stance for the art therapist to adopt might be that which 'view[s] all therapeutic relationships as meetings between cultures' as McNiff had it (1984: 128); this circumspect position is a useful one for art therapists to adopt.

Bibliography

Annoual, P. 1998. Art Therapy and the Concept of Blackness, in A.R. Hiscox and A.C. Calisch (eds) *Tapestry of Cultural Issues in Art Therapy*. London: Jessica Kingsley Publishers, pp. 13–23.

Banton, M. 1983. *Racial and Ethnic Competition*. Cambridge: Cambridge University Press.

Birtchnell, J. 2003. The Visual and the Verbal in Art Therapy. *International Arts Therapies Journal* 2. Available online at http://www2.derby.ac.uk/vart/vol-2-200203-international-arts-therapies-journal/42-refereed-articles-/58-the-visual-and-the-verbal-in-art-therapy-by-dr-john-birtchnell

Blackwell, D. 1994. The Emergence of Racism in Group Analysis. *Group Analysis* 27(2), 197–210.

Campbell, J., Liebmann, M., Brooks, F., Jones, J. and Ward, C. (eds) 1999. *Art Therapy, Race and Culture*. London: Jessica Kingsley Publishers.

Case, C. 1998. Reaching for the Peak: Art Therapy in Hong Kong, in D. Dokter (ed.) *Art Therapists, Refugees and Migrants: Reaching Across Borders*. London: Jessica Kingsley Publishers, pp. 236–62.

Case, C. and Dalley, T. 2006. *The Handbook of Art Therapy*. Second edition. London: Routledge.

Dokter D. (ed.) 1998. *Art Therapists, Refugees and Migrants: Reaching Across Borders*. London: Jessica Kingsley Publishers.

Farris-Dufrene, P. and Garrett, M. 1998. Art Therapy and Native Americans, in A.R. Hiscox and A.C. Calisch (eds) *Tapestry of Cultural Issues in Art Therapy*. London: Jessica Kingsley Publishers, pp. 241–8.

Geertz, C. 1993. *The Interpretation of Cultures*. London: Fontana Press.

Hiscox, A.R. and Calisch, A.C. (eds) 1998. *Tapestry of Cultural Issues in Art Therapy.* London: Jessica Kingsley Publishers.

Hogan, S. (ed.) 1997. *Feminist Approaches to Art Therapy.* London: Routledge.

Hogan, S. (ed.) 2003. *Gender Issues in Art Therapy.* London: Jessica Kingsley Publishers.

Hogan, S. 2011. Postmodernist but Not Postfeminist! A Feminist Postmodernist Approach to Working with New Mothers, in H. Burt (ed.) *Art Therapy and Postmodernism: Creative Healing Through a Prism.* London: Jessica Kingsley Publishers, pp. 70–82.

Hogan, S. (ed.) 2012. *Revisiting Feminist Approaches to Art Therapy.* London and New York: Berghahn.

Hogan, S. and Pink, S. 2010. Routes to Interiorities: Art Therapy, Anthropology and Knowing in Anthropology. *Visual Anthropology* 23(2), 158–174.

Holloway, M. 2009. British Australian: Art Therapy, White Racial Identity and Racism in Australia. *Australian and New Zealand Journal of Art Therapy* 4(1), 62–7.

James, R. 2010. Discussions: Questions About Interpretation and Assessment in Art Therapy (online debate). International Art Therapy Organisation (IATO) Linkedin page.

Kalmanowitz, D. and Lloyd, B. 1998. A Question of Translation: Transporting Art Therapy to KwaZulu-Natal, South Africa, in D. Dokter (ed.) *Art Therapists, Refugees and Migrants: Reaching Across Borders.* London: Jessica Kingsley Publishers, pp. 111–26.

Kuhn, T. 1962. *The Structure of Scientific Revolutions.* Chicago: University of Chicago Press.

Lala, A. 2011. Seeing the Whole Picture: a Culturally Sensitive Art Therapy Approach to Address Depression amongst Ethnically Diverse Women, in H. Burt (ed.) *Art Therapy and Postmodernism: Creative Healing Through a Prism.* London: Jessica Kingsley Publishers, pp. 32–48.

Lewin, M. 1990. Transcultural Issues in Art Therapy: Considerations on Language, Power and Racism. *Inscape* Summer, 10–16.

Lofgren, D. 1981. Art Therapy and Cultural Difference. *American Journal of Art Therapy* 21, 25–32.

McNiff, S. 1984. Cross-Cultural Psychotherapy and Art. *Art Therapy: Journal of the American Art Therapy Association* 1(3), 125–31.

McNiff, S. 2004. *Art Heals: How Creativity Cures the Soul.* Boston: Shamhala.

Modood, T. 2005. *Multicultural Politics: Racism, Ethnicity and Muslims in Britain.* Edinburgh: Edinburgh University Press.

Platt, L. 2007. *Poverty and Ethnicity in the UK.* York: Joseph Rowntree Foundation.

Rosal, M.L., Turner-Schikler, L. and Yurt, D. 1998. Art Therapy with Obese Teens: Racial, Cultural and Therapeutic Implications, in A.R. Hiscox and A.C. Calisch (eds) *Tapestry of Cultural Issues.* London: Jessica Kingsley Publishers, pp. 109–33.

Rowe, D. 1993. Foreword, in J. Masson *Against Therapy.* London: Harper Collins.

Schaverien, J. 1987. The Scapegoat and the Talisman: Transference in Art Therapy, in T. Dalley, C. Case, J. Schaverien, F. Weir, D. Halliday, P.N. Hall and D. Waller (eds) *Images of Art Therapy: New Developments in Theory and Practice.* London: Tavistock, pp. 74–108.

Schaverien, J. 1991. *The Revealing Image: Analytical Art Psychotherapy in Theory and Practice.* London: Routledge.

Schaverien, J. 1998. Inheritance: Jewish Identity, Art Psychotherapy Workshops and the Legacy of the Holocaust, in D. Dokter (ed.) *Art Therapists, Refugees and Migrants: Reaching Across Borders.* London: Jessica Kingsley Publishers, pp. 155–75.

Schaverien, J. and Case, C. (eds) 2007. *Supervision of Art Psychotherapy: a Theoretical and Practical Handbook*. London: Routledge.

Skaife, S. 2007. Working in Black and White: an Art Therapy Supervision Group, in J. Schaverien and C. Case (eds) *Supervision of Art Psychotherapy: a Theoretical and Practical Handbook*. London: Routledge, pp. 139–52.

Talwar, S., Iyer, J. and Doby-Copeland, C. 2004. The Invisible Veil: Changing Paradigms in the Art Therapy Profession. *Art Therapy: Journal of the American Art Therapy Association* 21(1), 44–8.

Chapter 10

Working as an art therapist with children

Annette M. Coulter

Introduction

Working with children is a natural form of art therapy, because making marks on the external environment is an innate drive in child development. This might be the delight of imprinting a foot or hand in mud or sand, making a shape from natural materials – a castle from sand, a man from snow – stroking their finger down a frosted window or marking the kitchen wall with a felt pen. Children have an innate urge to test themselves against their external environment – to experience their internal, subjective world of fantasy and dream, in relation to the external, objective world of reality and fact (Winnicott 1971; Case and Dalley 1990). Recent research in neuroscience notes that emotional expression through art therapy has links to the non-verbal parts of the brain (Hass-Cohen and Carr 2008; Siegel 2007; Lusebrink 2004). For art therapy to establish a scientific platform in the health sciences, the links between art, trauma and neuroscience are an area for further research (Coulter 2009). Emotional intelligence linked to cognitive processing with non-verbal parts of the brain and visual processes has potential implication for child art therapy in educational settings.

Art therapy provides an opportunity for the child's instinctual, emotional part of the brain, the amygdala, to make sense of conflicting experiences between inner needs, wishes and fantasies and the constraints of their external world over which they have less control. This is resolved through greater rational cognitive processing in the more logical part of the brain, the hippocampus. We now know that the child is born with a fully functioning emotional brain and that cognitive understanding is acquired (Siegel 2007). Childhood experiences vary based on the quality and consistency of parenting, early infant attachments to significant caregivers and the child's initiation 'into the emotional, political, and social world' (Case and Dalley 1990: 1).

Group work in child treatment settings is more cost effective than individual therapy because more children are seen at one time, and it can be conducted alongside and in adjunct to other treatment regimes being undertaken. For example, art therapy can be used effectively with children suffering suspected mental illness such as phobias, conversion disorders, eating disorders, unresolved trauma, depression, as well as for those with medically invasive treatments or developmental issues. Most art therapists are not trained to diagnose: however, they may work in a facility where clinical staff are expected to contribute to diagnostic formulations. When labelling children with a mental disorder, it is sometimes safer to use the more flexible codes (American Psychiatric Association 2013) until presenting symptoms are confirmed.

Funding for child art therapy is not always available and service provision is determined by the health scheme in place. The context in which the art therapist works with a child or young person becomes a determining factor in assuming a therapeutic role. Working in a state-funded mental health service for emotionally-troubled children or teenagers contrasts dramatically with a specialist school or a community-based non-government agency, where continuation of service-delivery is determined annually through performance indicators, statistics and funds availability.

Processing art work with children

The reason art is such an effective way to work with children is that it provides an alternate way to speak about feelings. Children generally do not know why they have made or drawn something a certain way. There are many ways to explore an image with a child individually, in a group, or in a family context.

Therapeutic art education

Possibly the best area for art therapists to consider practice with children is in education. The term 'therapeutic art education' was first used by Henley to describe the benefits of the art process in art education (Henley 2002: 16). Henley's ideas are developed from the work of Victor Lowenfeld, who believed the art process was inherently therapeutic for children's emotional learning (Lowenfeld and Brittain 1987). Lowenfeld's work supports the premise that making art involves aesthetic awareness and the gaining of skills, as well as offering therapeutic experiences that facilitate creative thinking, self-expression and interpersonal growth. An art therapist provides a specialist service in an educational setting regardless of their role or job title. As an art educator, a therapeutic slant is implemented in the lesson plan. As a school counsellor, individual and parental advice is offered or group therapy might be provided. As a 'specialist consultant' under contract, the art therapist can provide a preventative service, where problems are immediately addressed, before behavioural disturbance becomes more entrenched.

Edith Kramer proposed that art educators would benefit from clinical training in order to deal with the potential of what might surface in the classroom from non-verbal expressive language (Kramer 1971). This idea makes good sense, but is yet to be taken up by educational authorities. The use of art therapists, employed as skilled clinicians rather than special educators in school settings, remains an area of controversy within the profession. Incorporating art therapy techniques into essential curriculum studies offers educators an alternate way to stimulate a child's neural pathways, and current brain research supports the importance of the non-verbal visual expressive part of the developing brain.

When creative processes are mobilised in a classroom setting, art therapy can stimulate academic achievement (Rosal 1993; Stepney 2001). Rosal's research supports the beneficial impact of incorporating art therapy programmes into school-based settings. Her original doctoral research conducted in an Australian primary school examined the impact of an art therapy group work programme on classroom behaviour (Rosal 1985). Further research by Rosal successfully combined an art therapy programme with English curriculum studies 'to reduce school drop-out rates, to decrease school failure, and to improve students' attitude about school, family and self' (Rosal, McCulloch-Vislisel and Neece 1997: 30).

Conducting a children's art therapy group

Group themes

For the art task, focus on the group dynamics rather than the task. The task is designed to facilitate the group dynamic. A therapist can easily impose their agenda by deciding group themes; however, the challenge is to follow with relevant themes that facilitate the ongoing group process. It is useful to have a prepared choice of group theme options, so that individual and specific group relevance can be met. The following list of group work tasks can be a basis for an art therapy group-work programme. Some discussion of alternatives for different contexts is included.

Session one: free picture

In a structured group, the best time to have expressive freedom is at the beginning, when relationships are more cautious and less likely to cause damage. It can also be a time for art media exploration, working with accidental marks, exploring what materials have been made available and giving permission to relax conscious concern and control. Children respond to a less structured task because of their naturally more active emotional brain.

This task is used in several art therapy assessment procedures (Kramer 1971; Ulman 1975; Kwiatkowska 1978; Cohen, Mills and Kijak 1994) and involves drawing whatever comes to mind, letting the hand do the thinking or just playing with the art material. Later the therapist might suggest using the non-dominant hand. There is permission here, in the fact that there is no right or wrong way, that allows for an external locus of control (Rosal 1985) or how the child might adapt to an art task (Rosal 1996).

Figure 10.1 A picture of my name

Session two: something that introduces you to the group

This could include drawing your name (see Figure 10.1) and drawing a picture that tells something about you (see Figure 10.2).

Figure 10.1 is an example of a name picture completed in an in-patient art therapy group where the child has managed to include patterns and symbols to describe different parts of himself. In Figure 10.2, the child tells the group about their home. This child was witnessing domestic violence and had symptoms of trauma-related afflictions – sleep disturbance, physical aggression towards other children, refusal to attend school generated by fear and concern for his mother's safety and disturbed thoughts presenting as an inability to attend to tasks.

Session three: a self-focused theme

There are many options for self-image work (Liebmann 2004). Some useful themes are drawing yourself as a tree, an animal, a building, a plant, a toy, etc. The therapist can stick to one item for the whole group or give the children a choice.

To explore self-perception, older children enjoy making a badge for themselves (Liebmann 2004: 228) or drawing a life map to describe where they've come from and where they're going (Liebmann 2004: 230).

Figure 10.3 is a badge by a girl who was exhibiting oppositional defiant behaviour expressed in non-compliance with diabetic treatment. As she engaged in art therapy group work, her non-compliance settled down as her anger about her debilitating medical condition found an alternate expression.

Figure 10.2 A picture that tells us something about you

Figure 10.3 A badge for myself, by Vicky, age 11

Figure 10.4 A badge for myself, by Sarah, age 12

Figure 10.4 is a badge by a girl who was suffering trichotillomania, exhibiting non-compliant behaviour towards her treatment for diabetes. The central badge or shield is a clear 'mandala-like' centre point, framed to be separate from other marks external to the badge, which is quite a different style of media application. Her description was that 'this is me', indicating the centre point, 'and outside [me] is all the mess in my life'. Her parents had recently separated and her self-mutilation meant she had to wear a headscarf to cover her baldness.

Another suggestion is to draw *Me, Myself and I*, an art task which can evoke concepts of self as viewed from within the family and other extended life perspectives.

Session four: family theme

The individual self-perception tasks above can also be used to describe family or group members, who can be portrayed symbolically as animals, buildings, fruit, vehicles or any other group of objects. Whatever way the family or the group is portrayed, it stimulates the child's cognitive, thinking faculties.

Figure 10.5 is a portrait of a group of children with cystic fibrosis who have known each other since infancy and meet whenever they are admitted for medically-invasive treatment; the group is like a family away from home. The therapist has a significant place on the child's page.

Kwiatkowska points out the importance of establishing who is in the family (Kwiatkowska 1978) and that, depending on the prevailing culture, it might be particularly important to include the extended family.

Figure 10.5 The group as trees, by Michelle, age 13

Family portraits might be realistic or abstract family self-portraits or family members doing something together (Coulter 2007: 219; Kwiatkowska 1978: 95–106). Placement on the page can be significant and children can be assisted with the concept of abstraction (Coulter 2007).

Session five: dream images

Dream work provides opportunity for less conscious symbolic exploration and non-verbal brain activation. Some art therapists pre-draw a sheet of a figure sleeping in a bed in the bottom corner, connected to a think bubble in which the dream is articulated. If the child says they can't remember any dreams, ask them to think of a daydream.

Figure 10.6 was drawn by a young person who had been admitted to a child psychiatry unit suffering suicidal ideation. He described the picture as 'a repetitive dream I have of a person falling off the cliff… I wake up just before he hits the rocks – wish he would hit the rocks. He wants to die.' Later in the same session, he disclosed, 'It's me.'

Figure 10.7 was completed in Nathan's first art therapy group and was about his resistance to attending the group, during which he was fidgety and passive-aggressive. In both art works he is expressing different feelings behind his anger, related to his hospital admission and imposed group attendance.

Figure 10.6 A recurring nightmare, by Nathan, age 14

Figure 10.7 Boring, by Nathan, age 14

Figure 10.8 A volcano, by Darren, age 7

Session six: letting the monster out

Allowing children to acknowledge feelings that are difficult to verbalise – particularly negative, destructive feelings such as anger, fear, frustration and guilt – can be done through a collective group art instruction. There is a message given that it is okay to have not-so-good feelings and to learn that other children/people have these feelings also. Working symbolically provides space to reflect on feelings together that are less socially acceptable. Letting the monster out helps children deal with their shadow-self or darker side. To only focus on the positive to enhance a strengths-based approach colludes with the denial of negative thoughts and feelings. This does not help the more troubled child. Cox suggests the use of volcano drawings as a metaphor for anger (Cox 1985). Facilitated discussion includes when, how or whether to release angry feelings. The symbolic release of negative feelings prevents the festering of internalised themes of self-destruction and suicidal ideation.

In Figure 10.8, the boy, who is a victim of child sexual assault, symbolises his anger about the court case through the volcano that is in a state of overflowing.

Session seven: draw a miracle or a wish

This task builds on notions of hope and therapeutic goals in treatment. Consideration of a perspective of potential is challenging for some children. The child moves to a solution-focused frame of reference (Coulter 2011) and self-esteem is elevated as potential empowerment is the focus. The group is now halfway through and internal strengths can be built upon. In the previous task, the inner destructive self is released and accepted by the group. The therapist now facilitates a process of wish-fulfilment, acknowledging the possibility of change. Liebmann's suggested themes, any of which are appropriate for a children's group, include: where I would like to be right now? What would you do with a million dollars? What would you like to find in a treasure chest? What present would you like to receive or give? What's on the other side of the river? (Liebmann 2004: 239).

Session eight: free collage

This is particularly effective for older children who are more self-critical of their artistic merit. The use of photo collage frees up imagery choice and provides a sense of personal satisfaction, as difficult concepts are symbolically articulated through found images. Landgarten recommends two boxes of pre-cut images: people and miscellaneous items (Landgarten 1993: 5–7) that are 'culturally homogeneous' with the client group. Landgarten also provides a four-task assessment protocol that can be adapted to a group context (1993: 9–12; see also Chapter 12 of this book, pp. 158–9). Liebmann also provides collage suggestions for exploration in groups (Liebmann 2004: 231).

Session nine: group art task

Group art tasks are effective throughout group art therapy treatment (Liebmann 2004: 262–71), but when used towards the end of the group, they provide potential expression of established group cohesiveness as well as opportunity to symbolically address any group dynamic that may have arisen. The group begins to say goodbye and group mural tasks specifically focus on closure issues. Group mandalas are effective extensions to a group art task. Liebmann suggests group mandala tasks and Stepney modifies Liebmann's 'Mandala of Hands' (Stepney 2001: 81–2). A circle is divided into segments and participants outline their hand in their segment. Their hand is enhanced to convey their personality and then incorporated with the rest of the picture to create a group mandala. Children experience pleasure in this task because it externalises a portion of their phenomenal field, uniting them with others.

Session ten: a farewell experience

Further group closure continues in session ten. An opportunity for feedback from group members is offered. For example, a task such as *draw something that represents the group* gives individual members a prompt to consider and make comment to each other. The art therapist can direct a specific farewell task or provide time to explore what ending means for each individual member of the group. This structure can include making two drawings: something to take away and something to leave behind. Articulating what is being taken away assists individual validation of group life. Defining what is to be left behind considers what will be discarded from the group experience. This is a conscious verification that reflects on group process and considers what has been gained and let go, as part of self-learning. Unresolved issues of loss or grief often surface when groups end. Examples of ending themes that might come up at this time include: the death of a family pet; illness or death of a family member; an accident witnessed; or something seen on television or in a computer game.

Session eleven: gift-giving

Part of the group ending experience is to have opportunity to receive something to take away that has been given. An effective final group task is symbolic 'gift-giving'. The context of the group is significant to this task. For example, a group of adolescent girls suffering eating disorders might give each other representations of chocolate bars and other illicit foods amongst great frivolity. Generally, the 'gift' can be a tangible, concrete item such as in the above example, or it can be a thought or a feeling. The gift is either represented on paper or it can be a sculptural representation of an object or abstract notion. However the 'gift' is visually or sculpturally articulated; the task includes writing to whom it is intended and from whom it is given. It can also be wrapped or folded. Older age groups write an explanation, such as, 'I am giving you confidence so that you kick a goal next time' or 'I have made you a heart because I think you are brave'.

A world without words

Blake reminds us that not all children have the capacity to play when they first come to therapy (Blake 2008: 121). The therapist's job is to engage with the child and to be comfortable working with non-verbal primary processes and primitive states of mind (Case and Dalley 1990: 143). This requires that the therapist genuinely enjoys working with children who instinctively know when an adult is not being their true self because the child's right-brain intuitive faculty is highly developed. The adult therapist has often lost touch with their ability to play. Adults can be uncomfortable with the notion of sitting with 'not knowing', yet this is largely what one must do, at least at the outset of child art therapy.

Establishing a relationship

Children do engage in some way and most are open to giving the adult therapist a fair chance. A resistant, troubled child does not engage as easily but is likely to be subtly assessing the therapist in some way. In this situation, the therapist remains genuine to themselves and does not focus specifically on the child or gaining their trust, because a resistant child is used to adults trying to engage them – they have learnt ways to protect themselves. When the therapist is able to respond genuinely to the child, the child is instinctively curious about the therapist. Gradually, trust within the relationship will emerge. This trust, however, is dependent on the therapist's ability to maintain consistency and genuineness. Art therapy offers the less verbal child an opportunity to find expression through the image as object, finding links to feelings affecting behaviour. Withers takes the therapeutic application of art one step further, encouraging the child to find key words associated with the image and feeling (Withers 2009: 74–5).

The first contact is quite significant for a child and the therapist aims to make it count. Children want to trust significant adults in their lives. If their experience is that adults have betrayed their trust, then they are going to be more guarded in their first contact with the therapist, but this first meeting sets the scene for the ensuing relationship. If the first contact is difficult, the work is likely to be difficult. If the first contact is engaging and provokes curiosity, the therapeutic relationship is off to a good start.

A damaged adolescent will thoroughly test the therapist before they engage in the therapeutic processes. A younger child is less likely to test the therapist with the same degree of sophistication as a damaged adolescent. The most competent therapist can be caught off-guard when working with teenagers (Coulter 2011) and years of experience does not prepare the therapist for the next troubled adolescent. The sub-culture of the young person is ever-changing and it is unlikely that the therapist can keep up with this. The young person will be interested to test the therapist's knowledge of their sub-culture, and it is likely the therapist will fail this test. However, the young person can be surprised by the genuine concern the therapist has for their plight. In working with damaged adolescents, it is likely there will only be that first appointment to engage or lose the client. A solution-focused approach is recommended for this initial session (Coulter 2011) as the young person or their immediate problem is the target, not the personal history, an interest in the family system, or a focus on external others.

Therapeutic relationships with children

The complexity of the world of the child is never clearly defined nor fully understood. Maintaining a positive regard for the child's process is strongly supported (Axline 1969; Kramer 1971; Rubin 2005). Too much structure risks denying the creative potential the child brings to the therapeutic relationship. The child can remind and teach the therapist about lost creative transitional processes between less conscious states of mind and cognitive thinking.

It is not always easy to maintain positive regard for the child's process. The therapist needs to be able to set a limit, if the child is going to physically harm him or herself, the therapist, equipment or the facilitating environment. Being clear about limits provides a safe context in which a positive therapeutic relationship can flourish. The therapist's presence is part of the context of the external world. The therapist establishes only those limitations that are necessary to anchor the therapy to the world of reality and to make the child aware of their responsibility to the relationship (Axline 1969: 73–4).

Art play therapy

The way a child chooses to respond to using art materials indicates their ability to engage in the play process. Blake describes 'emotionally alive play' as 'play that bridges the subjective inner world, and outer objective reality is... fascinating to watch... time seems to fly. Alternatively, play that is emotionally disconnected feels boring and tedious' (Blake 2008: 121). Working with children demands an ability from the therapist to attend to their 'gut' reaction to the child's play. The process may not follow a logical sequence to the adult mind. It requires an ability to have faith in the process. 'Just moving toys around, drawing or telling stories' does not necessarily mean that the child is engaged in a process of play (Blake 2008: 121).

When a child is emotionally engaged with art-making processes, they are exploring the variable qualities of art media extensively. The art therapist focuses on what feelings the child is expressing through their engagement with art materials. The therapist observes the child's attitude towards the materials, how they are handled, as well as what is created. The therapist's presence is as witness to the child's art play process, validating whatever it is the child is engaged in doing.

This is Blake's account of spontaneous play:

> You feel the child is making it up as he or she goes along. It is not rehearsed... This enables thoughts to find a partner, a new combination that provides a new idea, the next piece of play... real play conquers depressive anxieties because it is pretend; nothing will really happen. Things will not be destroyed or damaged within the safety of play.
>
> (2008: 122–3)

In child art therapy, cognitive leaps are stimulated as creative risks are achieved. A wide range of playful approaches to art media are possible that lift the child beyond their comfort zone. In accepting and entering the child's world, the therapist enhances the child's confidence and self-esteem.

Child art processes provide a form of symbolic language that is an alternate means of communication. Through symbolic and metaphoric art play processes that are predominantly non-verbal, the child seeks expression of feelings, desires, fears and thoughts that are central to their inner experience, generated from their ability to create images based on past perceptions that are no longer present, but that are imbedded in their explicit memory.

Developmental awareness

Children go through stages of artistic development, and noticing developmental delay or advancement depends on the therapist's ability to identify these stages. Evans and Dubowski's research (2001) is thorough, supporting the work of Viktor Lowenfeld, who sees art activity as a valuable educational tool as well as a means to describe the child's emotional and social adjustments (Lowenfeld and Brittain 1987).

Art therapists should be aware of developmental stages of artistic development. Not all children manage to reach graphic milestones and are sometimes referred for therapeutic help (Levick 1983). For example, a child suffering intellectual delay may be stuck at a certain developmental stage of artistic growth and may be drawing repetitive spiral shapes. An art therapist can assist the cognitive perception of the child's world through following developmental sequence drawing to enhance more rounded shapes, in line with moving from random scribble to circular shapes. The behavioural responses of an intellectually disabled client are likely to improve when a developmental art therapy programme is implemented, simply because they begin to achieve the developmental stages of visual perception. However, this may take a long time and requires considerable patience from the therapist, who is motivated by the potential reward (Kellogg 1970; Lowenfeld and Brittain 1987; Rubin 2005).

Adolescent art therapy

Adolescence is a time of intense creativity, where self-expression through body art, music and fashion is an acceptable part of their psycho-social sub-culture. Engaging in expressive activities provides opportunity for self-motivated, personal narrative in the external world that is beyond the family of origin and is a continuation of internal processes linked to deeper-level struggles and concerns (Coulter 2011). Art therapy provides an expressive outlet for confusing emotions at this time, but other creative therapies are equally valuable in the psychosocial development of the adolescent brain, because non-verbal unexpressed parts now seek a language through which to be heard. Cognitive brain development is highly charged as their ability to think laterally increases. Group art work is particularly relevant because individual marks are achieved with peer support. The process of separation from the family of origin relies on the establishment of peer relationships enhancing a more autonomous world that exists externally to the family. Self-focused, open-ended art tasks shift from a narcissistic focus to decision-making processes that have a broader symbolic content. The art work can be stored for the future, the therapist accepting that the young person is not ready to discuss their work. Any form of interpretation is potentially destructive to the fragile sense of self and self-doubt, often contributing to low self-esteem.

Photo collage is a particularly useful medium to use with adolescent populations because photo images relate to popular external world culture, as well as to the fact that their use avoids any consideration of lack of artistic merit. Although Landgarten proposes two boxes of pre-cut images (Landgarten 1993: 20), pre-torn images are just as effective, if not more so, because the young person does the cutting which feeds their wish to not be treated like a child, that they can do things for themselves.

Art and childhood trauma

Traumatised children experience a range of emotions that are difficult to grasp, let alone express. Psychological problems such as anxiety, helplessness, fear, phobias, conversion disorders, depression and eating problems may all be symptoms of an unresolved childhood trauma. Children may be traumatised by removal from home as a result of domestic violence, being assigned to a foster placement or care home, or they may have been subject to kidnapping, natural disaster or a physical illness involving hospitalisation. Trauma may also result for child victims of verbal, emotional, sexual or physical abuse. Children can be witness to a natural disaster and other accidents or disasters. They can also experience vicarious trauma after witnessing televised media images of these (Stern 2003) or after inappropriate disclosures about former abuse from a disturbed parent.

Representational symbolic drawing of the experience of trauma allows an imaginative synthesis for perceived and imagined possibilities. Instead of carrying these images internally, they are externalised through art-making, which can help children to express feelings of grief and loss, resolve feelings of confusion and process strong emotions.

Art expression seems to be well suited as a modality with children in trauma as it is easier for them to use visual modes of communication before being able to talk about trauma. This is especially true for children who have been chronically traumatised, as they are less able to freely express themselves. They require time to adjust, to gain a sense of trust with the therapist and the therapeutic environment. The therapist may feel hampered by the short length of time available. However, when working with children, the therapist needs to be able to go at the pace of the child. This is well documented in a British training video in which an art therapy student is working with a child who is suffering from a brain tumour. The trainee art therapist engages in a process of 'automatic drawing' for several months (Rubin 2004). The therapist does not attempt to hurry the therapeutic process, recognising that it is a gradual one, and does not direct the child's actions or conversation in any manner. The child leads the way: the therapist follows.

The therapist must be able to sit with processes that may not be making any logical sense. Just because the referral asks the therapist to deal with a particular issue, does not mean this is in the child's best interest. The therapist has to let go of an agenda and be able to run with the child's emotional processes. This can be reflected upon later, but at the time, the therapist needs to stay with the processes of the child. This is unlikely to occur if the therapist is charged with purposeful intent. The child has a fully-functioning right brain and the therapist who can surrender to the child's innate expressive abilities can engage with the child's creative processing. It is necessary to have a faith that it will be possible to make sense of what is going on later in supervision (see Chapters 15 and 16). The therapist empowers the child to be confident, to trust the relationship, to cope better and to continue integrating with the external world.

Bibliography

American Psychiatric Association. 2013. *Diagnostic and Statistical Manual of Mental Disorders* (DSM-5). Fifth edition. Arlington, VA: American Psychiatric Association.

Axline, V. 1969. *Play Therapy*. Revised edition. New York: Ballantine Books.

Blake, P. 2008. *Child and Adolescent Psychotherapy*. Melbourne: IP Communications.

Case, C. and Dalley, T. (eds) 1990. *Working with Children in Art Therapy*. London: Routledge.

Cohen, B.M., Mills, S. and Kijak, A.K. 1994. An Introduction to the Diagnostic Drawing Series: a Standardised Tool for Diagnostic and Clinical Use. *Art Therapy* 11(2), 105–10.

Coulter, A. 2007. Couple Art Therapy: 'Seeing' Difference Makes a Difference, in E. Shaw and J. Crawley (eds) *Couple Therapy in Australia: Issues Emerging from Practice*. Kew, Victoria: PsychOz Publications, pp. 215–27.

Coulter, A. 2009. Mind Landscapes: The Creative Adolescent Brain. Presented at the Australia and New Zealand Art Therapy Association Conference *A Creative Landscape: Art Therapies by the Bay* at Waterfront Campus, Deakin University, Geelong, Victoria 31 October –1 November.

Coulter, A. 2011. Contemporary Art Therapy: Working with Transient Youth, in H. Burt (ed.) *Art Therapy and Postmodernism: Creative Healing Through a Prism*. London: Jessica Kingsley Publishers, pp. 83–93.

Cox, C.T. 1985. Themes of Self-destruction: Indicators of Suicidal Ideation in Art Therapy. Paper presented at the American Art Therapy Association Sixteenth Annual Conference, New Orleans, LA.

Evans, K. and Dubowski, J. 2001. *Art Therapy with Children on the Autistic Spectrum: Beyond Words*. London: Jessica Kingsley Publishers.

Hass-Cohen, N. and Carr, R. 2008. *Art Therapy and Clinical Neuroscience*. London: Jessica Kingsley Publishers.

Henley, D. 2002. *Clayworks in Art Therapy: Plying the Sacred Circle*. London: Jessica Kingsley Publishers.

Kellogg, R. 1970. *Analyzing Children's Art*. Mountain View, CA: Mayfield Publishing Company.

Kramer, E. 1971. *Art as Therapy with Children*. New York: Schocken Books.

Kwiatkowska, H.Y. 1978. *Family Therapy and Evaluation through Art*. Springfield, IL: Charles C. Thomas.

Landgarten, H.B. 1993. *Magazine Photo Collage: a Multicultural Assessment and Treatment Tool*. New York: Brunner Mazel, Inc.

Levick, M.F. 1983. *They Could Not Talk So They Drew*. Springfield, IL: Charles C. Thomas.

Liebmann, M. 2004. *Art Therapy for Groups: a Handbook of Themes and Exercises*. Second edition. London: Jessica Kingsley Publishers.

Lowenfeld, V. and Brittain, W. 1987. *Creative and Mental Growth*. Eighth edition. New York: Macmillan Publishing.

Lusebrink, V.B. 2004. Art Therapy and the Brain: an Attempt to Understand the Underlying Processes of Art Expression in Therapy. *Art Therapy: Journal of the American Art Therapy Association* 21(3), 125–35.

Rosal, M. 1985. The Use of Art Therapy to Modify the Locus of Control and Adaptive Behavior of Behaviour Disordered Students. Unpublished doctoral dissertation, University of Queensland, Brisbane, Australia.

Rosal, M.L. 1993. Comparative Group Art Therapy Research to Evaluate Changes in Locus of Control in Behavior Disordered Children. *The Arts in Psychotherapy* 20, 231–41.

Rosal, M. 1996. *Approaches to Art Therapy with Children*. Burlingame, CA: Abbeygate Press.

Rosal, M., McCulloch-Vislisel, S. and Neece, S. 1997. Keeping Students in School: an Art Therapy Program to Benefit Ninth-grade Students. *Art Therapy: Journal of the American Art Therapy Association* 14(1), 30–6.

Rubin, J.A. 2004. *Art Therapy Has Many Faces*. VHS/ DVD. Pittsburgh, PA: Expressive Media, Inc.

Rubin, J.A. 2005. *Child Art Therapy*. Second edition. Somerset, NJ: Wiley.

Siegel, D.J. 2007. *The Mindful Brain: Reflection and Attunement in the Cultivation of Well-Being*. New York: W.W. Norton and Company.

Stepney, S.A. 2001. *Art Therapy with Students at Risk: Introducing Art Therapy into an Alternate Learning Environment for Adolescents*. Springfield, IL: Charles C. Thomas.

Stern, P. 2003. *Standing Tall: Helping Children Cope with 9/11*. VHS film: Fanlight Productions.

Ulman, E. 1975. A New Use of Art in Psychiatric Analysis, in E. Ulman and P. Dachinger (eds) *Art Therapy in Theory and Practice*. New York: Schocken Books, pp. 361–86.

Winnicott, D.W. 1971. *Playing and Reality*. London: Tavistock.

Withers, R. 2009. The Therapeutic Process of Interactive Drawing Therapy. *New Zealand Journal of Counselling* 29(2), 73–90.

Chapter 11

Working as an art therapist with offenders

Annette M. Coulter

Documentation of the therapeutic use of art with offenders throughout the growth of the art therapy profession was sparse until Liebmann's *Art Therapy with Offenders* in 1994 and Gussak and Virshup's *Drawing Time: Art Therapy in Prisons and Other Correctional Settings* in 1997. These edited texts from either side of the Atlantic present an expansive account of situations where art has been effective in the treatment of prison inmates. Even prior to the establishment of art therapy, it was observed that victims of incarceration had a natural desire to make art with whatever materials were available (Prinzhorn 1972; Cardinal 1972, 1979). This natural urge to self-heal through engaging in the making of art is often counter-productive when conducted in an institution designed to control and contain. In this respect, prisons are not unlike long-term psychiatric hospitals (Goffman 1968) and 'especially for those who feel deeply unsure of their relation to themselves and to other people and are isolated from their surroundings, it [art therapy] can be a vital means of self-expression and communication often succeeding where words fail' (Nowell-Hall 1978: 39). However, the question arises how suitable is a form of therapy that promotes self-expression and individuation, when it is operating in a setting that desires compliance and promotes conformity and anonymity (Coulter 1986). Art therapists have to consider how to deliver a treatment programme that is going to satisfy not only the authorities but also benefit the inmates. Delivering an exciting self-expressive programme is not necessarily beneficial if the incarcerated individual begins to assert an independent attitude within the institution, challenging authority and the system in which they reside. Goffman writes that 'any group of persons... develop a life of their own that becomes meaningful, reasonable, and normal once you get close to it' (Goffman 1968: 11). Art therapists who work in prison settings adapt their skills and knowledge to an environment that is uniquely its own and foreign to any outside influences. Change is not encouraged and good behaviour is the measure of success.

Literature review

Gussak and Virshup discuss the economic demise and concerns for the dehumanising of individuals placed in penal services (Gussak and Virshup 1997: xv–xx).

There is an increasing trend to mix people with mental illness with criminals. Gussak and Virshup suggest that art therapy provides the opportunity for self-reflection and insight to take place on a less conscious level, without the need for this to be always addressed literally and consciously. They warn how 'unintended disclosure of issues or insight can be quite threatening' (Gussak and Virshup 1997: 2) but that art offers a vehicle of expression that does not have to be verbalised. The inmate must return to the prison after the session. He is therefore not left vulnerable: 'when a patient leaves a session... he is going back to the general prison population... treatment should focus on helping the inmate/patient increase the understanding of self while allowing necessary defences and masks to remain in tact' (Gussak and Virshup 1997: 2). After an art therapy session, the incarcerated individual must return to a world about which the therapist has no comprehension. Any institutionalised setting has its own culture and codes. As Gussak and Virshup remind us (1997) and my experience demonstrates (Coulter 1986), an individual's survival in a secure setting such as a prison or a psychiatric institution is dependent on their ability to conform with codes of anonymity, not individualisation through creative activity. The work of Laing and Boyle, while inspiring (Laing 1984; Boyle 1977), is more the exception than the rule (Gussak and Virshup 1997; Teasdale 1997; Liebmann 1994).

Working with anger and addiction

Offenders may often have addictive personalities; whether the addiction is to alcohol, drugs, gambling, aggressive behaviour or crime itself, the repetition of the compulsion to engage in behaviour that is deemed out-of-control by society normalises life for that individual. A mechanism of denial is operating that makes it difficult to accept there is a problem, so painful perceptions are denied. The purpose of art therapy is to challenge these cognitive distortions and to support the client to better understand the mechanisms of self-deception that are operating through the addiction.

Inmates are often dealing with extenuating problems connected to an offence – marriage or family breakdown, drug dependency, alcoholism, gambling and poverty. It is not the therapist's role to support and accept the prisoner's self-deception and perpetuate mechanisms of denial. The addiction is usually motivated by a need to escape painful feelings. The newly-qualified art therapist can be easily over-zealous to engage with their client, to understand and provide a warm, caring and supportive relationship. This is not always in the inmate's best interest. Through art, personal material can surface inadvertently. For client safety, it is not always in their best interest to encourage verbalisation (Gussak and Virshup 1997). Working with offenders, the therapy is in the making of art, the cathartic release of pent-up emotion and the expression of what is difficult to verbalise; 'since an "angry" work of art is not generally regarded as threatening, they [the inmates] can draw out their hostility and rage on paper, with little fear of retribution' (Gussak and Virshup 1997: 2). As Liebmann points out, 'often the actual offence is the tip of the iceberg and brings to light problems that have been left unattended for years' (Liebmann 1990: 134). Teasdale supports that while 'art therapy is not solely able to help deal with anger... it offers time for image-making and discussion through which they may want to share ideas about the reasons why thy have been so angry' (Teasdale 1997: 34). Offenders may genuinely want to solve their problems and agree to join an art therapy group to address alcoholism, gambling, anger management and other problem-focused groups.

A narrative approach with a solution focus

There are different theoretical approaches to process the therapeutic engagement with art materials. Liebmann has developed the narrative therapy approach of creating a storyboard to examine the events leading up to the crime (Liebmann 1990: 135; Liebmann 1994: 152–261). This approach is not dissimilar to Fisher's idea of encouraging the client to make a narrative map of their plight (Fisher 2005). Liebmann encourages the client to make a comic strip-sequenced disclosure of the crime, allowing an expression from their point of view regardless of evidence or court findings. There are several ways this technique can be developed further to assist a re-examination of the thinking in the distortion of the cognitive frame. For example, the storyboard can be drawn from another perspective to examine the incident from another's point of view who was maybe affected. The visual recollection of retained images from the criminal event provides a greater articulation of emotional memory.

The narrative approach can be collaboratively linked to a solution-focused approach (Cade 1995) by incorporating a plan for action that has a resolution to the problem (Coulter 2011). This resolution can be future focused – that destiny post-incarceration is within their control. Cade suggests that the therapist helps the client search for '*exceptions* to the behaviours, ideas, feelings and interactions that are associated' (Cade 1995: 1); in this case, to the recollection of the crime. Through the creation of a personal narrative in Liebmann's storyboard, 'exceptions are elicited, highlighted and explored in terms of how they came about and what was different at that particular time' (Cade 1995: 1). Through the storyboard examination of events, it may become clear that the influence of alcohol or the family argument that precipitated the event are factors that indirectly contributed to the event. As Cade suggests 'interventions build on what *has* worked or is *currently* working for the client(s), even if marginally or occasionally' (Cade 1995: 1).

In the solution-focused approach there are three questions to help the inmate consider their circumstances differently: (i) the 'Miracle Question' (de Shazer 1994: 95), where the client imagines that overnight a miracle happens so that when they awake in the morning, their situation is completely changed. They are asked to describe how things are different in as much detail as possible, the therapist eliciting questions about who in their circle of family and friends is affected by the change, how are they affected and precisely what would be different. It is often easier for the client to say what is no longer happening rather than what is happening. For example, if it is an alcohol-related crime, they may humour the therapist by saying they would no longer be drinking. It is more challenging if the therapist can respond with something like, 'so if you are no longer drinking, what are you doing instead?' – the therapist is implying for the client to describe what is the different activity in which they are now engaged that has replaced their alcohol consumption. The second technique in the solution-focused approach is (ii) to encourage the client to provide numerical value to their circumstances through asking scaling questions. For example, if 0 means not at all and 10 means as much as could possibly ever be imagined, what number would describe their potential to implement change to their current circumstances. If they respond with 2, the next scaling question encourages consideration of a future focus to improve this: 'So what would need to happen for you to move from a 2 to a 3?' The third question, (iii) is to highlight the client's ability to cope with adversity up until now. The client shares their resourcefulness and expertise, the client knows the solutions not the therapist. In the solution-focused approach, imaginative questioning encourages the client to describe practical solutions to their current dilemmas (Berg and Steiner 2003).

Another technique that is referred to as 'advocacy' in interactive drawing therapy (Withers 2006, 2009) is where the therapist draws for the client. It is important to only draw from the precise description the client presents and to not embellish this with anything from the therapist's personal pathology, but in doing an advocacy drawing for the client, the therapist can create the storyboard for the client, as the sequence of events is told. Advocacy is mainly recommended in situations where the client is reluctant to draw. In whatever way the image is created, it has the potential to provide emotional distance from the event for the inmate. As soon as possible, the picture is handed to the client to complete. Once engaged with the page, the client starts to continue the drawing (Withers 2006).

Another technique developed by Liebmann for an alcohol group can also be adapted to other art therapy applications with inmates. The page is divided into four frames. Liebmann dictates the content of the first and last frame for the alcohol group – drinking in the first and being arrested in the fourth. The group members are then asked to fill in the blank frames in between to show how they got from the first to the last (Liebmann 1990: 146). The same task can be applied for prison inmates with a scene before the crime in the first frame, then the crime on the last frame and then the inmate is asked to visually describe the events in between.

One last extension of the Liebmann storyboard technique is to impose a narrative intervention of finding an alternate story, not dissimilar to thinking about the Miracle Question (de Shazer 1994: 95) only in this alternate script, the focus is on 'news of difference' (White and Epston 1990), which is not dissimilar to the solution-focused notion of searching for exceptions (Cade 1995).

Art therapy offers opportunity for the inmate to examine painful feelings from a distance. Wilson uses art to manage feelings of 'shame' in her work with gambling addiction. There is a compulsion to commit the addictive behaviour in order to keep painful feelings at a distance, and the notion of being addicted or made out-of-control by the 'illness' of an addiction decreases the likelihood of feelings of 'shame' (Wilson 2003). With the offender feeling powerless and inadequate because of their addiction, the crime is justified. By engaging in the creative process through an art activity, denial is addressed as 'shame' reducing, and corrective work is begun. The art work production is an object that exists externally to the client but that relates to their internal sense of self. Through this creation of a bond between the internal/external worlds of the inmate, self-expression is promoted. The art work is a permanent, concrete record of the client's visual progress in therapy. It is easier to talk through the symbol or metaphor, and a contemplative process is encouraged because the making of art is relaxing – an opportunity to engage in a process of soothing, energising mindfulness and to play with imaginative possibilities. The creative process offers choices and solutions in the recovery process that the crime or the addiction does not offer.

Wilson believes there are five main considerations when using art therapy with people suffering addiction-related problems, which have parallels in working with offenders. These are: establishing safety and trust; understanding the nature of the addictive illness; breaking through denial; surrendering to recovery; and understanding the origins of shame (Wilson 2003). Each of these interventions will be examined, and examples given of practical therapeutic tasks.

Establishing safety and trust

The therapeutic aim here is to be able to risk self-disclosure. If trust and safety are to be established, there is the fear of being judged out-of-control for people addressing an addiction. Art provides an opportunity to develop a personal visual language of unprocessed shame reduction where thoughts or feelings can be transformed. 'If [the inmate] were to express anger verbally, those around him would react adversely because they interpret anger as an assault… but… they can draw out their hostility and rage on paper, with little fear of retribution' (Gussak and Virshup 1997: 2). At this stage the client is learning self-resilience, as mastering over what they choose to express relies on their ability to take risks and to trust the therapeutic process.

- Introduce yourself to the group (see pp. 66, 79–80).
- Draw the circumstances that brought you here (Liebmann 1990: 140–3).
- How do you feel about being here? (Wilson 2003: 285).
- Draw something about you that the group does not know (see p. 79).
- Draw a picture of your name (see pp. 79, 125).
- Draw whatever comes to mind (see pp. 57–8, 79, 156–7).
- Make a collage that describes you (see pp. 80–1, 135, 157–9).

Understanding the nature of the addictive illness

To move on from being controlled by the addiction, the fact that a problem exists must be acknowledged (Wilson 2003; Coulter 2011). In this process, the client is empowered to describe their experience through the personalised visual descriptions of their experiences and to become more accountable for their actions. As discussed above, sequencing events and considering the negative consequences of their actions assists the developing sense of an accountability – the addiction is named as an 'illness'.

- Draw your addiction (Wilson 2003: 285). If it could speak, what is it saying? (Withers 2006: 2).
- Draw being 'under the influence' of your addiction or impulsive behaviour (Coulter 2011: 88–90, Wilson 2003: 285).
- Draw the events (or sequence of events) that happen after you have succumbed to your addiction (Liebmann 1990: 137–43).
- Draw the feeling of 'being powerless' (Wilson 2003: 286).
- Draw other feelings related to your addiction.
- Draw the effects of your addiction on your family.
- Draw who I am/who I was/who I hope to be.
- Draw an outline of your house and fill in the internal and external effects of your addiction on that home (Wilson 2003: 291).
- Draw two pictures: one of yourself addicted, the other of yourself not addicted.

Breaking through denial

Art techniques as a therapeutic intervention are based on a non-verbal starting point. It is therefore often a more effective way to break through defences that mask shame and perpetuate denial. Through engaging with the creative process, defence mechanisms such as intellectualisation, rationalisation and minimisation (Moore 1983) are circumvented. A better understanding of what takes place is fostered as the client becomes more familiar with their issues.

- Draw the effect of the addiction on you, your family, the social systems that exist outside you and your family (one or all of these).
- Self-box/bag – 'the outside represents what you let people see and the inside is what you are afraid to let them see' (Wilson 2003: 287; see also pp. 80–1 of this book).
- Fantasy versus reality – what your addiction promises versus what you really experience (Wilson 2003: 286–7).
- Illustrate three forms of denial you use (Wilson 2003: 287).
- Draw a checklist of triggers (Wilson 2003: 288).
- Draw: who are you blaming?
- Draw a map of your addiction history and where this has led (Coulter 2007: 223).
- Draw when you are most vulnerable to your addiction – give it a context (Wilson 2003: 288; Withers 2006).
- Draw tools of recovery that help you deal with triggers (Wilson 2003: 288).

Surrendering to recovery

At this stage of treatment, a shift in the operating belief system is required so that the addiction loses its power. Wilson emphasises that at this stage, support from the therapy peer group, the wider community, family and friends needs to be harnessed (Wilson 2003). Depending on the circumstances, this support may also include back-up from a mentor. Wilson also refers to the need to structure a belief system or to develop a relationship with a higher external power of their choice, such as a return to an earlier belief system – an acceptance of succumbing to an addiction as part of being human assists shame-reduction. The support of a spiritual system from outside can be visualised as some distance away, but getting closer as their recovery progresses. There are alternate tasks that suit the same concept of a 'higher power' but less explicit, listed below:

- Draw your relationship to a 'higher power' (Wilson 2003: 290).
- Make a spiritual symbol – something to represent your new belief.
- Find and illustrate a symbol of strength.
- Draw a story about yourself talking to a 'higher power' (Wilson 2003: 290).
- Make a personal mandala that focuses on opposite parts of you.
- Draw a door of opportunity and a door of challenge.
- Draw your likes and dislikes.
- Draw what forgiveness looks like for you (Wilson 2003: 290).

Understanding the origins of shame

The final stage involves facing reality where the unspeakable is spoken. This means often exploring family-of-origin issues as problems of addiction start to connect to earlier childhood experiences. Alternatively, this may mean a need for self-regulation from a traumatic memory or a breaking through from myths and rules that are contributing to entrenched patterns sustained over the years as part of a need to control or a fear of change. This is a stage of self-realisation, empowerment and self-affirmation.

- Draw a portrait of your family, including yourself (see pp. 156–7).
- Draw an outline of your body and fill the inside with positive affirmations and images (Wilson 2003: 291). (This can also be used as a group task to draw the physical effects of addiction; Wilson 2003: 286; Feen-Calligan 1999.)
- Together, build a map or a road to recovery (Wilson 2003: 291; Coulter 2007: 223).
- Create an image of your inner child part being attended to by your adult part (Wilson 2003: 291; Withers 2006: 10–11).
- Make a doll or puppet of your inner child and create a safe place (Wilson 2003: 291).

- Make a group tree and leaves representing things you are thankful for and things you have lost.
- Make a mask – paint on the outside what people see and paint on the inside what different feelings are coming up for you.

Training workshops on addiction

When conducting training on working with addiction for allied health professionals, the following three workshops are effective experiential learning tasks. Visual diary work is part of any training workshop; in this example, the visual diary instruction tasks are included to demonstrate how to incorporate opportunities for privacy and self-care for workshop participants. Addiction work is confronting at times and the art therapist has a responsibility to provide techniques about how to self-process art work because they may only be with the training group for a short amount of time.

Art task 1: draw your addiction

Visual diary entry: journaling task

Draw something that is a debriefing from your addiction picture. This might be something reflective about the process, how you are feeling after doing this picture or thoughts that crossed your mind while doing the art task. Make any relevant notes. Entries are private and only viewed by another if or when you choose to share them.

Art task 2: family-of-origin

In any work on addiction, it is always useful to include something about the client's family. It might be their family-of-origin and how their addiction relates to their childhood experiences, or it might be their current family and how their addiction is affecting important people in their life. This task is adapted from the Kwiatkowska Family Art Evaluation Technique (Kwiatkowska 1978) but executed in a different form of art media.

Instruction 1

In plasticine, make a small abstract sculpture (approximately palm-size) to describe your family and the relationships within your family. Represent each family member considering colour, shape and any other principles of abstraction that are relevant for you. A list of abstract art considerations appear on page 74 as basic art principles. This list helps clients and therapists consider abstract concepts. The therapist can focus on a few or provide the whole list depending on the capabilities of the client or group. If plasticine is a difficult media, coloured paper can be used instead or one of the following tasks can be used as an alternative.

Instruction 2

If Instruction 1 is too challenging, think about abstract adjectives that describe each family member and try to convey those adjectives in colour, shape, size and texture. For example, three adjectives to describe one family member might be cheerful, active and reliable, and another might be irresponsible, mischievous and clever. Another family might have a member who is withdrawn, ambitious and deceitful, or someone who is depressed, anxious and indecisive. *See if you can make a shape that combines three abstract descriptive qualities for each family member through colour, form and texture, for example.*

The art therapist can brainstorm these examples if there is time.

Instruction 3

A further extension to this task is to include a family mapping activity. This can be done with the concept of a family genogram, or, in keeping with the visual art therapy demonstration, in a spatial format (Coulter 2007: 223). The small sculptures are placed in relationship to each other and a drawn or painted environment on which to place the family members may also be included.

Create a map of your family by placing them in relationship to each other. You may like to paint or draw on paper to add to this task. Consider the various relationships and demonstrate by line, colour or orientation of space, to emphasise the family system in which they are currently operating.

This task extension gives the abstract family portrait a context and provides opportunity for a narrative sharing as the story of a family-of-origin unfolds in small group discussions of three or four participants.

Instruction 4

A further extension to this task is to introduce a solution-focused task to consider possible changes to the current description. This is only relevant for those who would like some change to the map or context of their abstract family portrait.

Imagine that overnight, a miracle takes place and when you wake up the next day, everything has changed for the better in your family portrait. Rearrange your family sculpture into how it would be if a miracle happened. Alternatively, in order to not be quite so prescriptive to the solution-focused model, this could simply be *Rearrange your family portrait into how you would like it to be.*

After group discussion, another personal, visual diary entry is suggested to provide opportunity to debrief from this task.

Art task 3: build a map to recovery

Visual mapping tasks provide an elevated or diagrammatic view of the concept of a road to recovery, as an expansion of narrative storyboard construction. Visual maps in family work can be an expansion on the diagrammatic genogram or house plan (Coulter 2007: 223). They can also be a visual symbolic representation of a life journey (Liebmann 2004: 212). White's use of charting to re-author conversation maps provides a narrative approach (White 2007: 83–98) that can be adapted to the processing of a more visual art therapy task.

Trauma through imprisonment

The harsh reality of attending court and consequent imprisonment can be traumatic. Liebmann engages her probation clients in a narrative technique of storyboard work to deal with traumatic memory, including recollection of the crime (Liebmann 1990: 135–7). Over time, memory fragments convert into a coherent story, expressed through creating a comic strip account of the event, frame by frame. By creating a visual account, the events become experienced as past personal history that are no longer present. The subjective states of consciousness are converted into a visual text of non-verbal communication of traumatic memory image fragments. Through art therapy treatment all aspects of the trauma experience and responses are explored. Through externalised dialogues between the person and their dissociated states, there is a cognitive examination of the trauma. Images can evoke body memories and arousal of trauma flashbacks. These dissociated self-states gain consciousness through concretised images.

As well as resolving dissociation, art therapy attends to a victim mythology. Through the ritual of art, creativity and play, safety and trust are established and a sense of fear of the unknown and trauma damage is removed. There is an interrelationship between imagery and resistances as issues for surviving a dangerous world are addressed through the interaction of image and affect.

Alexithymia is a lacking of the words for emotions and is a manifestation of a deficit in emotional cognition. The person is unaware of their feelings or does not understand their significance, so they rarely talk about feelings or emotional preferences. They have a manner of concrete operational function and rarely use imagination to focus drives and motivations.

The essential feature of post-traumatic stress disorder (PTSD) is described by the American Psychiatric Association as:

> the development of characteristic symptoms following exposure to an extreme traumatic stressor involving direct personal experience of a event that involves actual or threatened death or serious injury, or other threat to

one's physical integrity: or witnessing an event that involves death, injury, or a threat to the physical integrity of another person.

(American Psychiatric Association 2000: 424)

This can also involve the person learning about such an event happening to a close associate.

Using art to process PTSD, concrete references to the trauma are transformed into symbolic images. There is right hemisphere-processing on multiple levels. Feeling experiences are essential to restructuring thinking and behaviour. Art therapy provides an interaction between right- and left-brain operations. There is a close connection between imagery and emotion. Art is now being identified as a vehicle for treating trauma and connecting feelings with thought, and effective management of emotion is enhanced (Coulter 2008).

Although art therapy offers victims of incarceration opportunity for self-expression, the benefits of this work need to be carefully considered in terms of the context in which the therapist is working. Enlightenment and self-realisation are not always the most productive goals if the individual is residing in an environment that discourages self-expression and self-assertion. There is no doubt that art therapy assists inmates to deal with issues of addiction. The benefits of art therapy in institutionalised settings help clients on a variety of levels as they come to terms with their addiction(s), face their fears and unresolved childhood issues and prepare for the retributions of change in their discovery of new strengths and convictions.

Bibliography

American Psychiatric Association. 2000. *Diagnostic and Statistical Manual of Mental Disorders* (DSM-IVR). Fourth edition revised. Arlington, VA: American Psychiatric Association.

Berg, I.K. and Steiner, T. 2003. *Children's Solution Work*. New York: W.W. Norton and Company.

Boyle, J. 1977. *A Sense of Freedom*. Edinburgh: Canongate.

Cade, B. 1995. The Future Focus. Unpublished training handout, Brief Interactional Approaches to Therapy, Epping, NSW, Australia.

Cardinal, R. 1972. *Outsider Art*. London: Studio Vista.

Cardinal, R. 1979. *Outsiders*. Arts Council of Great Britain.

Coulter, A. 1986. The Social Implications of Creativity with Reference to Art as a Form of Therapy Promoting Individuation. Unpublished Master's thesis. College of Art, Birmingham Polytechnic (now Birmingham City University).

Coulter, A. 2007. Couple Art Therapy: 'Seeing' Difference Makes a Difference, in E. Shaw and J. Crawley (eds) *Couple Therapy in Australia: Issues Emerging from Practice*. Kew, Victoria: PsychOz Publications, pp. 215–27.

Coulter, A. 2008. 'Came Back – Didn't Come Home': Returning from a War Zone, in M. Liebmann (ed.) *Art Therapy and Anger*. London: Jessica Kingsley Publishers, pp. 238–56.

Coulter, A. 2011. Contemporary Art Therapy: Working with Transient Youth, in H. Burt (ed.) *Art Therapy and Postmodernism: Creative Healing Through a Prism.* London: Jessica Kingsley Publishers, pp. 83–93.

Feen-Calligan, H. 1999. Enlightenment in Chemical Dependency Treatment Programs: a Grounded Theory, in C.A. Malchiodi (ed.) *Medical Art Therapy with Adults.* London: Jessica Kingsley Publishers, pp. 137–61.

Fisher, A. 2005. Co-creating Visual Maps Using a Narrative Approach around the Themes of Romance and Violence with Art Fisher. Unpublished notes from workshop held on 18 July at Coogee Surf Life Saving Club, Charing Cross Narrative Therapy, Sydney, Australia.

Goffman, E. 1968. *Asylums: Essays on the Social Situation of Mental Patients and Other Inmates.* London: Penguin.

Gussak, D. and Virshup, E. (eds) 1997. *Drawing Time: Art Therapy in Prisons and Other Correctional Settings.* Chicago, IL: Magnolia Street Publishers.

Hagood, M.M. 2000. *The Use of Art in Counselling Child and Adult Survivors of Sexual Abuse.* London: Jessica Kingsley Publishers.

Kwiatkowska, H.Y. 1978. *Family Therapy and Evaluation Through Art.* Springfield, IL: C.C. Thomas.

Laing, J. 1984. Art Therapy in Prisons, in T. Dalley (ed.) *Art as Therapy: an Introduction to the Use of Art as a Therapeutic Technique.* London: Tavistock Publications, pp. 115–28.

Liebmann, M. 1990. 'It Just Happened': Looking at Crime Events, in M. Liebmann (ed.) *Art Therapy in Practice.* London: Jessica Kingsley Publishers, pp. 133–55.

Liebmann, M. (ed.) 1994. *Art Therapy with Offenders.* London: Jessica Kingsley Publishers.

Liebmann, M. 2004. *Art Therapy for Groups: a Handbook of Themes and Exercises.* Second edition. London: Jessica Kingsley Publishers.

Moore, R. 1983. Art Therapy with Substance Abusers: a Review of the Literature. *The Arts in Psychotherapy* 10, 251–60.

Nowell-Hall, P. 1978. Marlborough Hospital, London, in *Inner Eye: An Exhibition of Work Made in Psychiatric Hospitals.* Oxford: Museum of Modern Art, p. 39.

Prinzhorn, H. 1972 (1922). *Bildnerei der Geisteskranken: Ein Beitrag zur Psychologie und Psychopathologie der Gestaltung [Artistry of the Mentally Ill].* Translated by E. von Brockendorff. Berlin: Springer Verlag.

de Shazer, S. 1994. *Words Were Originally Magic.* New York: W.W. Norton and Company.

Teasdale, C. 1997. Art Therapy as a Shared Forensic Investigation. *Inscape* 2(2), 32–40.

White, M. 2007. *Maps of Narrative Practice.* New York: W.W. Norton and Company.

White, M. and Epston, D. 1990. *Narrative Means to Therapeutic Ends.* New York: W.W. Norton and Company.

Wilson, M. 2003. Art Therapy in Addictions Treatment: Creativity and Shame Reduction, in C.A. Malchiodi (ed.) *Handbook of Art Therapy.* New York: The Guilford Press, pp. 281–93.

Withers, R. 2006. Interactive Drawing Therapy: Working with Therapeutic Imagery. *New Zealand Journal of Counselling* 26(4), 1–14.

Withers, R. 2009. The Therapeutic Process of Interactive Drawing Therapy. *New Zealand Journal of Counselling* 29(2), 73–90.

Chapter 12

Art therapy with couples and families

Annette M. Coulter

The use of art in family work introduces an alternative way for all members to communicate from a visual intervention, using a visual language of metaphor and image which are easily understood by all family members and can cut through complex verbal discourse. When family communication has a visual starting point, younger family members in particular are able to understand and relate to joint problem solving, challenge the system that is operating and develop a better understanding of others' perspectives. For some family members, it is easier to say through an art task how they are affected by current relationships. The inclusion of art in family therapy helps bridge generational barriers as parents and children work together to clarify different perceptions of the family issues. It is important for art therapists to be able to adapt their skills to suit all members of the family and to accommodate different thinking within family sub-systems, such as the couple relationship. The art therapist must maintain an unbiased approach in order to see each partner's perspective and to not ally themselves with only part of the family system, because one seems more reasonable than the other.

Family and couple consultation is a highly specialised field within art therapy, similar to intensive group work, but usually more toxic. Interactional dynamics are rich, entrenched and challenging. The focus is on current interaction patterns rather than gathering a comprehensive family history. Communication processes and patterns of interaction maintain the family system or couple relationship in a state of homeostasis. It is the aim of the therapist to implement a strategic intervention, designed to disrupt this system. An art activity offers the reluctant or resistant family member or partner a way to engage that has potential to introduce fun and a sense of humour to the seriousness of therapy, as well as an opportunity to express something through metaphor or symbol that is otherwise difficult to address.

Couples art therapy

Couples who seek therapy usually present a complex relationship history. If their problems were easy to resolve, they would not be requiring therapy but would have resolved their difficulties between themselves. There are entrenched patterns of communication that have been established over the years, laced with positions of misunderstanding and verbal impasses. Even if the couple are in a new relationship, one or both parties will have previous relationship experiences that may be impacting on their current new relationship. There is also the therapist's potential personal story of failed relationships or relationship difficulties that can impact on his or her response to a couple. Crago writes that 'the potential break-up of a committed adult relationship seems a matter of emotional "life" or "death"... *their* anxiety easily becomes *our* anxiety' (Crago 2006: 54; original emphasis).

Riley encourages the use of visual interventions in couples work because of the introduction of an expanded view: 'to "see" is not possible with words alone' (Riley 2003: 388). With a focus on visual mapping, the use of abstraction and other techniques, the couple's verbal process is enhanced as they examine their relationship in a different language, that of art (Coulter 2007: 215–19).

A basic principle from IDT (see pp. 82–3) that is effective when working with a couple is that the art therapist manages the process while the couple manage the content. If the therapist gets too caught up in the content, they feel drawn to take sides or to problem-solve for one or other party. In couple work, if the therapist has missed the point, it will surface again until the therapist addresses that issue. It is also likely that the surface issue being presented is symbolic of a deeper, less conscious problem or dynamic that is operating within the relationship. In managing the process, the art therapist comments on the phenomenon of repeated content and invites the couple to draw something about that repeated point. They can draw the same task each session to reflect on their relationship at that point (Coulter 2007; Riley 2003). By focusing on the couple's process, the art therapist aims to visually assist the amplification of difference. The visual concretisation of content means it is heard and seen by the other. Something that has an unconscious emotional momentum becomes externalised, allowing the couple to focus together on what is visually created, providing an opportunity to understand the problem from the other's perspective, which has been translated visually through symbol, metaphor or literal representation. The production of an image has the potential to highlight reflections, change or progress in the couple's relationship, and encourages the art therapist to listen to their own thoughts and feelings as they sit with the couple's emotional dilemmas.

For some clients, especially the men in relationships, it is particularly effective to provide a physical dimension to the therapeutic process. The notion of doing something together that is seen as constructive, such as an art task, helps contribute to an understanding of the system that is operating (Coulter 2007). Visual patterns of current circular causality assist in the recognition of an alternate view of the relationship difficulties. The aim of couple art therapy is to 'de-stabilize the cycle of misinformation that has interrupted their ability to understand each other' (Riley 2003: 389).

Family art therapy

The family art therapist focuses on the nature of the interactions between family members rather than on the sequence of events that lead to the problem in the first place. It is important to not regard the presenting problem as dysfunctional or a sign of weakness, but more as a system of recursive patterns of communication that maintain the interactional sequences (Bross and Benjamin 1982). Through the content and process of various art tasks, the family art therapist works to understand the family system that is operating and to also explore how this system is maintained. The family is seen as a self-regulating organisation that seeks to maintain itself despite external pressures and internal events such as births, deaths and developmental changes. Landgarten describes this process:

> The system is examined through the way in which the family functions as a unit while creating an art form together. The value of the art task is threefold: The *process* as a diagnostic, interactional and rehearsal tool; the *contents* as a means of portraying unconscious and conscious communication; and the *product* as lasting evidence of the group's dynamics.... *The invading device is the art directive, which contains the appropriate media and is clinically sound.*
> (Landgarten 1987: 5; original emphasis)

Children or adolescents who are resistant to family intervention engage more easily when a family art intervention is used to address a serious problem. Causality is a circular process based on the cybernetic concept of feedback. No matter where in the family system an interaction begins, the same result will occur. For example, where a family member is the scapegoat, regardless of what or who precipitated the problem or crisis, the operating dynamic is that this one person will be blamed, because that is their role in the dysfunctional family system. This pattern is entrenched and circular. The use of art as a systemic device is effective, clear and family inclusive.

Art therapy offers a reframe to take place in tangible form because by its very nature, an art work can be 'framed'. Physical reframing in art therapy, by cropping, transposing, destroying and repositioning, helps air family issues and facilitates viewing from an altered perspective. As Riley (1994) reminds us, framing can change a family's co-construction of the external world:

> To reframe ... means to change the conceptual and/or emotional setting or viewpoint in relation to which a situation is experienced and to place it in another frame which fits the 'facts' of the same concrete situation equally well or even better, and therefore changes its entire meaning. The mechanism involved here is not immediately obvious, especially if we bear in mind that there is change while the situation itself may remain quite unchanged and, indeed, even unchangeable. What turns out to be changed as a result of reframing is the meaning attributed to the situation, and therefore its consequences, but not its concrete facts....
> (Watzlawick, Weakland and Fisch 1974: 95)

The metaphor of change to the physical frame can lead to a parallel metaphor of change within the family system and joint reflection about how the dysfunctional homeostasis is being maintained. Therapist and clients engage in non-threatening communication through the symbolic quality of the metaphors/analogues. The art therapist uses both visual and verbal metaphors. When an intervention is presented through a metaphor, the client may not even realise the intervention has been made (Haley 1976). When the metaphor is visual rather than verbal, it is easy for all members of the family to grasp the new concept. The creation of tangible family symbols or metaphors add a physical potency to the therapeutic process. The family images provide the content of therapy; the art therapist provides processes by which those issues are addressed.

As well as systemic or strategic interventions, family art therapists can also integrate solution-focused brief and narrative approaches. When working with families, the art therapist is adapting to different personalities within the family constellation. An integrative approach provides a variety of theoretical approaches to be included to suit different personality types. For the logical structured thinker, the solution-focused brief approach engages even the sceptical or reluctant family member. A narrative approach allows opportunity for another perspective to be heard that may not have been heard before (Riley 1993). This 'news of difference' (White and Epston 1990: 61) can then be taken up by a solution-focused intervention creating a systemic intervention (Coulter 2011). The art-based nature of the activity is strategic in itself: art has a lot to offer the family in conflict.

For example, working in a women's refuge with mothers who are victims of domestic violence might include the provision of family art therapy that includes children and adolescents who are suffering vicarious trauma from their exposure to family violence. There could be an adolescent member of the family who is acting out a role model of violence to younger siblings or the adult parent. The systemic goal is to disrupt the multi-generational pattern of domestic violence. Through art, family members share their experience of domestic violence by the perpetrator who is now absent and the adolescent family member who is present. A narrative art task intervention might be to 'draw what it's like to be in your family' or 'what would you like to change in your family?' What comes to light may be that a younger child who is refusing to attend school is in fear that something might happen to their parent if they leave home. This becomes the narrative that was previously unheard. Individual art therapy may be required where anger management or separation issues are directly addressed in collaboration with family therapy. In adult psychiatry, the client suffering mental illness may have family members who require systemic treatment. Art therapy offers a way to examine and reflect on the system and the operating dynamics.

When working as part of a family therapy team, an image can be drawn by the team for the family to describe what has been discussed. Family members often say they cannot remember the discussions, but that they can recall the image the team drew and the metaphoric explanation. For example, a family member talking about their struggles might use the metaphoric phrase 'it feels like we're paddling upstream against the current and not getting anywhere'. The family therapy team then draw a river and a boat being paddled upstream, and include details such as the two sides of the river in contrast and some emphasis of a strong current. In doing a drawing, the team amplify a metaphor the family have raised in the content of the session. When this image is shared with the family, the therapist shows the team-generated image to the family by saying, 'the team behind the screen are wondering *if it looks a bit like this?*' Discussion ensues about why they are doing this, how they got there and what direction are they going in, and obstacles that are making their journey more difficult. In advocacy, IDT also promotes that the therapist draws a picture to describe something the client is talking about, the therapist is working as an advocate for the client's process (Withers 2006). Capturing a client's metaphor in the moment of a counselling session is a strategic intervention. The therapist is not imposing any agenda other than the content introduced by the client; what they are doing is managing the process by slowing things down and encouraging the family to examine what they're talking about, and so the finer details of a verbal discussion are explored. The family can change and correct the image or the therapist can hand the image to the client to explain or draw how it might be different.

The merits of a cognitive approach

While long-term art psychotherapy is an effective and satisfying way to work, it is reliant on a public health system that is robust enough to financially support this and does not fit for most parts of the world. An art therapist who has a psychoanalytic orientation needs to be flexible and be able to consider the integration of a more cognitive approach. Without this flexibility, their client numbers are reduced and limited to only the wealthy who are not reliant on state-funded services.

Designing an art therapy intervention

The real art of art therapy is the ability to be able to design an art intervention that is relevant to the moment and may be entirely unique to the client's therapeutic process and situation.

The simplest way to design an art intervention is to follow the client's content. For example, if a client is talking about feeling depressed and unmotivated, that their life is on hold and they're not enjoying things any more, a potential intervention might be to 'draw a feeling that is opposite to what you are feeling right now'. While this is interesting and has merit in some strengths-based situations, it is motivated by the therapist's need to dictate content and their agenda to 'cheer the client up', so the client leaves the session brighter and happier. A different intervention would be more prescriptive in terms of what the client originally spoke about, such as 'draw what feeling depressed looks like' or 'draw someone or something unmotivated'. The next statement, 'I feel like my life has been put on hold', is metaphoric and so has a visual ambiance. If a client is talking in metaphors, the therapist's intervention should be to concretise the metaphor, possibly providing a context where this is appropriate: 'draw something or someone being put on hold', for example, or 'what does being "on hold" look like?' In art therapy it can always be assumed that whatever a client draws in some way relates to them, regardless of the metaphor, diagram or symbolic content. By suggesting 'something' is on hold, a cushion or safety buffer is set up around the task so that the image produced is not necessarily to do with the client. Even though what they execute does relate to them, creating an emotional distance in the wording of the task assists the reluctant client (IDT Foundation Course, 2010).

Family art therapy training for allied health professionals

A visual intervention can be helpful if health professionals find themselves 'stuck' when dealing with entrenched patterns and circular processes of causality. There are two family art assessment interventions that can easily be integrated into a repertoire of skills. These are adapted from the work of US art therapy pioneers Hanna Kwiatkowska and Helen Landgarten (Kwiatkowska 1978; Landgarten 1993).

Art task procedure

There are always two therapists for a family art evaluation. Asking an allied health professional to be a co-therapist is an effective way to educate through experiential learning plus gain support from other members of the treatment team. The art therapist leads the art task sequence and the other therapist observes family interactions and their responses to the tasks. The co-therapist's role is similar to that of the co-facilitator for group work (see Chapter 14).

Each family member has their own set of pastels with a full colour range that includes black and white, plus six sheets of paper numbered 1 to 6. Each family member works in the same room but out of view of other family members. To achieve this, Kwiatkowska recommends working at easels, so that family members' distraction from the art task is minimised and they are able to focus more easily on their own work. Family members can talk to each other about the procedures as they unfold.

These six art tasks gradually increase in complexity and can be used as standalone tasks as well as part of the evaluation procedure (see pp. 57–8).

1   A 'free' picture: 'Draw whatever comes to mind' (see p. 57). This task is designed to be open-ended and to allow the person to draw wherever they are at the beginning of a family session.
2   A picture of your family, whatever is family for you. If the client asks who to include, the response is to draw it in whatever way they choose, and within one family this could produce quite different pictures (Landgarten 1987).

3   An abstract family portrait, the same as the above but symbolic (see pp. 127–8). This can be time-consuming but can be interesting, bringing up highly-charged feelings.

4   A picture started with the help of a scribble (see pp. 56 and 79). This begins with a physical warm-up exercise, loosening up before drawing a scribble with eyes fully or partially closed. Once an image is discerned, lines, colour and shape can be added to enhance the image.

5   A joint family scribble, as a group decision-making process. This task is a group decision-making process for the family to complete together. It begins with the same physical warm-up as above. Following the scribble-making production, the family members look at each other's work together and share what they see. They then choose one scribble and complete a joint family scribble picture. This is usually a successful family group task, though depending on the family dynamics, it can be a stumbling block for some families

6   A 'free' picture: 'Draw whatever comes to mind'. It is interesting to compare this last free picture to the first free picture. Titling art work is significant because of relevance to rest of the work.

Family portraits

Procedure 2 might be realistic family self-portraits (though stick figures are fine) where placement on the page, or a picture of family members doing something together becomes significant (Kwiatkowska 1978; Burns and Kaufman 1972). Abstract family portraits can be quite significant, if the child can be assisted with the concept of abstraction (Coulter 2007; Kwiatkowska 1978). The two 'free' pictures at the beginning and end of the procedure are compared. If the procedure has intensified family dynamics, it is likely to be indicated in how the second free picture compares with the first. For example, if the first free picture is a calm horizontal landscape and the last free picture an erupting vertical volcano or a dragon spitting fire, it is likely to conclude that feelings have been heightened for that family member.

Collage family assessment technique

A non-threatening task developed by Landgarten is useful for the client, family member or even allied health professional who is reluctant to draw (Landgarten 1993). Using found images alongside collage materials is an alternative, effective technique. Landgarten recommends two boxes of pre-cut images, one of people and one of miscellaneous objects, so that clients are not distracted to read magazine articles as they search for images. For the first box, Landgarten suggests pictures of people from different cultures, the majority of whom pertain to the client/family's culture; reality-oriented (only some to be stereotyped, glamorous images); male and female figures; people of all ages and different facial expressions, movement and static body positions; people from different economic conditions and walks of life, and in different environments, alone, in dyads, groups or family settings (Landgarten 1993).

The list of miscellaneous objects is not unlike a list of sand play objects and includes clocks, trucks, cars, clothes, computers, dishes, furniture, tools, medicines, houses, animals, bottles of liquor, fires, plumbing, food, jewellery, scenes from nature, rubbish, demolished homes, broken glass, guns, pills, and destroyed, broken, fragile items. Additional materials include newsprint, coloured paper, glitter and fabric scraps.

Landgarten alerts the family art therapist to consider: how are pictures handled? Were they torn, cut away or trimmed before they were pasted down? How was the glue handled – messily, neatly, obsessively? Was placement of the found images careful, haphazard or reasonable? What was the pictorial content? Did specific themes appear or get repeated?

Assessment procedure 1

Invite each family member to look through the images and pick out ones that catch their attention, paste them onto the paper, then either write directly onto the paper or tell anything that comes to mind about each picture.

Rationale: this introduces the assessment procedure. Few instructions make the task easy to master and there are no boundaries on the number of pictures and a lot of freedom for the selection process.

Assessment procedure 2

Invite each family member to pick out four to six pictures of people and paste them onto paper, then write or tell what they imagine each person is thinking and what he/she is saying.

Rationale: this reveals trust regarding themselves, someone else or the therapist. There is a specific number – how does each family member deal with limits being set or an authority figure? It relates to congruencies or disparities about what people think and say. There is sometimes a resemblance between the picture and someone they know.

Assessment procedure 3

Invite each family member to pick out four to six pictures of either people and/or miscellaneous items that stand for something good and something bad, paste them down and write or tell what the picture means.

Rationale: this is purposely ambiguous regarding something good and something bad.

Leeway is given in the choice of image selection. There is a choice between people (more emotional content) or objects (distancing). Humorous pictures may be avoiding feelings or may be a testing of the therapist. If this is the case, it would be addressed later in the treatment phase.

Assessment procedure 4

Invite each family member to pick out only one picture of a person, paste it down and write or tell what is happening to that person. Then ask, 'do you think the situation will change?' If so, find a picture illustrating the change or tell what will make it change.

Rationale: evaluates a negative/positive outlook and reveals attitudes, ability to cope, whether problem-solving is part of their lifestyle.

Landgarten has devised all four tasks (above) for free association and personal projection. There is flexibility within each task to reflect individual personality, with minimum constraints imposed by the family art therapist.These procedures may appear simplistic, too prescriptive and cause discomfort for some art therapists to consider. However, they are useful for allied health professionals, and the techniques are effective and safe for most therapists.

Couple art therapy training for allied health professionals

Again, safe, clear tasks provide a positive experience for both the art therapist and allied health professionals. The line conversation (Coulter 2007: 218) is now used in the context of a couple conversation. In a training workshop, there are two participants to one piece of paper, preferably representing a couple. They may even have a particular client in mind to possibly role-play in the line conversation. Make the second line conversation a conflictual one; again, possibly role-play a particular client with whom you are working or someone you know.

Joint scribble picture

Participants pair up in role as a couple – they can discuss a scenario or they can be themselves.

Each person makes a scribble on the page. Together, view each scribble and choose one to make a joint scribble picture. Enhance this shared image with colour, and add details such as eyes, texture and any additional features or qualities.

Abstract description of a relationship

Make an abstract sculpture using plasticine or clay to describe the relationship. (This can be a personal relationship, or a difficult client relationship with which the worker is familiar.)

The Expressive Therapies Continuum can also be discussed (see Chapter 6).

For the therapist

These points are designed to quickly impart basic best practice guidelines for couple and family therapists.

Establish guidelines before sharing

Issues of confidentiality and ownership of the art work must always be addressed before art work produced in a therapeutic context is discussed and shared with other family members or partners in relationship counselling. Such guidelines help to provide psychological safety.

- Listen to the language used: clients' word symbols not the therapist's
  The fact that client art work needs to be respected is always an important point. Emphasising the significance of language as word symbols will resonate for other family therapists because use of client language is a core understanding to best family therapy practice. Where this point expands is the notion of words as another symbolic system in relationship to the art work that is produced in the family or couple therapy session. Interactive Drawing Therapy (IDT) is a drawing tool that focuses on the interaction of words–image–behaviour (Withers 2006). For therapists who do not wish to complete an art therapy qualification, further training in IDT provides a basic methodology for best practice.
- Avoid assumptions
  This point is a reminder about how easy it is for the therapist to impose themselves onto the client's art work. The same applies for other family members imposing their view on another member's drawing.
- Do not talk while art-making is in progress: allow internal dialogue
  This is another reminder of a basic art therapy principle. When working with families, it is not always relevant or possible to impose this guideline because family members are so familiar with each other and the multi-generational aspect means younger members will want to interact with parents and older siblings spontaneously and in order to deal with their anxiety about an art task. At the same time, it is possible for children to understand a time for art-making and a time for talking (see Chapter 10). It is up to the art therapist's discretion how relevant it is to try to enforce this guideline in a family consultation.
- Do not impose a 'therapist's agenda'
  This point re-emphasises the idea of following the family's agenda rather than something imposed on the family by the therapist. Art therapists are trained to understand their own psychopathology and to avoid countertransference when viewing and facilitating exploration of client imagery. However, because allied health professionals are not so schooled, this point helps them to consider what might be influencing their involvement in the family

systemic dynamic. It is easy to be drawn into a toxic family operating system but it is also easy to have an unexpected reaction and response to client art work. This point reminds the therapist to stay with the family process and to remember not to impose themselves in the family interactional patterns in response to personal wants and needs.

- Do not be satisfied with obvious responses
  This is a reminder that when the client responds in an expected way, the therapist may be satisfied and moves on to another aspect of the image too quickly. It is important to double check predicted responses to ensure there is not something being missed. By consciously managing to hold a moment in the processing of a drawing, the allied health professional is more likely to not miss something significant in the content of the art work.
- Seek permission when handling art work
  Art work is regarded as a physical extension of the maker. When processing in the context of the family there is expected personal intrusion between family members, but the facilitating therapist models a respectful regard of the art work by bearing in mind boundaries around touching and group displaying of work in family processing.
- Provide adequate workspace
  Some techniques such as the family art evaluation (Kwiatkowska 1978) require that the collaborative art works are completed in private view, away from other family members to avoid contamination of individual engagement with the art materials or task. Easels can assist this but are not always easily included in a family therapy space. Family therapy usually takes place in a small group room or a larger than usual consulting room; however, there is often limited space for other equipment. Alerting the allied health professional to consideration of space helps planning and preparation with limited physical resources.
- Document and store art work
  This point is another reminder of the therapist's responsibilities. Documenting art work (with name, date and title on the reverse) is crucial to best practice. The family is unlikely to remember all that was shared pertaining to the art work, and the therapist's record of what was stated assists families to recall difficult moments in the session. The titling of art work is especially important as this can often generate family metaphors and symbols to which all family members can respond. Without good documentation, successful moments in the couple or family sessions can be lost.
- Try out tasks beforehand
  To understand how a task is to be received and responded to, and to gain familiarity with the client's process, the allied health professional needs to test out the intervention, where possible, on themself first. This is not always possible if the intervention is a spontaneous, in-the-moment response to a family situation during an art therapy session. However, where an art

task or an array of tasks is being considered in preparation for a couple or family session, trialling these tasks beforehand is highly recommended. Going through some ideas personally is always possible, but better still, asking other staff to trial an intervention and provide feedback is equally useful.

Clinical supervision and ethical practice

When sharing art therapy skills with other health professionals, the art therapist is also available to offer clinical supervision for the family or couple art consultation. Alternatively, supervision can be provided by a family or couples therapist clinical supervisor. Supervision helps monitor transference and countertransference in relation to the use of art therapy interventions as they are designed and trialled. It is educational for allied health professionals to learn that clinical supervision is required for art therapy and that this is not just the provision of playful diversion for couples and families. As they use art more frequently in their work, therapists realise that art therapy directives can be a treatment intervention in itself or can be used as an adjunct to verbal family therapy to address specific clinical issues and needs as they arise.

Art crosses generational and gender barriers, bridging family members to co-construct a new family story. A solution-focused approach provides opportunity for brief goal-directed art interventions for resistant families who may not attend therapy for many sessions. Their experience is positive and productive, allowing opportunity and motivation to return to therapy in the future.

Bibliography

Bross, A. and Benjamin, M. 1982. Family Therapy: a Recursive Model of Strategic Practice, in A. Bross (ed.) *Family Therapy: a Recursive Model of Strategic Practice*. New York: Guilford.

Burns, R.C. and Kaufman, S.H. 1972. *Actions, Styles and Symbols in Kinetic Family Drawings (K-F-D): an Interpretative Manual*. New York: Brunner/Mazel.

Coulter, A. 2007. Couple Art Therapy: 'Seeing' Difference Makes a Difference, in E. Shaw and J. Crawley (eds) *Couple Therapy in Australia: Issues Emerging from Practice*. Kew, Victoria: PsychOz Publications, pp. 215–27.

Coulter, A. 2011. Contemporary Art Therapy: Working with Transient Youth, in H. Burt (ed.) *Art Therapy and Postmodernism: Creative Healing Through a Prism*. London: Jessica Kingsley Publishers, pp. 83–93.

Crago, H. 2006. *Couple, Family and Group Work: First Steps in Interpersonal Intervention*. New York: Open University Press.

Haley, J. 1976. *Problem-Solving Therapy*. New York: Harper and Row.

IDT (Interactive Drawing Therapy). 2010. *Foundation Course: Unit One and Unit Two, Version 9*. Auckland, NZ: IDT Ltd.

Kwiatkowska, H.Y. 1978. *Family Therapy and Evaluation through Art*. Springfield, IL: Charles C. Thomas.

Landgarten, H. B. 1987. *Family Art Psychotherapy: a Clinical Guide and Casebook*. New York: Brunner/Mazel.

Landgarten, H.B. 1993. *Magazine Photo Collage: a Multicultural Assessment and Treatment Tool*. New York: Brunner Mazel, Inc.

Riley, S. 1993. Illustrating the Family Story: Art Therapy, a Lens for Viewing the Family's Reality. *The Arts in Psychotherapy* 20, 253–64.

Riley, S. 1994. *Integrative Approaches to Family Art Therapy*. Springfield, IL: Magnolia Street Publishers.

Riley, S. 2003. Art Therapy with Couples, in C.A. Malchiodi (ed.) *Handbook of Art Therapy*. New York: Guilford Press, pp. 387–98.

Watzlawick, P., Weakland, J. and Fisch, R. 1974. *Change: Principles of Problem Formation and Problem Resolution*. New York: Norton.

White, M. and Epston, D. 1990. *Narrative Means to Therapeutic Ends*. New York: Norton.

Withers, R. 2006. Interactive Drawing Therapy: Working with Therapeutic Imagery. *New Zealand Journal of Counselling* 26(4), 1–14.

Chapter 13

Group work with adults and the group-interactive art therapy model

Susan Hogan

Group art therapy

In Chapters 8 and 9 an overview of this approach was given, which will now be elaborated in further detail. Earlier chapters have highlighted the fact that there can be different styles or emphases within this model. At one end of the interactive spectrum (or continuum) can be located approaches that focus much more on explorations of transference reactions, or analyses of group interactions, with an emphasis on talking about these. At the other end of the spectrum are approaches which are more focused on the person as an individual in the group, and in facilitating their relationship to their own art work, with minimal attention to group dynamics (bringing the style of working closer to that which I have described above as art therapy support groups). Some art therapists attempt to position themselves pretty much in the middle of the interactive model of working and attempt to work with all elements. However, as has already been noted, some choice about what aspects to focus on is unavoidable, as 'there is a wealth of material which can sometimes seem overwhelming and thus difficult for the group to process and make use of' (Skaife 1990: 237).

Groups can vary immensely and develop different personalities. Some groups can be particularly conflict-ridden; others nurturing and highly sensitive to an almost stifling degree; other groups can be vastly reticent, depending on the personality make-up of its participants. Groups develop unique identities, which then change over the course of their life. I have been running art therapy experiential groups since 1990 and get fond of my groups: they are like an intimate friend who is often cranky and hard work, but often generous and immeasurably brave too. The analogy works quite well and individuals in the group can experience the group as an entity too, and 'project' emotions onto it.

Group-interactive theory

The distinctive aspect of the group-interactive model of art therapy today is that, as the name suggests, it is interested in looking at how people interact in the group with a view towards interpersonal learning:

Group interactive psychotherapy [from which interactive art therapy has derived] focuses on the actions, reactions and characteristic patterns of interaction which constrain people in their everyday lives and for which help in modifying is sought in the group... A fundamental of this approach is that each person constructs an individual inner world which is continuously being reconstructed through interactions with others and which determines that person's view of himself and others and affects the expectations of others.

(Waller 1993: 22)

It is immediately obvious that this is a rather particular way of conceptualising what people are and how they are constituted in comparison with a more traditionally psychoanalytic view, which insists that our personality traits, or neuroses, are developed early in childhood. Rather, this model of thought provides a sharp contrast, proposing instead that we are continuously shaped and re-shaped, and that, to some extent, our identities are in a state of continual flux and re-construction. Philosophically, this is potentially at odds with orthodox psychoanalytic models, though some interactive art therapists (including Waller) try to incorporate some analytic features into their work, notably work with 'transference' and processes of 'projective identification' (members' feelings about another person, or the group as a whole, not generated by their here-and-now experience, but triggered by habitual reactions which are then stimulated). Therefore, childhood experiences are not overlooked, but are not the main focus of the group's attention.

A more behavioural understanding is also possible as:

In group therapy, the individual gradually realises how inner assumptions may determine the patterns of interaction that develop. Exploration of these patterns and willingness to modify them in the safety of the group enables the person to try out new ways of relating in the 'outside world'. Clearly, then, the model places *the main source of change in the interaction between group members* and depends upon the participants learning from each other.

(Waller 1993: 23; my emphasis)

This model has an emphasis on the capacity for change, and an idea that human actions are not predetermined and that we have both choice and responsibility. It also assumes that existentially we are looking for meaning in our lives (Ratigan and Aveline 1988: 45). However, our habitual ways of being may not be very evident to us. The anthropologist Pierre Bourdieu has highlighted this tendency and called it *habitus*. This is an 'embodied history, internalised as a second nature and so forgotten as history – is the active presence of the whole part' (Bourdieu 1990: 56). An important aspect of the group work is to increase personal self-awareness of this *habitus*; this is done through active participation in group processes:

Members do not simply talk about their difficulties in the group but actually *reveal them through their here-and-now behaviour*. In this model, the 'here-and-now' is where the therapy takes place and 'reporting' on past experiences is discouraged. Disclosure does, however, take place: that is, revelation of 'secrets' or significant events from the past and present outside the group and this may be important in understanding the behaviour of that individual in the group.

(Waller 1993: 23; my emphasis)

I'm not sure I'd use the word 'discourage', as there may be an inner compulsion to reveal past traumas, and I think that doing this and being accepted by the group is potentially curative. Traumatised individuals often hold the irrational belief that they will be rejected, or that people will be repelled by them if they tell... Exorcising deeply internalised feelings of guilt and shame is helpful. However, as Waller points out above, the focus is more on the here-and-now of the group and how the past informs the present. Participants are encouraged to gain a sense of their influence upon events in the group. The aim is that group members will move from unproductive ways of being and relating to being able to take on more responsibility for their lives, including their symptoms and difficulties (Ratigan and Aveline 1988: 45). This is achieved by giving participants constant feedback (hence the group work is analytical).

In art therapy the individual learns how his or her assumptions (conscious and unconscious) determine patterns of interaction and may have led to problems in relating.... Taking responsibility for one's participation in the learning experience of the group, having a sense of one's influence on events, and learning to give feedback are prerequisites.

(Waller 2003: 314)

To give a simple, and simplified, example, Jonathan (a pseudonym) had been abused as a boy, but he had learned to be tough, to defend himself and he had been involved in physical assaults and knife crime. Now quite a large man, he was verbally aggressive to other members of the group, engendering antagonistic responses and then accusing the group as a whole of rejection (what revealed itself to be a pattern of behaviour). However, it was possible to point out aspects of his threatening talk and demeanour whenever it occurred, to make him more aware of the fact that his own aggressive communication style was keeping other people at a distance and preventing him gaining the intimacy with other group members which he strongly craved; the group, though tempted, was not permitted collectively to reject ('scapegoat') him. His aggressive manner acted also as a catalyst for other group members to explore how they felt about being threatened and how they felt about male violence, so added usefully to the overall group process. As Waller puts it:

If we accept that patterns of behaviour are learned and that it is possible to unlearn or relearn more effective or rewarding ways of being, then there is much to be learned from interpersonal interaction within the boundaries of a group.

(Waller 1993: 25)

Enacted patterns of being are scrutinised. This can also take place on a more conscious and self-conscious level in the group. Waller advances the following as an example:

Participants are encouraged to explore irrational belief systems (i.e., if I don't get married, pass an exam, get promotion by 30, then I am a complete failure.

(Waller 2003: 314)

The model also attempts to respond to 'social, political, and economic realities including discrimination and racism and how internalisation of these realities can lead to feelings of despair and powerlessness' (Waller 2003: 314).

Waller (1993) endorses Bloch and Crouch (1985), who suggest that there is an important therapeutic factor created through interaction, which they call 'interpersonal learning' or 'learning from interpersonal action'. Interactive groups offer two important aspects, according to Yalom (1985: 77), which are that the group functions as a 'social microcosm' and second, that it offers the opportunity for a 'corrective emotional experience'. Waller (1993: 26) expands on this concept:

'Social microcosm' refers to a group process which resembles customary everyday functioning, in which patients tend to behave in their usual maladaptive way. It is by observing and drawing attention to these behaviour patterns in the group that the therapist and other group members can have a 'corrective emotional experience', thus helping each other to change.

So, in other words, the group becomes a place where participants can learn about patterns of behaviour which are causing them distress and result in disturbed inter-personal relations. Group members may *see* these for the first time in a revelatory way or perhaps dimly perceived aspects will come into focus. Increased awareness permits the possibility of change, and changed ways of relating can be rehearsed or 'tried out' in the group; as Waller emphasises, feedback from the therapist and other participants, in addition to self-observation, enables an expansion of self-awareness:

Feedback from members of the group and the therapist, illuminating aspects of the self which have become obvious to others, but which are not recognised by oneself, is essential. To be effective it must be well timed and delivered with sensitivity. In this respect the therapist is an important role model, demonstrating a positive clinical approach as opposed to a negative

and judgemental one, observing and commenting on behaviour and images
and their effects on the process of the group.

(Waller 2003: 314–15)

New ways of being are taken outside of the group process by participants, who
can then 'report back' to the group on how aspects of their lives are changing.
Bloch and Crouch (1985: 78) suggest that an 'adaptive spiral' is developed. Waller
(1993: 35–7) identifies a number of interrelated features of group work, which
she suggests are generally regarded as 'curative features'. These are in summary:

1   the giving and sharing of information;
2   what she calls 'the installation of hope' regarding the process of participation;
3   mutual aid;
4   the discovery that other participants have the same kind of anxieties, problems
    or fears, and that the individual is not alone in having this problem (or there
    may be someone who has overcome this particular issue and who can provide
    inspiration);
5   the group can work as a reconstruction of the family, allowing potential family
    dynamics to be recognised and worked out;
6   catharsis is an important aspect whereby a person admits to feelings and
    thoughts (often of which he is deeply ashamed) or re-experiences a traumatic
    experience with the group, and then usually experiences a strong sense of
    relief or even release; such intimate disclosures often precipitate similar
    'confessions' from other participants, which, in turn, allows the group to
    become more intimate. The containment of these feelings also makes the
    group feel safer;
7   participants learn more about how they interact with others and get feedback
    in relation to which they can try out different ways of being;
8   the safety of the group as a place where deep feelings can be shared without
    fear of reprisal allows group cohesiveness to develop;
9   through interpersonal learning, old ways of relating can be examined and
    changed.

There is both visual and verbal expression in interactive art therapy and, as I
have pointed out above, the focus can move from the art to an interaction, in a
back and forth manner. Maclagan has articulated that:

Art therapy represents a potentially dangerous encounter with the irrational
and the uncontainable. It also involves a shift of competence, from a verbal
domain that is to some extent an instrument of rationalisation and control,
to a non-verbal (or marginally verbal) area that is unfamiliar… [addressing
itself] to those very areas of experience (dream, fantasy, imagination) that are
usually kept hidden behind veils of literal and anecdotal subject matter.

(1985: 7)

Whether or not we agree that art-making necessarily gives easier access to 'irrational' material, it is certainly non-verbal and non-linear and presents a fundamentally different, but very rich, way of communicating to others and with oneself. One aspect of art work which is importantly different from verbal language, which was also highlighted earlier, is that art works can contain multiple and conflicting discourses simultaneously, exemplifying irreconcilable ideas or impulses. As Waller points out, image-making can be akin to 'free association' or 'dreaming into paper'. Skaife discusses what the art activity adds to the interactive group work, allowing:

> ... feelings to be expressed in an alternative way and metaphorical and symbolic language to stay on in the group in a concrete form. As well as this, feelings that are not easily expressed in words can be played with in their symbolic form, for instance colour and shape, and thus worked on in a way that can make them more accessible to language and thus to consciousness. As in other art therapy settings group members are encouraged to use the art materials to express themselves freely; this work is then looked at as both belonging to the history of the individual and [potentially] as an expression of the dynamic of the group.
>
> (1990: 237)

The art work can become the focus of attention in group work, so that conversations between participants may become indirect and via art works. Also, the art work can become the focus for projected material and can be destroyed and repaired. Members can show empathy towards each other by adopting a similar pictorial style or particular symbols or motifs, and this has been called 'group resonance' by Gerry McNeilly (1984); this is an idea (taken from physics and used metaphorically) to describe the way images can seemingly influence each other and 'resonate' or reverberate together. Certain themes can be held by the art and art works can be brought out over and over again and reworked. This process could take place over weeks or months. Making a picture can feel less threatening to some people than having to talk in a group, and playful aspects of art making can come to the fore. Many British people 'did art' at school, so there is sometimes a regressive dimension to using art materials, especially in initial sessions. The actual physical art object is in some sense a record of what has taken place, but is also a future stimulus for reflection and disclosure. Although the image is a disclosure in pictorial form, the maker of the image may decide when to share content with the group, so, depending on the nature of the image (which may be more or less pictorially revealing), the pace of disclosure can be controlled by the participant; arguably, this gives power to the art therapy participant in having control over when they wish to make disclosures to the group. Group processes can be intensified through the use of group painting, and group conflicts can be articulated and explored. Finally, as noted in previous chapters, the pictorial struggle itself (the mess made or the effort in articulating a concept) can be tremendously revealing.

The shape of the group

Waller argues that some fundamental processes of an interactive group are enhanced by the addition of art-making:

> These include projection, mirroring, scapegoating, parataxic distortion, and projective identification. Projection involves group members having feelings and making assumptions about other members which are not based on their here-and-now experience. For example, one member might experience another as his critical mother and make assumptions about that person's feelings toward him. Mirroring entails a member having strong feelings and emotions about another's behaviour, which is in fact an aspect of the member's behaviour. Projection and mirroring are often accompanied by splitting – by experiencing a group member, the facilitator, or the whole group as all good or all bad. Scapegoating occurs when the group tries to put all its difficulties onto one member and to get rid of them. The members' tendency to distort their perceptions of others (parataxic distortions) provides valuable material for the group to consider. An important and often disturbing phenomenon is projective identification, which can result in one member projecting his or her own (but actually disowned) attributes onto another toward whom they may feel 'an uncanny attraction-repulsion' (Yalom 1985, p.354). These attributes may be projected so strongly that the other person's behaviour begins to change.
>
> (Waller 2003: 315)

Regarding the latter, our emotional antenna may be finely tuned so that we find ourselves reacting without being clear about why. Consequently, the long experiential training group is an integral part of art therapy training. Arts therapists work more or less with these elements, depending on their style.

Although Waller does not see the use of themes as in any way antithetical to a group interactive approach (Waller 1993: 29), this chapter will concentrate on non-directive approaches. It will identify two slightly different ways of approaching a non-directive stance. As noted in Chapter 9, there are two main models of working: one, which I will call 'regulatory' (or time-regulated) and another, which is not regulated and is 'group-led' or 'open'. Both are non-directive, insofar as the therapist is not offering themes or tasks. Both would be scheduled at the same time each week. The length of the group would not alter. In the 'time-regulated' model, the art therapist divides the time between talking and art-making: a common structure would be a short period of talking on arrival in the group (generally how people feel about being back in the group, a sharing of any unresolved feelings about the previous session which feel too pressing to 'keep' to the end, or clarification of something which the participant feels might have been misunderstood), followed by between 20–60 minutes of art-making (depending on the duration of the session, which is commonly two hours) and the remainder of the session analysing the images made. There is often a minimal break between the art-making and the final discussion part. With a group of two-and-a-half hours' duration, there is time for a short 'coffee' break. This is a secure model (because participants have a definite time frame), but doesn't allow for spontaneity of movement from talking to painting, and group members may have to break off what they are doing in order to join the circle when it is time to talk about the images, regardless of whether the majority feel ready for this.

In contrast, working with the group-led ('open') non-directive interactive model, the 'shape' of sessions can vary from the above model, though as Skaife and Huet (1998) observe:

> ... when we allow the group to develop their own culture for art-making each session usually, though not always, follows a similar pattern. The group usually starts with spontaneous verbal interaction, followed by art making, followed by analysis and relating of the first two... [a] pattern similar to that discussed in groups where the therapist has set the structure.
>
> (1998: 21)

And:

> ... our groups have tended to establish a culture for how long they spend making art, which is usually something between twenty and forty minutes. At times this is negotiated, but at other phases in the group's life there may be a gradual stop, with one person beginning to clear up, thus giving a signal to others who may or may not respond by also finishing.
>
> (1998: 26–7)

We can see from the above quotation that groups tend to adopt a particular way of working, though some groups may be more erratic than others.

Arguably, the group-led approach gives greater responsibility and power to the group to direct itself; because I am involved in teaching advanced group-work skills to art therapy trainees, this is the model I use as it is more complex, challenging and potentially 'messy', with more intense and immediate opportunities for learning. However, for therapeutic work with clients I favour the more contained, and containing, time-regulated model. All of the issues I am about to outline can arise in the time-regulated model too, but sometimes in a less immediate way. They are more acutely felt in the group-led or 'open' approach, because these issues *must be resolved;* they are pressing and immediate.

In an earlier chapter, I suggested that there are productive therapeutic opportunities generated by this group-led approach, in which tensions can arise about how much time to spend talking and how much time to spend art-making, and when that transition should occur. In negotiating this, group members illustrate habitual ways of being and behaving with regard to a variety of issues. Therapeutic material can be generated from an exploration of conformity versus individuality in the group process, including members' feelings about compromise; or, fears of being alone and lonely can be explored. Desire for or fear of dependency, including exploration and articulation of irrational fears about engulfment, or rejection, are useful to consider.

Skaife (1990) elaborates the positive aspects which can emerge during this process:

> ... the factors experienced in the process of making decisions as a group become a means by which the group members can reflect on their own contribution to the decision-making process, thus developing a greater understanding of their own particular means of negotiating social relations. As well as this, issues particular to 'creative activity', such as the ability to 'let go', tolerate chaos, and so on, emerge frequently for discussion as the responsibility for action is placed firmly with group members.
>
> (1990: 238)

Attitudes towards authority figures, and what should or should not be expected of them, invariably arise. Feelings of disappointment (at not being 'told what to do'), some of which may be transference and relate to significant others in participants' lives, can be explored and expressed verbally and in art works. Consequently, 'the group makes use of the tensions around the change in activity to play out issues of power and authority' and this is something that can occur throughout the life of the group (Skaife and Huet 1998: 25). Waller puts it thus with reference to the opening of the group:

> The first moments in a group when the members are trying to decide how to proceed are often tense and the members want the therapist to tell them what to do.... Individuals will quickly fall into habitual patterns: being the one to suggest projects, withdrawing, moving away from the group into an isolated corner, disagreeing with whatever is suggested, quietly or not so quietly sabotaging the work, or being the peacemaker. All this is useful material for the therapist to note for comment and to later reflect to the group.
>
> (Waller 2003: 316)

Skaife and Huet (1998) note that it is the 'transition' from one activity to another which is sometimes difficult:

> We have observed that the 'push pull' dynamic between art therapy and group interactive therapy is at its most intense at the times of transition between phases. Breaking away from the group, the circle of chairs and from the familiarity of words to the physicality of working with materials on one's own is not easy. Finding the right time to stop making art may be artificial, and finding a way to talk about art work can be difficult.... There may be a long period of group time spent coming to some kind of consensus about

whether it is time to go and make art work. This can create an uncomfortable tension for the art therapist, as during this time she has no clear role. Her usual role as commentator on the group process would only serve to extend the talking time, putting her vote, as it were, behind the verbal rather than the change to art-making…

(1998: 22–6)

Skaife and Huet also observe (1998: 27) what I have also observed myself, and that is that there is a general desire on the part of participants to speak about what they are feeling. Participants often also want to receive acknowledgement from others on their art work; occasionally this may simply be showing a work and saying, 'I don't feel able to talk about it yet', but much more frequently there is a desire to explain the work and how it relates to their experience. Sensitive questioning or comment making is also very much appreciated, and serves as a symbolic and real acknowledgement of the work – it says, 'Yes, I really have understood this work, and I can demonstrate this by my appropriate and valued remark'; it also says, 'Yes, I really have been attentive, and you really have been heard, and this remark is evidence'. Not getting a response to a disclosure can feel very disconcerting. We all respond slightly differently to anxiety caused by not knowing. Some of our self-reflection in the group can be analysis of this discomfort. The group can also explore moments of collective reticence. Sometimes silence is deemed as a 'respectful' response to a powerful disclosure, for example. However, the silence may be misconstrued by the participant who has made the disclosure and is waiting for a response as not caring, or as disengagement! (Here cultural differences can come into play too and expectations and assumptions can be explored.)

Alternatively, empathy may be expressed more directly through another participant offering a disclosure: 'Yes, that happened to me too' or 'I feel that too' (though potentially that may move the group's focus away from the first speaker and on to the next). On a different level, trainees must practise their facilitation skills, so it is entirely appropriate that they practise responding to disclosures made. Occasionally, participants will ostentatiously hide, or fold up, an art work, which could draw attention to them because of a desire from group members to make sure that person is okay, or out of curiosity, or even irritation at the lack of exposure (the latter, especially if it's part of a pattern of behaviour of not showing). All this exploration takes up time from the art-making process.

The facilitator's primary role in both modes of interactive group is to solicit feedback from participants on group processes; to facilitate analysis of the pictorial content of art work; to ensure safety, by maintaining and reinforcing the group's boundaries; to intervene *in extremis* when the group gets 'stuck' (though this is rarely necessary, as most groups can resolve their own issues); to ensure participant safety by helping to facilitate acknowledgement of material which might be overlooked or ignored to the detriment of a member or sub-group; and to point out attempts at scapegoating, if not discerned and articulated during reflection on group processes (ideally, the group, not the facilitator, can do this work). With the more regulated of the two non-directive approaches, the facilitator also plays a time-keeping role, rather than just flagging up the beginning and end of the group. A mature group can run itself with little intervention from the art therapist.

In this chapter I have outlined the basic theory underlying group-interactive art therapy. I have examined the pros and cons of working with two slightly different, fundamentally non-directive, group-work styles: 'time-regulated' and 'group-led'. The chapter then moved on to look in more detail at how art work functions in this model of working.

Bibliography

Bloch, S. and Crouch, E. 1985. *Therapeutic Factors in Group Psychotherapy.* Oxford: Oxford University Press.

Bourdieu, P. 1990. *The Logic of Practice.* Cambridge: Polity Press.

Maclagan, D. 1985. Art Therapy in a Therapeutic Community. *Inscape Journal of Art Therapy* 1, 7–8.

McNeilly, G. 1984. Directive and Non-directive Approaches in Art Therapy. *Inscape: Journal of Art Therapy* Winter, 7–12.

Ratigan, B. and Aveline, M. 1988. Interpersonal Group Therapy, in M. Averline and W. Dryden (eds) *Group Art Therapy in Britain.* Milton Keynes: Open University Press, pp. 43–64.

Skaife, S. 1990. Self Determination in Group Analytic Art Therapy. *Group Analysis* 23(3), 237–44.

Skaife, S. and Huet, V. 1998. *Art Psychotherapy Groups: Between Pictures and Words.* London: Routledge.

Waller, D. 1993. *Group Interactive Art Therapy: its Use in Training and Treatment.* London: Routledge.

Waller, D. 2003. Group Art Therapy: an Interactive Approach, in C.A. Malchiodi (ed.) *Handbook of Art Therapy.* New York: Guilford Press, 313–24.

Yalom, I.D. 1995. *The Theory and Practice of Group Psychotherapy.* Fourth edition. New York: Basic Books.

Chapter 14

Art therapy and co-therapy

Annette M. Coulter

An aspect of art therapy practice about which there is limited discussion is the issue of co-facilitation of art therapy groups. Frequently constrained by limited financial resources or the idea that the co-facilitator must be another art therapist, art therapists may tend to run groups on their own. However, in both ongoing training groups and art therapy treatment groups, working in co-therapy is advantageous to both the group and the art therapist, with an educative aspect as well as support for funding applications and in case-management discussions. Furthermore, in most treatment situations, it is irresponsible to not work with a co-therapist due to practical reasons, such as a group member needing to leave the therapy space. Part of the co-therapist's role is also to be available to assist with any extraordinary group situation. In such circumstances, the availability of a co-therapist for best practice becomes imperative.

Contracting a co-therapist

In co-therapy situations, it is not only group members who have a group agreement. Another group-related contract is that of the co-facilitator's commitment to the group. Most responsible co-facilitators already understand that becoming the co-therapist for an art therapy group is a commitment for a certain number of weeks, but it is crucial that the art therapist has a written contract of understanding with their co-therapist that clearly states their agreement to participate, including the commitment to a time frame.

Some groups have no set time frame because they function as part of an ongoing treatment regime. In some residential treatment facilities, such as a women's refuge or refugee detention centre, art therapy groups can be part of the weekly programme to address ongoing trauma-related issues. To do this work alone is irresponsible. Art therapy groups facilitate the expression of thoughts and feelings where verbal or local language may be limited. In these settings where art therapy is part of the ongoing treatment regime, groups are open to whoever is in residence at that time. Group membership varies as clients are admitted or discharged from the facility, and the operation of the ongoing group becomes the consistent factor, rather than the group membership. The two co-facilitators are part of this residential treatment consistency, and contracting the co-therapist's involvement ensures that this is a clear understanding.

Contracting is better if it is in a written format. This does not have to be a lengthy document but does outline the co-therapist's commitment. They must also understand the likely impact of their absence from the group and the importance of their role in 'holding' the group 'frame' (Schaverien 1989; Bull 1985; Vinogradov and Yalom 1989).

Successful art co-therapy

The most successful co-therapy situation is where the art co-therapists have a similar training background or are grounded in a similar working model of art therapy practice. Where co-therapists have an intuitive understanding of each other's art psychotherapy interventions, the other's non-verbal communication is understood and the co-therapists are able to complement each other's interventions. This is supported by good supervision, preferably from a more experienced art therapist or otherwise from an experienced group or family therapist, preferably someone who has some psychodynamic training so that they can facilitate a productive examination of any difficult dynamics that may arise between the two co-therapists.

In residential situations when a co-therapist has a greater knowledge of the individuals and any interpersonal dynamics that are operating outside the group, they are able to inform and complement the skills of the art therapist in facilitating group work. Finally, mutual respect for each other's skills will also assist successful co-therapy.

Co-therapy for treatment groups

Generally, one therapist is the primary group leader and the other is the co-facilitator. Usually the more experienced therapist leads the group and in the case of an art therapy group, it is the art therapist who is the primary group leader or facilitator. It is advantageous for one therapist to focus on maintaining the structure and to address inclusion issues as they arise. Inclusion issues include aspects that affect the core structure and holding of group trust, such as group membership, group contracting especially around such issues as confidentiality, time frames and group boundary maintenance, as well as violations. While one therapist works with what is the conscious agenda of the group, the other therapist focuses on the group's less conscious processes. This is done by particularly attending to other group members not in the line of focus of the group leader, who is dealing with a particular issue with a particular group member or members. While the group are making art together or individually, it is preferable that the co-therapists, as well as the group members, do not talk. Non-verbally and with discretion, they may draw the other's attention to something of significance, but group participants' engagement with the art-making processes should not be distracted or compromised – they are engaged in an internal dialogue between themselves and the emerging art work.

The presence of a co-therapist provides an opportunity to present an alternative view in situations where group members are divided over an issue. Co-therapists can work together to present different perspectives and model the resolution of conflict, using phrases such as *'I can hear what you're saying* (the other perspective can even be repeated back to demonstrate that it has been heard) *but my problem with this is…'* and an alternate view can be presented. Co-therapists can also role-play group members' thoughts (for example, 'I can understand why Scott thinks Johnny should… but he doesn't agree').

Considering gender balance: male and female co-therapists

Having a co-therapist who is the opposite gender to the art therapist provides an opportunity to recreate the primary parental configuration. This allows group members to project parental issues into the group situation, as well as observing the role-modelling of a male and female working together collaboratively and respectfully. There will be fantasies about the relationship between male and female co-therapists, but this configuration can be highly effective and reassuring for group members where parental issues are unresolved or difficult to access. For example, in a male ward of a psychiatric hospital, two female art therapists worked with two male charge nurses and so helped constellate a mother-and-father-projected presence in the co-lead group facilitation. This continuity of gender balance and co-facilitation provided a unique service, and might have been less successful had there simply been two female art therapists, imposing something onto the community from the outside. In addition, by involving co-therapists from within the therapeutic community, group continuity was maintained.

Similarly, the impact of a female co-worker working with a well-established men's group raised a variety of beneficial issues for everyone involved. Observing this collaborative partnership was significant for group members to varying degrees, and the combination of male and female co-therapists working in collaboration provided therapeutic gains, mobilising group material that might otherwise not have been raised.

Agency collaboration in co-therapy

Another co-facilitation scenario is where two therapists decide to pool their patients to form one larger group in their clients' best interest. The two agencies involve two members of staff to work collaboratively to facilitate a group. This can be a gender-balanced partnership or a same-sex partnership. For example, an organisation that specialises in family dispute resolution forms a partnership with another organisation that provides mental health services to troubled adolescents. A group for parents of those adolescents is then established to address behaviour management issues and to provide support as members discover they are not the only ones experiencing problems with their teenager.

Another collaborative co-facilitated group is the example of a nurse therapist working with new parents in a paediatric hospital, and collaborating with an art therapist who specialises in couple work. The group examines issues that are coming up as the couple prepare for the arrival of their firstborn child and for their new role as co-parents. The use of art facilitates the expression of feelings, particularly for young fathers within the group who may not have the same ability as their partners to articulate the array of feelings coming up about their imminent parenthood. The young mothers have had more contact with each other, meeting throughout the pregnancy with various paediatric services, establishing supportive relationships, but the fathers-to-be are more isolated. Co-facilitating with a nurse specialist provides the medical knowledge that is required to any questions group members may have and the art becomes a way to express difficult emotions about taking on fatherhood responsibilities and everything that this brings up. The group becomes psycho-educational as affective and practical matters are aired and addressed by the varying skills of the co-therapists.

In a youth refuge, an art therapy group is co-facilitated by one residential staff member who better understands the dynamics of the group and the art therapist who has the art specialist expertise. If one young person becomes emotionally overwhelmed and leaves the room in a distressed state, the co-therapist can accompany them to ensure their safety, calm any emotional turmoil and to encourage their return to the group, which may require considerable internal effort. Attending to them upon their immediate return is not recommended. In the post-group peer debriefing session, the co-therapist can inform the art therapist about issues that may have triggered the young person's inability to tolerate remaining in the group room, and they can discuss the merit of follow-up in a future group session.

The art therapist as a co-facilitator

If the art therapist is the co-facilitator of the group, their main role is to support the group facilitator.

The group may not be an art therapy treatment group. The art therapist as co-facilitator may be invited to provide adjunct therapeutic interventions on occasion to facilitate the ongoing group process (Kerr 2008: 159). Such variables dictate whether the art therapist is the co-facilitator or the group leader. Art therapy is a useful tool as an intervention in its own right at a certain point within a group process. For example, in the ongoing men's group, co-facilitated by a psychotherapist and an art therapist, the main modality is verbal psychotherapy. Art therapy is not used every week, although the use of the visual diary at the beginning and sometimes during or at the end of the group is increasingly encouraged. A visual diary entry at the commencement of the group, for the first ten minutes, facilitates an inward focus, a letting-go of outside world distraction and an entry into the therapy space. Sometimes art is used to provide a creative intervention to clarify thinking during the group where a particular issue is causing confused thoughts and feelings.

Frequently, this is to address strong emotions whose source is unclear. The group leader might initiate a request to the art therapist, or the art therapist might offer a suggested intervention or simply the space to do something reflective in their diary about what just took place. For each group member the experience is different, and engaging in an art task mobilises around a certain issue. At times this helps dissipate verbal confrontation and facilitates constructive use of volatile emotions such as anger. For example, a guided interactive drawing therapy (IDT) (Withers 2006) session about going on a journey facilitated powerful metaphors on a recent men's retreat (Coulter 2012). Art therapy provides opportunity to express thoughts and feelings but is not the main modality of therapy – its use is on occasion and as required by the group process.

Some art therapy groups may not have a 'group leader' as such, but simply have two group facilitators of equal responsibility and involvement. In these situations one facilitator may alert the group to a dynamic issue and the other facilitator supports this observation and assists pursuing that particular issue, theme or observation. An example might be that one group participant is cautious to participate in a group discussion. There may be a number of reasons why their participation is not forthcoming – the subject may have no relevance; the subject may be very relevant and they do not want to expose their dilemma in relationship to the discussion; or they may want to participate but simply have no idea how to participate: the words just are not there. It is not the group facilitator's role to do the hard work for this group participant, but it is their role to notice their non-involvement and to consider what might be going on. One facilitator may notice their non-participation and the other facilitator may link something they have said previously to their current reticence. Working in co-therapy allows opportunity for the therapists to interact within the group as they initiate and co-facilitate the exploration of a group's themes, dynamic issues or observed group behaviours.

An allied health professional co-therapist

As mentioned in the various situations described above, the co-therapist for a treatment group does not necessarily have to be a qualified art therapist to be effective in an art therapy group. The co-therapist for an art therapy group can be a nurse, a psychiatric registrar or psychologist intern, a social work or occupational therapy student, psychotherapist or another allied health professional. A family art therapy assessment procedure might also have a more senior clinician as the co-facilitator, such as the child psychiatrist or family therapist team leader.

Having an allied health professional as the co-therapist is an opportunity to educate staff about art therapy in clinical practice. Although this is experiential art therapy education, the art therapist can provide preparatory reading material for the co-therapist to read as a pre-requisite before co-facilitating an art therapy group. Allied health professionals usually have a commitment of interest and enthusiasm to extend their skills repertoire. They are keen to gain knowledge and do whatever is required for their co-therapy to be productive. For some co-therapists it is beneficial to know more about their role and potential expectations from the art therapist group leader. The art therapist must decide whether or not pre-group reading material advantages the allied health professional in their co-therapy role. For some non-art therapist co-facilitators it is better to first experience an art therapy group, so that what they later read has an experiential context. In the rare circumstance where more than one member of staff is interested to be the co-therapist for an art therapy group, meeting with each allied health professional individually and asking each the same set of questions to help make a decision is advisable, although it is likely to be clear who is most suitable. Contracting a minimum limited number of group work sessions allows opportunity for other staff to also participate later. Assistance to conduct ongoing group work facilitates a better understanding about the effective benefit of art therapy, even as simply 'another approach', 'a tool' or 'a technique'.

The co-therapist's role in art therapy treatment groups

One of the co-therapist's main tasks is to support the art therapist. Although supporting the other therapist seems a simple role, this task is increasingly complex as the co-therapists each become caught up in the group's dynamics. If one therapist believes the other has not been supportive, this needs to be discussed immediately after the group and if not resolved, taken to a joint supervision session as soon as possible. It is important to address a perceived lack of support immediately because if unchecked, this can damage the group potency. Group participants unconsciously tune in to any cracks/chinks in the interpersonal dynamics between the co-therapist group facilitators.

Being supportive means maintaining a number of responsibilities. Most importantly, if one therapist is directing discussion and is focused in one direction, the co-therapist is required to watch what is happening in another direction. Seating positions of the co-therapists should never be side by side, but they should be within easy range of the other's vision. Co-therapists develop non-verbal communication skills as they get to know each other and this is most effective if it is less obvious to the group participants. The co-facilitator may observe more subtle interactions that take place in another part of the group, away from the main focus of the group. It is not their role to highlight these observations but they should note them. It may be appropriate later during the group to mention an observation but more importantly, it is to advise the other therapist of any subtle dynamic that was observed in preparation for future group work. The co-therapist can also assist with time-keeping issues. Part of the seating arrangement may include discrete observation of a clock in the room, to which the co-therapist attends. Frequently, something major will come up towards the end of the group because this is a safer time to raise something complex, without having to deal with it. If a contentious issue is raised, the co-therapist can remind the group of the time constraints, intervening with a statement such as, 'I'd just like to remind the group that we have eight minutes left.' Going over time is counter-productive to effective group time management, and the co-therapist helps keep such things in check.

Another inclusion issue is group membership. The co-therapist assists with pre-group interviewing to assess client suitability for art therapy group work. As mentioned above, they might also be bringing a number of clients to the group in circumstances such as a collaborative group work initiative of two services. It is valuable to have both therapists present so that a decision, such as to not accept a potential group member, is a joint decision made in consultation with the co-therapist. Pre-group interviews also provide an opportunity for group members to meet both co-therapists prior to the commencement of the group. This helps potential group members feel more at ease about joining the group. This is not relevant if it is an ongoing open-ended group, for example in a residential setting, but if the group is being conducted for a specific number of sessions, it is useful to involve the co-therapist in preparatory logistics such as pre-group interviewing.

Another role of the co-therapist is to assist with feedback to other staff members. Depending on group circumstances, this is usually the role of the group facilitator; however, in a residential setting, for example, feedback to the rest of the team from the nurse co-therapist or the residential care worker contributes to an understanding of a resident's post-group mood or behaviour. Joint feedback can also occur if the co-therapists attend the same case management meetings about clients. Where the co-therapists are presenting collaborative feedback to other workers, they may be able to make the same point in different ways. One approach might be slightly more acceptable than another. For example, if the co-therapist is a psychiatric registrar, their opinion might gain more respect from the medical members of the treatment team. It is sometimes more convincing when two therapists share the same opinion. Back-up from the co-therapist when explaining a client issue can assist a difficult treatment decision.

Co-therapists also assist where a client may need to leave the group therapy space. Although the group guideline is always that participants try to remain in the room for the duration of the group, there are exceptional circumstances where this may not be possible. In the case of a young person, there is sometimes the risk of an urge to self-harm or self-damage in light of a group interaction. Having a co-therapist available to ensure no one is injured while absent from the group is part of the group facilitator's duty of care. It is far better if the client can disclose when self-destructive feelings arise without the need to leave the group therapy space, but this is not always possible. Their abrupt walking out of the room, or tearful fleeing is often provoked by a state of overwhelm that can be short-lived, if they can have some quiet time – a few minutes away from the group. Where a group is conducted with a high-risk group, the group dynamics can be quite volatile particularly while group cohesiveness is being established. Leaving the room might be part of a personal anger management protocol instigated by their therapist, as part of a self-monitoring regime or it simply might be that something has been triggered and the person requires time out to compose themself. Group members leaving the therapy session should be discouraged; however, in exceptional circumstances the group co-therapist's presence can be of assistance. If the client is distressed, the co-therapist engages only minimally with the client outside the group. Their brief is to accompany the client to ensure their safety and to suggest their return to the group as soon as this is deemed appropriate or possible.

The co-therapist also assists with setting up and cleaning up of the group room space. An art therapy group can be quite messy at times. Encouraging clients to assist with cleaning up art materials is counter-productive where it distracts from post-group self-reflection about personal issues that are the reason they are attending the group in the first place. Clients often need time to stay with group material and to not be distracted, so it is better that they leave the group room to have time to self-reflect immediately after the group, unless the need to tidy up is part of the treatment goal, such as the need to encourage a child to be more responsible. Tidying up the therapy space post-group provides time for the co-therapists to informally discuss their group work before formally making notes together. The other option is to make notes first and tidy up art materials afterwards.

Note keeping and documentation

Contributing to group work documentation is another role of the co-therapist. Their input can be useful, particularly where they have been observing more subtle group dynamics while the other therapist was focusing on and facilitating a dominating group issue. The co-therapists can refer to their previous group documentation and might jointly decide on a structured task or group directive that might facilitate exploration of a particular group issue. Through joint note making, co-facilitators offer each other opportunity to debrief from their group facilitation. They can also take turns to lead the group. This might affect continuity of a closed group but works well for some open group situations because the co-therapists learn about each other's way of working.

Use of art in group co-facilitation

A general principle of art therapy co-facilitation is that the co-therapists do not produce art work. Their role is to observe the art-making processes and to provide technical assistance if required. However, there are exceptions to this. For example, co-therapists making art can help settle children into a group. Working with a co-therapist in a classroom setting, Prokofiev would allow the teacher 'to join in the art activity if she wished but… I would be an "engaged observer" with responsibility for the professional running of the group' (Prokofiev 1998: 63). Such decisions need to be carefully considered and always with the best interest of the group participants in mind.

While co-therapists do not usually make art during the group, they can use art as part of their post-group debriefing and joint reflecting. The use of images to recall thoughts and feelings of the co-therapy experience assists note making of group work – a form of visual documentation of the group process. This might be diagrammatic to record weekly seating variations, with arrows to indicate directions of conflict or to represent focused scenarios or alliances within the group or geometric force-field clusters operating as part of the group dynamics. Visual documentation might also provide opportunity for co-therapists to express their impressions or experiences as group facilitators – this could be by literal, symbolic or metaphoric representation. If the group is newly formed, or is a short training course, visual documentation might include quick portraits or caricatures of group members to assist facilitator's visual memory of participants. Co-therapists can include art making as a regular part of their group work documentation to process their interpersonal relationship as co-therapists in the context of conducting group work together. Such use of art therapy processes can enhance co-therapists' understanding of each other and contribute to self-learning and the therapists' personal growth in the context of experiential clinical work. Peer debriefing through an art task also supports best co-therapy practice. Co-therapist tasks might include:

1 Draw how we each feel after today's group.
2 Draw a good moment and a not so good moment from today.
3 Regarding a particular group interaction that took place today – from your impression draw how this affected the group.
4 Draw how this incident affected you or us.
5 Draw how we see our co-therapy relationship at the moment.
6 Draw how our relationship has changed.
7 How could our co-therapy relationship improve? Represent this in some way.
8 How does your co-therapist impact on your ability to facilitate the group? Is this positive or not so positive? Is there a way to represent this symbolically?

Any of these suggestions could be discussed in supervision or as part of co-therapy peer supervision.

Art therapy students as co-therapists

In agencies that might be considering employing an art therapist, an art therapy student might work there on a clinical placement or internship. There are three possible ways to expose other staff to the effectiveness of art therapy in situations where an art therapist trainee is available for co-therapy:

1 The trainee art therapist runs a group with another member of the team as their co-therapist. The student has support and help from the training institution, and also the opportunity to develop group work skills while on

clinical placement. The other staff member can use this as an opportunity to observe the student's group work skills and provide written feedback to the training programme.

2 The trainee art therapist is co-therapist for an ongoing group that is conducted at an agency and provides spontaneous art task interventions as required by the other co-therapist group leader. This other staff member is likely to be part of the permanent team and provides feedback to others about the benefits of recruiting an art therapist.

3 If the agency can provide digital media equipment and the group members sign consent forms agreeing to be recorded, the trainee art therapist can document the art therapy group. This can be played back with their clinical supervisor as a training resource.

Agencies are often keen to consider establishing an art therapy position but do not know enough about this to go ahead with funding applications. A student art therapist can help promote and educate allied health professionals about the therapeutic benefits of incorporating art therapy into their agency's treatment regime.

Interviewing for a co-facilitator

Art therapists are interviewed for both short- and long-term art therapy groups. An advertisement indicates that a co-therapist is required and art therapists with reasonable credentials are considered. The following questions are used to assist the selection of an art therapy group co-facilitator.

What is your experience of art therapy groups?

It is preferable that co-facilitators have some group work experience and have completed a group work component as part of their training programme, though in some countries it is a compulsory component of regulated training.

Have you any previous experience working in co-therapy?

It is not necessary to have worked in co-therapy previously, although it is an advantage if the two art therapists work in the same approach. However, if one co-therapist is less experienced than the other, there is opportunity to develop group work skills while working as a co-therapist.

What is your understanding of co-therapy for an art therapy group?

Does the applicant place importance on supporting the other group facilitator or do they see their role as one of co-leadership? It is often a misunderstanding that co-facilitators co-lead. The best co-facilitation is where the two therapists can take on group leadership when required, can concede to another's leadership and can back up a group work intervention, even if they disagree at the time. This basic understanding of group co-facilitation is core to successful art therapy group work.

How do you feel about working with another art therapist?

This question may not be relevant if the co-therapist being interviewed is not an art therapist: it is to explore how one art therapist regards working with a peer professional. There may be one art therapist who has more group work experience but the other therapist may have an understanding of the client group or knows specific group members. This combination is usually successful because each offers the group something unique – there is no competition or potential for group ownership issues to emerge.

What would you do if you thought the co-therapist had affected an unfortunate outcome in the group dynamic?

This is not an uncommon group dynamic event and it helps to know the potential group facilitator's opinion on this point. The co-therapist hopefully knows to wait until the group has ended and brings the matter up in the facilitator's debriefing session. If they are unable to agree, the matter can be taken to supervision. When working together over a long period of time, there are parallels to being in a relationship together, not dissimilar to being like a married couple. This is a good concept to keep in mind and there may be parallels to other relationships in the life of the therapist.

What would you do if you became aware the group was engaged in splitting the group facilitators?

It is better to have a co-therapist who expects this is part of the group process. The mechanism of splitting co-facilitators is a drawback to co-therapy but if the therapists understand this mechanism and can handle this dynamic when it occurs, it is a learning situation for both group participants and facilitators.

Are you prepared to attend supervision with the co-therapist?

If the co-therapist does not appreciate supervision as part of best group work practice then there is a problem, as supervision is important to sort out between what is group material and what is the co-facilitators' personal business intruding into their co-therapy relationship.

Can you commit to the term of the group life?

A responsible therapist understands the therapeutic contract is a commitment for the life of the group or the term of the group members' contract to each other.

Do you have personal support systems in place?

Although supervision is provided, when personal material comes up for therapists it is helpful to be able to discuss material sometimes with partners, family or close colleagues/friends. It is unlikely a co-therapist does not have personal support systems in place, but it is still an important question to ask rather than to make an assumption. A scenario could be that the therapist is socially isolated and might want to co-facilitate a group because they are lonely.

Do you have any questions?

It is important for potential co-therapists to ask their own questions. They need to know about the structure of the course or therapy group and more about the context of the co-facilitated group component of the training or the expectations for therapy provision.

It is strongly recommended that art therapists consider working in co-therapy where possible, as the advantages of co-therapy with either another art therapist or a supportive allied health professional far outweigh any disadvantages.

Bibliography

Bull, A.S. 1985. The Psychotherapeutic Frame. *Australian and New Zealand Journal of Psychiatry* 19, 172–5.

Coulter, A. 2012. The Use of IDT on a Men's Retreat. Unpublished presentation for InSightIDT Conference, New Zealand.

Kerr, C. 2008. Experiential Family Therapy and Art Therapy, in C. Kerr (ed.) *Family Art Therapy: Foundations of Theory and Practice.* New York: Routledge, pp. 151–66.

Prokofiev, F. 1998. Adapting the Art Therapy Group for Children, in S. Skaife and V. Huet (eds) *Art Psychotherapy Groups: Between Pictures and Words.* London: Routledge, pp. 44–68.

Schaverien, J. 1989. The Picture within the Frame, in A. Gilroy and T. Dalley (eds) *Pictures at an Exhibition: Selected Essays on Art and Art Therapy.* London: Tavistock/Routedge, pp. 147–55.

Vinogradov, S. and Yalom, I.D. 1989. *A Concise Guide to Group Psychotherapy.* Washington, DC: American Psychiatric Press.

Withers, R. 2006. Interactive Drawing Therapy: Working with Therapeutic Imagery. *New Zealand Journal of Counselling* 26(4), 1–14.

Chapter 15

Starting supervision – vulnerability in supervision

Aspects of hopelessness, inadequacy and anxiety in the initial stages of a supervisory relationship

Susan Hogan

This chapter will focus on some important aspects of good and bad practice in the very preliminary stages of supervision groups. It will draw on notes from two psychodynamic student-led post-graduate art therapy supervision groups conducted on-site in an art therapy training institution (not the one in which I currently work, incidentally). The chapter will make reference to the challenges, fears and doubts expressed by trainee art therapists in their initial weeks, as well as their successes. It documents their evolving understanding of art therapy processes in this very first phase of supervisory work.

Art therapy training is complex. Students undergo experiential group-interactive art therapy sessions in which they make art work and talk about it. This group work can often become very intense. They receive supervision from a placement supervisor where they are placed for their clinical work experience component. They also attend a university-based supervision group with their peers, in which their placement work is further scrutinised. Furthermore, they are required to undergo personal therapy throughout their training. Generally, this latter requirement is the responsibility of the student who enters into a private arrangement with a registered practitioner. Where things 'fit' – whether best into group work or personal therapy, or supervision – is not always immediately obvious.

The role of supervision

In any kind of supervision arrangement, a clear contract is always advisable. In training institutions this should already be in place, but for those supervising other professionals, part of the first session can be used to clarify the parameters of the work.

The main focuses of university supervision is the supervisee's ongoing presentation of their client work, with a view to improving the service to the client, and a learning experience for the student, leading to enhanced clinical competence. Their casework presentations comprise a description of what they are doing, an elaboration of the interventions made and a justification of these. There should be an elucidation of the process underway. I don't mean a 'justification' in a defensive way, but a reflection on their own emotional and intellectual responses, which led them to make a particular intervention. There is a self-critical component here – was the intervention too hasty? Was it too clumsy? Was it too dogmatic, not leaving room for other forms of interpretation? Was my own emotional discomfort at that moment having an impact on my decision-making? Necessarily, an analysis of emotional responses to the content of art therapy sessions is an element of the important process of critical self-reflection on the part of the supervisee.

There are different models of working, but I favour a psychodynamic model in which students feel increasingly able to share personal responses to their therapeutic work. Like Edwards (1997), I don't feel it is appropriate to bracket off emotions and tell students to 'take them to personal therapy'.

At the outset, the group will help in alleviating anxiety about the placement and prospective clients, and, as will be outlined, aspects of the supervisory relationship can be scrutinised. Assumptions and fears can be aired, and students learn to articulate potentially embarrassing or painful questions.

Clearly, the supervisee must feel very safe in the supervisory relationship in order to be able to open out their professional practice for scrutiny in this manner, so establishing a climate of trust and safety, with clearly defined boundaries in terms of confidentiality, is essential.

As Malchiodi and Riley (1996: 60) point out, part of this process involves the experienced professional (or trainee) looking at their attitudes and prejudices as part of the process of analysing their clinical work. Again, being willing to be a little vulnerable in the supervisee role is essential to get the most from supervision. The therapist (or trainee) must be willing to reveal aspects of themselves which they may worry another might find distasteful.

More straightforwardly, supervision is the place where trainees (or indeed professional art therapists) should be able to say, 'I think I made a mistake', and then to go on to analyse what was happening in the group or at that moment with an individual which caused that error to occur. Not letting egotism get in the way allows the useful exploration to take place. Clearly, the supervisor has a great responsibility to respond to disclosures with the same level of sensitivity and tact that they would with clients' disclosures in the therapy room.

With openness comes the realisation that there is an opportunity for reparation too, and it is liberating for trainees to realise that they can return to something they feel they missed in a therapeutic session; in a literal way, 'I've been reflecting on what X said to Y...' and thus something important (or bungled) can be revisited.

Mollon (1989: 113) points out that:

> Trainees inevitably suffer injuries to their self-esteem and self-image when finding they are floundering; the capacity to withstand these narcissistic blows, perhaps with the aid of supervision, is a crucial factor in whether or not the trainee can learn to practice effective psychotherapy.

The supervisor can draw on their own emotions, as well as intellect and theory, in order to make responses which will help the supervisee's reflective processes: 'that makes me feel...'-type responses can often be helpful.

If a 'group interactive' approach is being used in the therapeutic work being undertaken, the supervisee can elaborate on the group's dynamics and solicit their supervisor's reactions. Getting a 'second opinion' in this way is useful, especially when the group processes involved are very complex. Or, the supervisor, or another group member, may simply 'read' the situation differently and notice something the trainee or supervisee may have missed.

There are advantages to supervision taking place in a group setting, because participants can learn from each other. It is cost effective and as Case and Dalley (2006: 208) point out, 'There is less likelihood of supervisor and supervisee sharing blind spots or of an authoritarian/dependence relationship being established'.

Edwards (1993: 33) notes some common strategies employed by students in supervision in order to help them contain anxiety. These include flattering the supervisor (be nice to me because I am nice to you); attempting to redefine the relationship as a social relationship in order to evade a potentially negative evaluation; or indulging in extreme self-criticism aimed at eliciting sympathy and minimising the opportunity for the supervisee's work to be critically examined by others, including the supervisor.

To feel a little fearful and vulnerable in supervision, especially as a trainee, is entirely reasonable. I have argued that it is essential for supervisees to be willing to be emotionally open with their supervisors in order to use supervision effectively. Inviting supervisees to articulate their fears and fantasies may be part of the process of supervision. This chapter will now elaborate further on this topic.

This account provides an excellent resource for would-be art therapy supervisors. It also gives the trainee art therapist a useful insight into what they are likely to encounter in the outset of their clinical placement, which forms an important part of their art therapy training. I hope that in seeing the struggle and the anxiety inherent in the opening stages of the supervision groups, trainee art therapists will gain confidence and prospective supervisors will have a better idea of what to expect. Of course, the precise content of sessions will vary, and this is a 'taster' rather than a definitive summary; furthermore, groups vary in what they bring, but the anxiety and uncertainty will be a feature. For prospective supervisors the account will give an insight into the issues that arose in the first few weeks of supervision. Students' apprehensions were to the fore.

Some of what we are dealing with is imagined, as the supervision in art therapy training commences before students are actually in their work placements; various 'what if' scenarios can be articulated.

Supervision tools and structured note taking

There are various guides for helping students to reflect on their clinical work, which range from very simple to very complex. Some supervisors may wish to

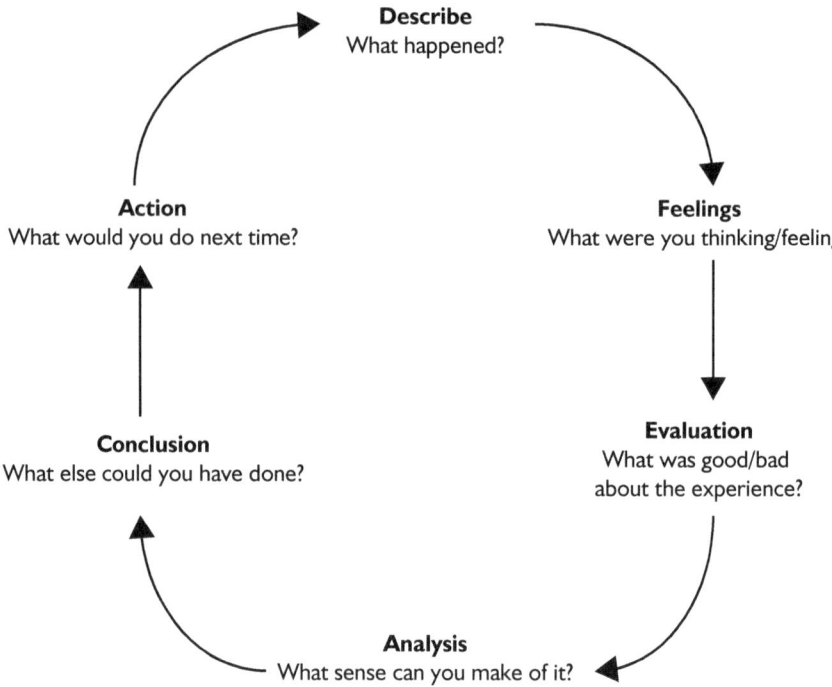

Figure 15.1 The Reflective Cycle (used by permission of Gibbs 1988)

run through several of these at the outset of supervision to enable students to pick a model they wish to work with. Other supervisors may provide a supervision sheet with a standardised format which students are expected to use to help them structure their thoughts about the clinical work. When the student starts clinical work, these standardised supervision sheets are completed prior to supervision by students and brought in with them as a reference. I increasingly feel that such structures are helpful for students, so long as it is made clear that students should try to think beyond whatever format they have been given, rather than allowing it to restrict their thinking.

Complex tools may not be introduced at the outset, but rather later on when they will be more relevant, perhaps a few weeks into the supervision group's life. The Reflective Cycle may be a good starting point (see Figure 15.1).

The role of the art work in supervision

Art can be used to help the analysis in supervision. For example, when using plasticine or clay, it might be useful to make representations of all the members in an interactive group and to then place them in relation to one another to help the analysis. How group members are represented can be illuminating and how they are positioned in relation to each other can be explored very easily using a medium such as plasticine. The figures made can be moved around, which can also be helpful when exploring what has happened in a session. Using a malleable medium such as plasticine can even allow the figures to be modified as they change their position, so for example, a rather brittle and spiky-looking 'creature' might undergo a metamorphosis when placed next to a representation of someone whom they feel is particularly supportive. This is in addition to clients' art work being brought in and analysed.

Students, in the initial sessions of a supervision group, may be asked to complete brief art works to depict their mood, or to be used in client–therapist role-play sessions. There are different ways of doing this, but client/therapist/observer can work very well as an educational technique. Students work together in groups of three, taking turns in the different roles of being the 'client' (talking about the brief art work just made), being the 'therapist' (who practises facilitating the 'client') and the observer (who will give feedback to the therapist apropos of their demeanour, how they asked questions and what they missed in the image).

The observer will be asked to comment at the end of the role-play session on the demeanour of the therapists, which could include the body language of the protagonists: for example, 'you asked really sensitive questions, but you had your arms crossed and you were leaning back in a rather defensive posture', or, 'you kept biting your lower lip and you looked rather stern'. A student concentrating on what the client is saying may not think about what their posture may be communicating.

The observer can also comment on the types of interventions made by the 'therapist': 'are you aware that you interrupted your "client" twice?' The language used may be scrutinised: 'you made a statement of fact about X rather than asking an open question'. The tone of a question or the pace of questions may be of relevance. Perhaps the 'therapist' rather over-interrogated the 'client'. Whether content was missed can be noted ('you didn't comment on the sea at all') and so forth. This is extremely useful training to help build trainees' confidence prior to them starting work with real clients.

Later on, students may also (with their clients' and on-site supervisors' permission) bring in examples of their clients' work for discussion in the group. The art works can help aid the student's memory, so they can point to a bit of the picture and reiterate what had been said about it. However, having the art works in the session is more than a mere *aide-mémoire* as the group members and the supervisor will ask apposite questions: 'did you ask the client where that bird is flying?' for example. Then the student can admit, 'no; actually, I didn't think of that'. Consequently, their analytic skills can be strengthened in this process. Many compositional elements can be considered, such as the relative scale of objects and how they are juxtaposed. Metaphors and analogies may have been overlooked. Missed opportunities for detailed scrutiny can be considered. Of course, this is always done in relation to thinking about the client's manner. It may be appropriate not to ask too many potentially intrusive questions, depending on the client's mood. So this is a two-tier analysis of what might have been appropriate at the time, as well as a process of learning to interrogate images in further depth. Just because many art therapy trainees have an arts-based background (all present a portfolio at application, regardless of the subject of their first degree, at least in the UK), this sort of analysis of images is not something that all trainees can do without practice.

I want to distinguish between analysis and interpretation here, as we are honing the student's analytic skills, not encouraging them to offer interpretations of the art work to their clients (though it is reasonable, and inevitable, to formulate ideas about the art which then help form open questions which do not foreclose meanings); multiple meanings contained within one symbol and tantalising ambiguity is part of what may be represented. As many art therapists have pointed out, art works can contain multiple meanings that may be quite contradictory (Malchiodi 2006: 12) and it is hard for trainees to understand that not knowing may be the most appropriate response to a particular work.

As noted, the type of language used by the trainee can be thought about. 'You might have asked a more open question at that point' might be possible feedback. New art therapy trainees need to think about not foreclosing meanings by being too unequivocal. Other things the trainee might have said can be envisaged. Focusing techniques can be explored, such as, 'if you imagine yourself in this purple space, what does it feel like?' or 'what does this animal feel?'

The actual construction of the piece can be thought about. How was it made? What has been covered up or obliterated? How was this acknowledged or explored in the session?

The use of the therapeutic space as a whole can also be thought about. How did the client or clients position themselves in relation to the trainee whilst making their work? Did they sit in a corner with their back towards the trainee or were they performative? (I had one client spend an entire session sculpting my face in a portrait, before, when it was her 'turn' in the group to speak, pulverising the sculpted head in front of the group, releasing angry feelings about someone I reminded her of. This was a strong example of a 'transference reaction' to the therapist.) How the image is modified, displayed or destroyed is always an important element to be considered.

The on-site supervision and university-based supervision interface

University supervision groups have the general purpose of assisting students with their learning whilst they are out on placement. Some students start off their clinical placements in an observation role prior to the allocation of clients, so they will sit-in on sessions and watch without taking on the role of therapist; others act as an 'assistant' to the practising art therapist from the outset, prior to being allocated their own clients. This will depend on the nature of the client group, the model of art therapy being used, as well as the preference of the supervisor. If possible, a period of observation can be extremely helpful in building the student's confidence.

During art therapy training, supervision is provided in the placement setting by a registered art therapist or another professional who has an understanding of, and an interest in, art therapy. As well as this on-site supervision (or 'mentorship' as it is sometimes called), students attend a weekly art therapy supervision group in the university setting, usually facilitated by a registered art therapist. In the latter group, students are encouraged to air their concerns about and reactions to their placement setting and their clients. Sometimes the relationship between the student and the on-site supervisor can become strained:

> Art therapists can experience problems if the supervisor is unfamiliar with working with images. Either party in the relationship can feel mystified, devalued or defensive about her own or the other's approach. It is helpful if these difficulties are resolved within the 'here and now' of the supervision relationship.
>
> (Case and Dalley 2006: 208)

This may be easier said than done, depending on how defensive the relevant parties are. Sometimes, there can be a personality clash or tensions about what are appropriate 'boundaries' in terms of the confidentiality of the group work. Sometimes, an on-site supervisor will agree one thing and do another. Occasionally, a placement supervisor will sabotage their student's work. Problems about the on-site supervisory relationship can be brought to the university supervision group and discussed. The university supervisor may give the student opportunities to resolve matters before intervening. A strategy may be formulated within the group and the student would then 'report back' on the ongoing situation.

It can be useful for the university supervisor (or placement visitor if this is not the same person) to hold separate meetings with the student and the supervisor on placement visits and to hear the different (and possibly conflicting) 'stories' of each and to look for areas of disparity, which can indicate where there are conflicting expectations or misunderstandings. Then a joint meeting can be convened where these conflicts are highlighted to the parties by the university supervisor. These problems tend not to surface immediately and are unlikely to arise in the opening weeks of a new supervision group.

The placements available to trainee art therapists in this setting are wide ranging and include working in established art therapy departments. A wide spread of community-based placements are available with a variety of client groups. Some very interesting work is also being carried out in pre-operative and post-operative care using art therapy, in hospital settings and by voluntary organisations.

Contracts and formal assessment

The practical task of negotiating placement contracts with on-site supervisors may or may not be conducted by the same member of staff facilitating the university-based supervision group, but in either case the contacts established for student placement work can be brought in to the supervision sessions in the initial stages and scrutinised, so that all aspects of the contact are understood. Students must be confident that they understand the paperwork. Doing this practical work can also help to allay students' fears about the unknown; on the other hand, the assessments do look daunting at first sight. Standards of practice for UK-based art therapists are available from the Health Professions Council (HPC), and all courses tailor their assessments to meet these standards of proficiency. These may be subject to change in the future, so rather than reproduce them here I refer readers to the Health and Care Professions Council website which has the 'Standards of Proficiency' for art therapists listed.

Many institutions divide the assessment up into various chunks. To give an example from my own institution, one might be entitled 'personal skills' which could look at the student's ability to respond to feedback, their capacity for critical self reflection and whether they are dependable or not. Their professional demeanour is assessed also, along with their capacity to work under pressure.

Because assessment is quite difficult, the criteria for assessment have been carefully described to try to make the process easier for supervisors and students. So to take the example of the student's ability to think about their work and respond to constructive criticism, there are various columns in the placement assessment document which try to describe what is meant: 'the student is unable to self-reflect in an open and honest way and respond to constructive criticism appropriately without significant guidance' in the far left-hand column, which would be a very poor 'score' (and a fail), moving to, 'the student can sometimes self-reflect in an open and honest way, and can respond to constructive criticism appropriately with guidance' (which we also have as unsatisfactory – fail, because only being able to do this 'sometimes' would not render them fit to practise), followed by, 'the student can self-reflect in an open and honest way; and respond to constructive criticism appropriately with guidance' (a pass), and so forth, through to 'the student is excellent in his or her ability to self-reflect in an open and honest way; and can respond to constructive criticism appropriately' (which is an A). All of the HPC Standards of Proficiency are 'benchmarked' in this way to assist in the assessment of clinical work.

A discussion about all aspects of the assessment is important as students need to be aware precisely how they will be assessed, and to be as clear as possible about what will be expected of them. Obviously, thinking about the assessment can raise the students' anxiety levels, so it may be worth starting with some other less daunting tasks before scrutinising the assessments. Looking at ethical regulation documents and discussing them, undertaking some simple role-play exercises, as previously mentioned, and discussing the role of supervision itself can be better things to do at the outset of the supervision group (though the timing of this must be determined by when students are timetabled to do clinical work, as clearly it would be inappropriate to allow clinical work to commence before the assessment procedures had been properly scrutinised).

Another important aspect of early supervision is in discussing different models of analysis and tools for note taking. However, in the initial weeks of a supervision group it can be helpful to allow time for some open discussion.

Issues which arose in initial student-led sessions

Drawing on transcripts, I shall now highlight some of the issues and concerns that arose at the outset of the supervision groups. As the sessions were student led, issues were discussed as they emerged in a fairly ad hoc manner.

Anxiety

Anxiety about the prospect of starting a clinical placement was at the forefront of students' minds at the beginning of the supervision group. Issues around their capacity to explain themselves arose along with anxiety about how they would cope starting an art therapy session.

Giving oneself time to settle into the placement and discover its ethos, philosophy and working practices were considered to be important. Students expressed their sense of pressure in having to get started. It was thought they would be better able to do this having first got a grasp of how the organisation functioned.

In some placement settings students would not have a specified group to work with but would have to recruit clients by advertising their services within the organisation, by word of mouth, or by other means, including the production of posters and brochures. We agreed that advertisements could be brought into the group for comment and discussion. Using language in the advertisement which we ourselves would not find alienating was thought to be a good strategy, rather than phrasing ads along the lines of: 'Have you got a problem?' or 'Depressed? Try Art Therapy!'

Supervision can respond to concerns directly as they arise. For example, in this situation a ten-minute role-play on 'introducing yourself and the concept of art therapy' to each member of the group in turn could help turn anxiety into self-confidence.

Moral issues and 'therapeutic boundaries'

A considerable amount of discussion focused on the importance of explaining what art therapy is to clients before engaging in any work with them and not foisting art therapy onto clients under the guise of an art class or other creative activity. The British Association of Art Therapists' guidelines on ethics and professional conduct were read by the group and discussed. The code of ethics is clear that at the start of treatment a clear contact between the client, or the client's representative, and the art therapist will be agreed with respect to the boundaries of the therapeutic relationship, and different types of contract were discussed.

What constituted 'therapeutic boundaries' came under scrutiny as some students were placed within a therapeutic community and other settings where clients and staff engage in a range of activities together, such as socialising and eating together. I suggested that in such a setting one would not discuss the content of art therapy sessions in any other context than the art therapy session. One anxiety that was expressed was what would happen if a client raised an issue from the art therapy session outside of the session? The supervision group felt that it might be possible to gently suggest that the issue raised be taken up in the next art therapy group. The idea that one could be straightforward was advised. A response such as, 'Well, that's an art therapy issue so we can follow up on it in the next session' was promoted. The importance of containment in group work was discussed. The added complexity of working in a therapeutic community setting was acknowledged. The relationship between trainee art therapist and client is obviously much more straightforward if they only meet in the context of the ongoing art therapy group work.

Bumping into clients on the street was also discussed. In a large city, this was relatively unlikely to happen, but it was felt that a polite 'hello' without further conversation would be the best response. It could be counter-productive to 'blank' a client. A colleague of mine, who works in a very small community where she is known as the local therapist and where she frequently bumps into her clients all over the place, asks them in the first session if they would like her to acknowledge them or not outside of sessions.

Photographing the work

Whether or not to ask to photograph work at the outset of therapy was discussed in the group. Since art therapy students have to produce an illustrated case study on one of their clients during both years of the two-year training, this was thought to be an important issue. I felt that it was reasonable for them to explain their trainee status and the requirements of the course at the outset though this might feel quite awkward. Offering a simple permission slip for the client to sign was recommended (ethical protocols suggest that this should contain a paragraph about the client's right to withdraw the permission and that the client should retain a copy). Asking to photograph work after sessions had started could result in a refusal from the client and disappointment for the trainee art therapist. However, asking fairly early on in sessions to photograph work rather then at the outset was thought a viable alternative, as it should be possible to keep very detailed notes on several clients for the first few weeks before selecting whom to write the case study on. This has the advantage that it gives students time to select a case they find particularly interesting to write about.

Writing up case notes

It was suggested that an hour between sessions should be set aside for the task. As trainees, it is useful for students to record as much detail as possible about the sessions so that they are forced to reflect on the work, and it can then be analysed in depth in the supervision group.

Other paperwork

Therapeutic work with clients should not commence until institutional permissions are in place. Most training institutions have now developed a set of protocols (standardised forms and procedures) to enable students and on-site supervisors to expedite permissions, and these are all completed and signed off before students start any clinical work. Obviously, if not scrutinised elsewhere, initial supervision sessions for student trainees can involve looking at such paperwork.

Location

The location of art therapy sessions is always a recurring issue as not all art therapists work from a designated art therapy studio space. One student was due to see clients in a playroom and felt this was potentially confusing for the children who associated the room with a certain type of activity.

Do not disturb

Staff members interrupt sessions for various reasons. These include practical reasons, because the room is where certain things are stored, or in a well-meaning but disruptive way, because they want to know how the art therapist is getting on. Establishing confidential boundaries in some institutions, in terms of ensuring sessions are not interrupted, can feel quite difficult. Other disruptions to art therapy sessions can be from other clients. Some students resolved to work with staff teams to emphasise the importance of confidentiality and creating a 'safe space' in which strong emotions could be expressed within their placement settings. Giving a talk or running a workshop for staff was discussed. Others decided to put up 'do not disturb' notices while they were working!

Has the client got a problem?

A number of issues were raised in this session around a student's ambivalent feelings about seeing clients as 'other'. One group member expressed her desire to work with clients as though they were entirely 'normal' human beings, this prompted by a positive desire to treat clients with respect, to engender and promote their sense of self-respect in the process. However, she worried that her stance might lead her to overlooking genuine difficulties. This led to an interesting philosophical discussion about the nature of normalcy. I then asked the group to reflect about how they might feel if they were to work with someone who was very identified with their psychiatric diagnosis, or to imagine they were working with a prisoner whom they felt was genuinely evil!

The group then focused on one student's experience of being told that her prospective client was considered to be a 'problem client' before she had even met her. This raised expectations and anxieties before art therapy had even begun as well as fear of failure since the student was being given a 'difficult' case. Whether students working with prisoners should know what crimes they had committed was raised. Art therapy students said that initially, at least, they would rather not know since this could colour their perceptions of and subsequent relationship with the client.

What can art therapy offer and does it work?

One student attended a case conference in a psychiatric institution at which a number of different professionals were gathered. The client in question seemed to have intractable problems and was seemingly unable to be cured. This made the student wonder what good he could do and trepidation was felt at the prospect of starting art therapy sessions.

How to explain art therapy in a non-condescending manner was raised as part of this question. What kind of language should be used to explain what art therapy can offer to self-referring clients? Will certain kinds of language alienate certain people? We discussed using language that was natural for us to use, since if the client didn't like the way we expressed ourselves, they might not like working with us. On the topic of professional demeanour, we talked about being 'ourselves' in the art therapy session, and the importance of not putting on a pretence or using language that we wouldn't normally use.

Confidentiality

Problems of confidentiality were again raised. For example, working as an art therapist in a prison setting, would there be other people in the art therapy room? What would happen to the art work? Would it end up on the governor's desk? Would a prison psychiatrist get to see it? Institutional norms vary. On-site supervisors need to make students aware of the code of ethics in place in each institution prior to them starting work with clients.

Sometimes confidentiality was problematic. Not wanting to disclose certain information to a supervisor was an issue for one student. The student said, 'He knows the men so well that I might as well name the person under discussion, as he knows who I'm referring to'. The student was able to explore his fears that if the supervisor knew who he was referring to, then the supervisor might make a remark about a disclosure made in art therapy in another setting; it was suggested that the trainee explore these fears with the supervisor directly and that the limits of confidentiality of the supervision agreement be re-stated. Clearly, being able to talk about individuals openly with the supervisor in the on-site supervision sessions would be advantageous to the student's learning as the supervisor had a lot of insight about the individuals concerned. The issue here was one of a lack of trust.

Another student was uncertain about the ethical problem of getting agreement from a woman with senile dementia who forgot who her art therapist was in-between sessions. Extra confusion was caused by the location of the sessions, which were in a kitchen area. Again, the institutional supervisor should be able to advise the student what permissions are required prior to therapy commencing (which may be from the next of kin). There may also be larger questions about the appropriateness of the referral.

The importance of setting out a clear contract at the outset was emphasised as important in terms of making it apparent to clients who will have access to their art work and how art therapy will be conducted. Obtaining clarity about supervision, and other arrangements, which might involve the student disclosing information about therapeutic work, needs to be negotiated and agreed and then articulated to potential art therapy clients.

Clients should be aware of whom information disclosed in a session will be shared with. The limits of confidentiality should be clear to both therapist and client at the outset of therapy. Setting the boundaries might require some research or negotiation on the part of students who may need to find out from their placement supervisor what norms apply within the institution. For example, some institutions have inter-disciplinary case meetings at which they would want to view art therapy work and discuss the therapy in progress. The university's supervisor can always be brought in to negotiate on their behalf, if necessary, if institutional norms are such that art therapy would be untenable.

Setting the pace

Anxiety about how to set the pace of an art therapy group was expressed. How does the art therapist influence the pace of the group? What about the 'chemistry' of different people in a group? How much should be exposed by clients and, if exposed, acknowledged and dealt with? How does the art therapist deal with the client's resistance to the idea of the art therapy? Students fantasised sentiments such as a client saying, 'she is trying to get into my head' or, 'art therapy is for nutters, isn't it?' These are quite difficult questions to answer, since groups vary tremendously. Certainly, acknowledging disclosures made was considered important, though clients themselves need to become aware of the meaning of what they have made. Sensitivity is required on the part of the therapist to give clients time to assimilate what they have done and this might mean holding back for some time until an invitation is extended to them directly from the client, or the client somehow indicates that she or he is ready to speak. These subtleties of practice are daunting for the new trainee and can be explored in supervision in a succession of 'what if'-type scenarios.

Settings vary tremendously. Some students were based in therapeutic community-style settings in which a lot of trust had already been established and clients already knew each other. In such settings the art therapy had 'taken off' very fast with disclosures of a very personal nature being made from the outset. This raised anxiety for some students about whether they would be able to 'handle' the pace of the work, and cope with the strong emotions being expressed.

Almost the opposite occurred for some students with very different client groups such as people with physical illnesses or prisoners, as it was possible, or had already occurred, that clients from an art therapy group had left or been removed. In the prison settings, in particular, it was possible that a prisoner would be moved or given an appointment with another person or placed on a work duty, which would prevent him or her attending the art therapy session. These problems were not confined to prison settings though.

Students expressed a concern about a prisoner 'opening up' and then not being supported in an ongoing manner because they had been scheduled elsewhere. These experiences also provoked frustration in students when their clients simply failed to turn up, no one in the institution having bothered to inform the trainee. It was felt important to note the missing person's absence in group work. In one institution a client had been withdrawn from the art therapy group (which he loved) as a punishment for disruptive behaviour.

Trust

Are you believed in or are you working with a client group who has been promised much and delivered little? Clients' expectations are clearly relevant in terms of how art therapy has been 'sold' to them.

The usefulness of communicating about the art therapy sessions with other members of staff was noted. For example, one student said that her conversations with a head teacher about a child's background had given her vital information necessary for understanding the content of the child's pictures. Again, good and open working relations with the on-site placement supervisor cannot be overstated in their usefulness.

Establishing trust is pivotal to the success of therapy work.

Us and them

A clash of cultures was evident in some placement settings with an 'us and them' attitude firmly entrenched in one particular prison setting. Professional territorialism was noted in several settings, with one art therapy trainee getting a very cool reception from the on-site clinical psychologist. Whilst promoting good relationships with other professionals, giving presentations to raise awareness of art therapy practice and attending multi-disciplinary case-assessment meetings are part of the grist of an art therapy placement, it is often very daunting for the new trainee, especially if some of their reception is frosty.

Boundaries and having others in the room

The benefits of being placed with an experienced art therapist were noted. One student who felt great anxiety found he gained a lot of reassurance from working alongside a therapist.

The presence of a clinical nurse, in a room of particularly challenging psychiatric patients, was described by another student as a help in allaying her anxiety. We discussed the pros and cons of inviting the nurse or support worker to paint and join in the group discussion. It had been decided that in this case she would simply sit as unobtrusively as possible in the corner.

We discussed how a silent observer could have an impact on group dynamics. On one occasion, I had worked with a deaf women who had a sign-language translator and I recounted how his behaviour had begun to have an impact on group dynamics – how he sat, his gestures, whether or not he glanced at his watch (clearly waiting for the break or the end). Secondly, fantasies began to develop around what he might be thinking about in the group.

Another reaction to fear of failure or a sense of personal danger was a sense of relief expressed that an art therapist or other professional was to sit-in on sessions. In prisons, a prison warder was often on call outside of the room. All art therapy students were advised that they should not work in an isolated situation, though sometimes this would occur by chance. One student who had formally worked as a care worker recounted how in the psychiatric hospital she had worked there were many locations on the wards that had panic buttons, but that when they were pressed by staff, help had not always been forthcoming. Safety precautions should be articulated in placement contacts and signed by both on-site supervisors and their trainees, but they are not always honoured and unfortunately sometimes placements have to be withdrawn.

Being put at risk by a lax on-site supervisor

A number of factors can potentially have an impact on the ability of students to fulfil their contracts with clients. In one prison session a 'lock-in' was used to enable prison officers to get together for a meeting. The art therapy student on placement at the prison elected to be locked in with her art therapy group and then experienced anxiety when one of the prisoners left the art room and wandered off in the department. This left the trainee feeling very 'responsible', yet she felt unwilling to 'interfere'. Clearly, without her placement supervisor on-hand, the student had been put in an untenable position.

What do art therapists do?

Some students faced overt or subtle misunderstanding about their role from staff at their placement institutions. For example, some students were extended invitations to give lessons in art techniques. Others sensed an expectation that beautiful objects were to be produced. Another student was handed a book about model building (a strong hint that this is what was considered to be appropriate with her male client). Rehearsing how to describe art therapy can be part of the preparation for trainees.

The absent supervisor

One student noted that though she had established a regular appointment time with her supervisor that he was often absent, busy on the wards, leaving her feeling very unsafe, very unsupported and alone. (Supervisors sign a contract offering a certain amount of supervision time to their trainees, so this would be a matter the university would pursue on a formal level; however, it is also useful for the trainees to be able to share their feelings about unsatisfactory supervisory relationships.)

Contracts and 'ground rules'

Students working with disruptive children felt that a clear contract with them was imperative to determine what behaviour was not acceptable in the art therapy room. Drafts of contracts were brought into the supervision session for discussion and included items such as, 'the client and the therapist agree not to be rude to one another' or 'the client and the therapist agree not to hurt one another'.

The ugly client

Students can find it useful to fantasise about what kind of people they may or may not be able to work with. Feeling unsafe is a recurring theme of early supervision work. The physical appearance of a client could make a trainee feel unsafe. It was also felt that knowing a client's background could set up anxiety. This ranged from working with a small child renowned for biting, to working with a formerly violent prisoner. The advantages and disadvantages of knowing the client's history was debated, with a number of students deciding that they would rather not know about their client's past at the outset of therapy; rather that they would rather commence the relationship in the 'here and now'.

Storage

The disposal and storage of art work is an important issue that needs to be resolved at the outset of therapy. For example, if a group of clients makes a large group work, what will happen to it? If there simply is no storage available and the work needs to be dismantled at the end of the session, clients will have feelings about this. This is more than merely a practical question. Some outpatient departments give clients a choice to store work or take it home at the end of sessions. Making sure clients understand what is on offer in terms of disposal and storage is always a point that needs to be clarified.

Ending sessions

Even early on, students start to think about how to end art therapy. So even though this chapter is looking at the outset of supervision, this issue is likely to come up.

Issues around loss can crop up near the end of groups, so betrayals, bereavements and feelings about mortality can become group themes towards the close of groups.

Summary and conclusion

As noted, students felt the need to bring drafts of client contracts and advertising into the sessions for discussion in the initial stages. They also rehearsed describing what an art therapist is. Standard client contacts can be included in placement handbooks which students can modify, as necessary, to make the whole process easier. Placement contacts can be considered, and codes of professional practice and ethics assimilated.

In this chapter, I have suggested that it is essential that supervisees, be they professional practitioners or trainees, feel able to share their feelings of vulnerability with their supervisors in order to benefit fully from the supervision process.

Many fears and fantasies can be expressed and explored prior to trainees commencing their clinical hours. Giving clear permission to students to feel able to express their vulnerability is profoundly important in order for them to learn to use supervision effectively; appearing professional, though important in their placement settings, is not the point when it comes to participating in supervision. As I noted at the outset of this chapter, supervision is where students must be able to share their sense that they may have made a mistake in clinical work. Supervisees may need to deal with their feelings of humiliation, embarrassment or shame in order to make such disclosures, but when sensitively handled by their supervisor these disclosures are transformed into positive learning experiences. Becoming a safe practitioner means being able to use supervision effectively.

In the initial stages of supervision for art therapy trainees, it is helpful for them to be able to openly express their doubts and fears. Students newly out on training placements, as demonstrated, experience a wide range of issues and concerns. Not all trainees have the luxury of a placement in a well-established art therapy service, or they may be working peripatetically, so negotiation about service provision, promotion of the art therapy service and establishing therapeutic boundaries are an important part of the learning experience.

At the outset of the supervision group, familiarising students with rules for professional conduct and codes of ethical behaviour, looking at placement documentation, informing students as to how their clinical work will be assessed, rehearsing how to explain and define art therapy, sharing leaflets and promotional material as well as conducting client-therapist role-play exercises, are all useful constructive activities, which help to counteract the students' initial feelings of despondency, frustration and apprehension. Later, when the supervision process is more advanced, the work of the supervision group can become more concentrated on therapeutic interactions and interventions, but at the outset, as illustrated, a lot of time can be spent usefully addressing trainees' feelings of hopelessness, inadequacy and anxiety about prospective clinical work and clients, which also acts as a rehearsal for how to use the supervision group.

Bibliography

Carrigan, J. 1993. Ethical Considerations in a Supervisory Relationship. *Art Therapy: Journal of the American Art Therapy Association* 10, 130–5.

Case, C. and Dalley, T. 2006. *The Handbook of Art Therapy.* Second edition. London: Routledge.

Edwards, D. 1993. Learning About Feelings: the Role of Supervision in Art Therapy Training. *The Arts in Psychotherapy* 20, 213–22.

Edwards, D. 1997. Supervision Today: the Psychoanalytic Legacy, in G. Shipton (ed.) *Supervision of Psychotherapy and Counselling.* Buckingham: Open University Press, pp. 11–23.

Fish, D. (ed.) 1998. *Turning Teaching into Learning.* London: West London Press.

Gibbs, G. 1988. *Learning by Doing: a Guide to Teaching and Learning Methods.* Oxford: Oxford Further Education Unit, Oxford Polytechnic.

Gilroy, A. 2006. *Art Therapy, Research and Evidence-based Practice.* London: Sage.

Hawkins, P. and Shohet, R. 1992. *Supervision in the Helping Professions.* Buckingham: Open University Press.

Hogan, S. (ed.) 1997. *Feminist Approaches to Art Therapy.* London: Routledge.

Ishiyama, F.I. 1988. A Model of Visual Case Processing Using Metaphors and Drawings. *Counsellor Education and Supervision* 28, 153–61.

Malchiodi, C. 2006. *Art Therapy Source Book.* New York: McGraw-Hill.

Malchiodi, C.A. and Riley, S. 1996. *Supervision and Related Issues: a Handbook for Professionals.* Chicago, IL: Magnolia Street Publishers.

Mollon, P. 1989. Anxiety, Supervision and a Space for Thinking: some Narcissistic Perils for Clinical Psychologists in Learning Psychotherapy. *British Journal of Medical Psychology* 62, 113–22.

Schaverien, J. 2007. *Supervision of Art Psychotherapy: a Theoretical and Practical Handbook.* London: Routledge.

Smith, H., Hogan, S., Newell-Walker, U. and Stein, N. 2008. *Art Therapy Clinical Placement One: Assessment Form.* Derby: University of Derby.

Wilson, L., Riley, S. and Wadeson, H. 1984. Art Therapy Supervision. *Art Therapy: Journal of the American Art Therapy Association* 1(3), 100–5.

Chapter 16

Models of supervision and personal therapy

Annette M. Coulter

Introduction

A newly qualified art therapist enjoys the availability of peer supervision and psychotherapy supervision. There is a culture of support and experiential learning which also includes the provision of on-site clinical supervision for art therapist trainees on clinical placement. However, when working in more remote locations there may be quite a different understanding about clinical supervision arrangements and requirements. Motivated by an awareness of professional isolation, the art therapist's request for supervision may elicit unexpected employer responses such as, 'Why, don't you know what you're doing?' indicating a different understanding about supervision requirements. This response is a reminder that the concept of clinical supervision is relatively recent and cautions against making assumptions about supervision availability when setting up a new art therapy service in a different country. There is also the risk that the employer may be motivated by economic convenience and cost cutting, wanting the clinical supervisor to be appointed from the local community – suitability and quality become of secondary importance. The supervisor must have more expertise than the supervisee but what does an art therapist do when their employer determines that they see a supervisor with less experience or less expertise?

Defining supervision

As Hogan has already described in the previous chapter, art therapy supervision gives an opportunity to scrutinise ongoing clinical work, to ensure safe practice and to enhance the level of clinical practice. Pedder's metaphoric description of a good supervisor's relationship with their supervisees in the learning experience is that:

> they are not empty vessels into whom we pour from a jug; not inert lumps of clay to be fashioned after our own image. We are facilitators, gardeners, accepting the plants that spring up in our gardens and doing what we can by pruning.
>
> (Pedder 1986: 2)

This idea is of the supervisor's role being one of working with what the supervisee brings, rather than imposing themselves onto the supervisee's skill set; the supervisee has a large part to play. This view fits with Carroll's position that supervisees are active in determining supervision to meet their requirements. Carroll lists the rights and responsibilities of supervisees. Rights include those to 'see your supervisor's report on you with opportunity to comment on content'; to 'give clear and focused feedback to your supervisor'; and to 'appeal decisions made in supervision with which you have problems' (Carroll and Gilbert 2006: v). Responsibilities include 'preparing for supervision'; 'being aware of other stake holders in the supervisory arrangements' (for example, clients and their families, taxpayers and organisations); and 'being aware of cultural, religious, racial, age, gender and sexual orientation differences between you and others'.

Finding a supervisor

It is the supervisee's responsibility to find a suitable supervisor, someone from whom they will learn more, extend their skills, with whom they will be able to reflect with about their work and with whom there is a rapport of potential trust, honesty and mutual respect. If the employer is insisting on a supervisor who is deemed by the supervisee as inappropriate, it is the supervisee's responsibility to educate the employer about their professional needs and requirements. The most obvious way to do this is to quote professional standards of practice, arguing that in order to complete professional registration requirements, an art therapy supervisor with considerably more experience is recommended.

However, in circumstances where the job title is not a designated 'art therapist' position, it is not always viable to argue for an art therapy supervisor. Art therapists may be employed under such job titles as 'counsellor', 'clinical coordinator', 'team leader' or 'family counsellor', for example. In these circumstances, the employer may argue that the position in which the art therapist is employed is not a designated 'art therapist' position and therefore does not require an art therapy supervisor. In this situation, the art therapist has several options: as part of educating their employer, the art therapist may decide to deliver a talk about the specialist nature of their work (see Chapter 5); where post-training registration requirements demand art therapy supervision, the art therapist may choose to pay for their supervision privately (either in conjunction with supervision provided by the employer or not); or the art therapist may choose to write a paper on the merits of clinical supervision, arguing for the need to travel for supervision. In a rural or remote location, this may entail negotiating time to travel and arguing the need to attend supervision in the city because local expertise is inadequate. When working in a clinical role that stretches beyond the role of 'art therapist' it is sometimes necessary to find a supervisor who can provide expertise that stretches between the parameters of cognitive goal setting and the unpacking of unconscious material; clinical supervision is most effective when it caters for all contingencies the workplace demands.

Supervising allied health professionals

Experienced art therapists are available to supervise allied health professionals, in particular those who have chosen to use art as part of their casework. An art therapy supervisor provides expertise in the use of image-making processes as part of therapy and as occasional therapeutic intervention.

While on clinical placement or internships, art therapist supervisees are often called upon to educate their allied health professional supervisor about art therapy. They may also be asked to present to the rest of the agency in the form of an introductory talk, a case presentation or about their training course (see Chapter 5). Talking intimately to their on-site supervisor is quite different to presenting to a larger audience or clinical team. Art therapy can enhance the supervision relationship regardless of whether the supervisor is an art therapist or an allied health professional (Durkin *et al.* 1989).

Supervision contract

The supervisee has a right to negotiate the terms and conditions of the supervisory arrangement. A written agreement of understanding makes provision for this right, as well as clarifies from the outset 'what is not negotiable in the contract' (Carroll and Gilbert 2006: 27). According to Carroll, there are four types of supervision contracts:

1 Two-way contracts between the supervisor and the supervisee that include time and space to bring work to reflect upon.
2 Three-way contracts include the organisation that is employing the supervisor and to whom the supervisor may be also reporting. Being clear here on limits of confidentiality and boundaries of the supervisory relationship becomes important.
3 The business contract is the administrative aspects of the arrangement.
4 The psychological contract defines the expectations of both the supervisee and supervisor.

(Carroll and Gilbert 2006: 27–8)

One contract could incorporate different aspects of these four types of contracts, which are not mutually exclusive.

Art therapy tasks in supervision

From the outset, art therapy tasks can be used to enhance the supervisory relationship. When negotiating the supervision contract, the supervisee may not understand and be fearful that in signing something this might be held against them later. They may also have ambivalent feelings about the intention or purpose of a contract. Prior to concretising the supervision contract agreement, art can be used to explore fears, ambivalent feelings and to visually conceptualise the desired learning relationship. A task such as 'draw an effective supervision contract' helps the supervisee to visually describe what they regard as important in the supervisory relationship.

Art can be used to establish group supervision cohesiveness. Art tasks could include drawing 'how I see the purpose of this group'; 'what do the supervisor/ other supervisee group members expect of me?'; 'feeling safe in this group'; 'how I would like this group structured'; or 'my understanding of how this group is to operate'. Such tasks help group members negotiate their needs and wants at the commencement of group supervision. Art therapy can be used to facilitate processes of getting to know each other, determine group supervision goals, explore hopes, expectations and ambivalences, as well as how the group is to operate and be structured.

Based on the experiential learning cycle of activity, reflection, learning and application (Kolb 1984), there are a number of experiential art tasks that facilitate the supervisee's learning process. These are more likely be used in a one-on-one, face-to-face supervisee–supervisor relationship but could be adapted to a group supervision setting.

1 In the first stage of Kolb's learning cycle, the supervisor and the supervisee examine how the supervisee does their work, with an art task such as 'draw how you do your work' or 'draw yourself doing your work'. Where the supervisee is an art therapist or an allied health professional who is learning to use art more effectively with clients, the task describing the activity of therapy or counselling can be more specific, such as 'draw how you use art with clients' or 'draw yourself using art in your work'. It is up to the supervisee to determine how they approach such a task, but suggestions are that it could be diagrammatic, literal or symbolic. For some, a diagram is a much easier way to describe what they do than a more descriptive, complex image.

2 In the reflection stage, art tasks could include 'draw something that reflects on an aspect of what you do with clients' or 'think about what we have been discussing today and draw about your relationship with this client/group'. A reflective art task is about developing the ability to step back from the intensity of the clinical work or to focus on a particular aspect or incident in the content of a session. The use of art at this learning stage provides opportunity to examine therapy content and processes from a reflective distance. Supervisors use art-making to facilitate this reflective process. Creating a concrete image, something that represents whatever is being reflected upon, gazing at that image, then receiving back from that image, is not unlike phenomenological perceiving (Betensky 1995: 17–20). The art work allows what is less conscious in the therapist–client relationship to emerge. It also provides opportunity for countertransference issues that were not previously clearly evident to also emerge. The use of art-making at this stage of the supervision learning cycle enhances the supervisee's ability to step back from the case and see it from a more objective place.

3   What the supervisee sees or becomes aware of while in reflection becomes core material for the third stage: learning. Art tasks can concretise what has been learnt; for example, 'based on your reflective drawing, what have you learnt in this session? Is it possible to visually describe what you now know? Draw what this session has taught you' or 'draw some wise advice for yourself' (Withers 2006). This task is based on what the supervisee has learnt in the process of reflecting from the session through creating an image. The supervisor attends to the supervisee's learning process and notes their ability to grasp self-awareness, heed advice and gain knowledge of themselves and their relationship with a client, group or family while self-reflecting on process and content (Carroll 1996). The art task can also examine their relationship with the supervisor: 'draw something to represent what you have learnt in this supervision session' or 'how do you feel in relation to me after today's supervision session?'

4   The application stage challenges the supervisee to consider how they are going to apply what they have learnt in the earlier stages to their work. An art task reflective of this could be 'draw how you intend to integrate what you have learnt' or 'draw yourself in relationship with this client or with me (i.e. your supervisor) with this new information'. The intention is to integrate what has become conscious, or changes in self-awareness, in the process of reflection and learning stages.

Working in professional isolation

Chapter 5 explored the challenge of finding oneself located far from any other art therapists and possibly any other counsellors or psychotherapists. Particularly in countries where distances are great, art therapists are often working in complete professional isolation, or they may be part of a relief team in an area of natural disaster or conflict, risking exposure to vicarious trauma without adequate supervision. In such circumstances, it is important to have a flexible attitude to supervision and to think creatively about what other options are available, such as peer supervision and self-supervision. For some professional associations, however, neither of these options may count towards supervised hours credentialling requirements. This is unfortunate, because supervision with other allied health professionals who are also part of an isolated community offers art therapists in sole-worker positions a viable alternative that is arguably effective and well considered. From a more global perspective, a future view of art therapy as a fully integrated profession might allow consideration of both peer supervision and self-supervision as offering a credentialing option over more traditional methods.

Peer supervision

Art therapists can offer each other support through shared group supervision. Peer supervision is effective in situations where income does not stretch to include clinical supervision, such as when a newly-qualified art therapist is unable to find immediate employment, but has an opportunity to provide minimal therapy.

In peer supervision, 'each participant becomes co-supervisor and supervisee at different times' (Carroll and Gilbert 2006: 11). Participants might also include non-art therapists (Laine 2007). When working in professional isolation, the art therapist can be part of a peer-support group made up of professionals from the local community, such as nurses, doctors, clergy and teachers (Crago and Crago 2002: 83). Crago and Crago suggest that instead of asking, 'is this person my professional equal?' the therapist should consider, 'would this person be able to give and take, in an atmosphere of mutual respect and safety?' (Crago and Crago 2002: 83). For professionally isolated art therapists, community-based peer supervision provides an opportunity to educate and promote art therapy through a group of professionals who have significant roles in the community, even though 'this supervision may end up coming from right outside the network of similarly trained and credentialed professionals with whom most of us identify' (Crago and Crago 2002: 83).

It is important to ensure that the type of supervised hours, including peer supervision, are recognised as meeting supervision requirements by most associations. Where this includes therapists trained in quite different or quite specific models, such as a Steiner or transpersonal orientation, a cognitive-behavioural bias or a psychoanalytic psychodynamic approach, there is a wealth of peer educational opportunity, exposure to new theoretical models and challenging, thought-provoking discussion. For peer supervision to be beneficial, formal professional roles need to be replaced by mutual respect, an openness towards a sharing of self-disclosure and an honest self-expression in one's responses. The goal is to establish trust and safety over time.

Hawken and Worrall (2002) suggest a reciprocal mentoring model of peer supervision (Hawken and Worrall 2002: 43–53) in small groups of not more than two or three where each participant is both supervisee and supervisor at different times. Responsibility is to the collegial relationship and there is no hierarchical line-management accountability. A reciprocal learning relationship is fostered, based on 'mutuality and equality' that 'recognises wisdom, skills and knowledge of each person' who gives as well as receives, and 'these partnerships have exponential potential as they proliferate throughout organisations' (Hawken and Worrall 2002: 43–53).

Peer supervision allows opportunities for the integration of knowledge from other fields such as the acceptance of art therapy by allied health services and the relationship 'provides reliable and candid personal feedback, emotional support, career strategizing, and on-going confirmation of each individual's competence and potential' (Kram and Isobella 1985: 121–4). An optional structure is a reciprocal mentoring arrangement which allows freedom to choose a supervisee partner. The purpose is to engage in a non-hierarchical, non-evaluative relationship where there is an equal commitment to time and process. A contracted formal relationship of reciprocity and mutuality is established where trust, honesty and transparency are promoted through structured sessions, where reflective learning takes place. Hawken and Worrall (2002) describe meeting fortnightly and rotating both the venue and who starts. They have a break in the middle of a three-hour session where they change roles from supervisor to supervisee. Their contract includes boundaries regarding confidentiality and they are intentional about not identifying clients or organisations. There is no managerial accountability – trust and honesty have encouraged a deep and close relationship to evolve over time. They are able to challenge each other safely and respectfully: 'we leave supervision feeling heard, understood and with a much clearer perspective on our professional lives… we give what we would like to receive' (Hawken and Worrall 2002: 50).

Supervision and the internet

Peer supervision can also be through an internet hook-up such as Skype. A reproduced image to be discussed and any prepared notes can be sent in advance to an art therapy peer group. This group may even be made up of art therapists from outside the local area or country to include overseas members. This is not the same as face-to-face contact, but is a compromised alternative where no other option is available. McNiff mentions 'distance art therapy' practice as a future direction for art therapists to consider, including clinical supervision and digital storage of art therapy records and images (McNiff 2000: 98). The discussion of images in supervision by distance requires that both the client's art work and the supervisee's preparatory art work (see below) is sent in advance to the supervisor. On Skype, images can be held up to indicate a certain aspect or to point to something in particular. A phenomenological viewing and description can help with this logistic (Betensky 1995).

Stages of supervision

In one view of the supervisory relationship, the supervisee moves from unconscious incompetence, to conscious incompetence, to conscious competence, to unconscious competence (Robinson 1974). Another way to describe this is as moving from relying on your own internal critic, to the 'internalised' supervisor, to developing your own 'internal supervisor' (Carroll and Gilbert 2006: 45–7). The 'internal supervisor' is able to integrate what has been learnt in supervision with individual style and clinical experience. The supervisee is able to effectively assess their own work and to trust their practice in a more instinctive, intuitive way that does not necessarily follow known rules and systems. 'Unconscious competence' means that skills and knowledge have been fully integrated and the therapist conducts their practice with an inner confidence, knowing what to say and do without any conscious thought.

Visual diaries in supervision

Visual diaries provide a means to personally debrief from client work and offer an alternative to the more traditional means available to supervisees' presentation of material: verbal reports, process notes, session verbatim accounts, audio taping or filming, role-play and client evaluation feedback. Visual diaries can also be used to present aspects of verbal and physical communication between client and art therapist, the supervisee's perspective of what might be going on in the client's mind or what is going on in their own mind – a personal perspective on the transference and countertransference relationship, to be shared with the supervisor.

Completion of a quick, spontaneous image after a difficult session provides cognitive relief and an opportunity to express feelings of counter-transference that are difficult to access and to immediately verbalise. The therapist sometimes experiences a personal issue that is triggered by a session, or an unclear emotional response comes up in reaction to client work. Sometimes the therapist is aware and insightful of what personal issue has surfaced for them, but they may be unaware or uncertain. Art provides an opportunity to self-reflect which is especially valuable when clinical supervision is not immediately available. In circumstances where supervision is monthly or fortnightly, visual diary work offers an alternative way to prepare for the next clinical supervision session, with both spontaneous diary entries as well as journalling tasks that explore the therapist's responses to client issues (see pp. 83–5).

When planning a journalling task, the therapist's intention might be to explore counter-transference material that they are aware has emerged. Through this documentation, the supervisee assists the supervisor in addressing things that are continuing to emerge in relation to their case material, but which are remaining unclear for the supervisee. This visual diary work provides an alternate way for the supervisee to engage in advanced casework preparation and processing involvement before supervision takes place. It allows for 'reflective distancing', described by Kagin and Lusebrink (1978: 172) thus: 'reflective distancing is an integrative experience where body sensations take on perceptual organisation and are then given meaning... [and] a cognitive distance between the art experience and the individual's reflection on that experience'. Visual diary work can also be a warm-up to facilitating a self-supervision session as a way of processing a difficult session when supervision is not immediately available.

Self-supervision

Regular clinical supervision is a requirement ideally built into the art therapist's weekly work for best practice (Case and Dalley 2006: 203). Self-supervision is where the art therapist has a discussion with themselves regarding an interaction with a client, family or group. The therapist presents the problem as they would to a clinical supervisor, then asks questions and explores aspects as if they are the clinical supervisor. By setting this time aside for self-examination, an opportunity for daily debriefing is provided. Self-supervision is also an interim measure if supervision is not available because of cost or geographical isolation. Through the making of art work, the art therapist is able to provide self-reflection and transference examination. The notion of self-debriefing through art allows time to consider difficulties in clinical work before going home to family, friends or social situations. This provides a 'stop-gap' measure until supervision can take place. Sometimes an issue will resolve itself through this process and sometimes the preparatory work that has taken place must be taken to supervision. There should always be an arrangement that the supervisor can be contacted between sessions, if necessary, for emergency/crisis cases that cannot wait until the next supervision session to be discussed and resolved. This is likely to be a discussion over the phone, and again such crisis contact with the supervisor can be enhanced by self-supervision preparation.

Documentation

As in all counselling and psychotherapy practices, art therapy files can be subpoenaed. A case note account that comments weekly on the 'black blob' (as a euphemism for the client's anger/character in their art work) requires complex, possibly subjective, explanation. Art therapists are at risk of cross-examination about the intent of such documentation and its wider meaning or 'interpretation'. It is far better to write in the official case file that the client is 'working through issues of anger' and quote the client's verbatim statement about the art work directly into the case notes, if the therapist believes this to be relevant and important. Subjectivity is hearsay in legal proceedings: it is strongly recommended to only state facts in case notes. Case notes and anything written down is a legal document. For example, someone becomes angry in a session. Rather than writing, 'he became aggressive', it is better to state 'he came to the counter and said to the secretary, "where's the bloody counsellor?"' and to record that the secretary responded in a calming tone with 'please take a seat and someone will be with you shortly' and that he then responded, 'no fucking way. I want to see that bloody counsellor right now'. Saying the client was 'aggressive' is a subjective statement: it is an opinion only. Documenting actual facts, and what the client said during a critical incident, preferably verified by a witness, leaves it up to the magistrate to determine whether or not the client was aggressive.

It is always good to document art therapy work and a more detailed explanation might be attached to the back of the art work. This allows direct material from the client's perspective to be recorded as part of the post-session documentation. The art therapist's official case files are best written with minimised language that only states facts. Because of the sheer size of art work, client art work is often stored away from the case file but some art therapists maintain client art work records on file as digital images. The art therapist must always consider the viability of art therapy documentation in the event of a client file being subpoenaed.

Some clients might also maintain their own explanatory account of their work in a specific exercise book or visual diary, depending on their ability to work with insightful processes. Visual diary processing between sessions is also useful for most clients. Between sessions the client is encouraged to record dreams, events and feeling states as they arise. In this way, the client is supported and empowered to continue their own personal therapy process. This is also preparing clients for post-therapy after termination when the client has greater autonomy and is more self-reliant. The visual diary provides opportunity to self-reflect on issues away from the art therapist. Diary entries are private – there is no expectation these images must be brought to the next session. The use of the visual diary between sessions provides a private space that maintains the client (Coulter 2008). An ongoing visual diary at the beginning and end of each session can be used by the client as part of a self-monitoring of the treatment experience. There should be an initial intake form in which basic client information is recorded. Several art therapy and other publications provide examples for intake information (Malchiodi and Riley 1996; Edwards 2004) and these can be adapted to suit specific workplace situations.

Every art therapy session requires entry into the general client case notes file – in most countries, this is a legal requirement. The art therapist must determine how much to write but usually briefer notes are preferred: five to eight hand-written lines are adequate. Other staff read the case notes, so lengthy accounts are not appreciated – staff want to know the client attended art therapy and that it went well, or that a particular issue came up and was dealt with, or that the client has concerns or plans regarding something.

Personal therapy, suicide risk and supervision

It is always good to experience therapy from the position of being a client. All therapists benefit from engaging in personal therapy. This is not only to experience being a client, but also the more the therapist knows about themself, the less likely personal material is going to contaminate the relationship with clients or the client's transference onto the therapist. It is important for the clinical supervisor to be clear about the boundary between what is material for supervision and what is personal material arising within the supervisory process. Although the supervisor is not there to provide personal therapy to the supervisee, the overlap and parallel processes that may be taking place during supervision and in relation to a client's processing may need to be addressed as part of the supervision session (Case and Dalley 2006: 205). The better understanding the therapist has about their own psychopathology, the more effective their casework is likely to be.

On British art therapy training programmes, personal therapy is mandatory, undertaken independently from the training programme via an independent practitioner; this is in addition to the supervision provided by the university setting which Hogan describes in Chapter 15. When dealing with a form of therapy that is stimulating unconscious processes, there is a risk that the therapist or clinical supervisor cannot always know of or understand the irrational thought processes that may be taking place in the mind of the supervisee (Yorke 2005). Likewise, the importance of being clear about the supervisee's responsibilities in supervision, especially their education in emotional competence in relation to issues such as suicidal threats, can be enhanced through what one learns in personal therapy (Carroll and Gilbert 2006: 95–100).

Personal therapy is encouraged both during training and as a practitioner, because it benefits both the therapist and the client. The therapist is more aware of their own psychopathology and what personal issues may be triggered by transference and projection from the client. The therapist's competency is enhanced if they are self-aware and possess self-knowledge as a result of several years of personal therapy. They have developed humility and respect for the client's process because of their own 'client' experience.

The supervisee has areas of responsibility in organising, monitoring and managing their supervision and this chapter has outlined some options to consider when resources for supervision are inadequate or unavailable. Effective practice includes the designing of forms for the documentation of work for supervision as well as clinical practice. Standardised forms are used for the gathering of referral information, consent to be taken in supervision, including art work, exchange of information, and discussion of both session content and processing client art work with an art therapy supervisor.

Bibliography

Betensky, M. 1995. *What Do You See? Phenomenology of Therapeutic Art Expression.* London: Jessica Kingsley Publishers.

Carroll, M. 1996. *Counselling Supervision: Theory, Skills and Practice.* London: Cassell.

Carroll, M. and Gilbert, M.C. 2006. *On Being a Supervisee: Creating Learning Partnerships.* Kew, Australia: PsychOz Publications.

Case, C. and Dalley, T. 2006. *The Handbook of Art Therapy.* Second edition. London: Routledge.

Coulter, A. 2008. 'Came Back – Didn't Come Home': Returning from a War Zone, in M. Liebmann (ed.) *Art Therapy and Anger.* London: Jessica Kingsley Publishers, pp. 238–56.

Crago, H. and Crago, M. 2002. But You Can't Get Decent Supervision in the Country! In M. McMahon and W. Patton (eds) *Supervision in the Helping Professions: a Practical Approach.* French's Forest, NSW: Pearson, pp. 79–90.

Durkin, J., Perach, D., Ramseyer, J. and Sontag, E. 1989. A Model for Art Therapy Supervision Enhanced through Art Making and Journal Writing, in H. Wadeson, J. Durkin and D. Perach (eds) *Advances in Art Therapy.* New York: Wiley, pp. 390–431.

Edwards, D. 2004. *Art Therapy.* London: Sage Publications.

Hawken, D. and Worrall, J. 2002. Reciprocal Mentoring Supervision: Partners in Learning: a Personal Perspective, in M. McMahon and W. Patton (eds) *Supervision in the Helping Professions: a Practical Approach.* French's Forest, NSW: Pearson, pp. 43–54.

Kagin, S.L. and Lusebrink, V.B. 1978. The Expressive Therapies Continuum. *Art Psychotherapy* 5, 171–80.

Kolb, D. 1984. *Experiential Learning.* Englewood Cliffs, NJ: Prentice Hall.

Kram, K. and Isobella, L. 1985. Mentoring Alternatives: the Role of Peer Relationships in Career Development. *Academy of Management Journal* 28(1), 101–32.

Laine, R. 2007. Image Consultation, in J. Schaverien and C. Case (eds) *Supervision of Art Psychotherapy: a Theoretical and Practical Handbook.* London: Routledge, pp. 119–37.

Malchiodi, C.A. and Riley, S. 1996. *Supervision and Related Issues: a Handbook for Professionals*. Chicago, IL: Magnolia Street Publishers.

McNiff, S. 2000. Computers as Virtual Studios, in C.A. Malchiodi (ed.) *Art Therapy and Computer Technology: a Virtual Studio of Possibilities*. London: Jessica Kingsley Publishers, pp. 86–99.

Pedder, J. 1986. Reflections on the Theory and Practice of Supervision. *Psychoanalytic Psychotherapy* 2(1), 1–12.

Robinson, W.L. 1974. Conscious Competence: the Mark of the Competent Instructor. *Personnel Journal* 53, 538–9.

Withers, R. 2006. Interactive Drawing Therapy: Working with Therapeutic Imagery. *New Zealand Journal of Counselling* 26(4), 1–14.

Yorke, V. 2005. Bion's 'Vertex' as a Supervisory Object, in C. Drive and E. Martin (eds) *Supervision and the Analytic Attitude*. London: Whurr, pp. 34–49.

Chapter 17

International perspectives

Annette M. Coulter

This chapter is written with the reader in mind who has migrated overseas, set up art therapy training or a national association in a new country, or had to work in unsupported professional isolation. These 'outsider' art therapists work on the fringes of the known art therapy world. For the reader who has not worked outside Britain or North America, the content of this chapter is likely not to resonate and might be difficult to grasp.

For the purpose of this chapter, the reader has to consider the possibility that the current international community of art therapy is very broadly polarised into two 'camps' that are biased towards either side of the Atlantic. Although this gap is lessening, the purpose here is to define this positioning so that it is better understood in terms of a global view of current art therapy perspectives. These camps encompass a North American/Canadian as opposed to a British/European position, which will be referred to as 'US' versus 'UK' perspectives respectively. Both offer rich and contrastingly unique information, practical structures and theoretical challenges (Hagood 1993, 1994).

The professional development of art therapy is influenced by differing cultural, political and educational systems that affect training, mental health services and professional governance. As more countries establish art therapy, this 'transatlantic' divide is increasingly examined and appreciated (Betensky 1971; Coulter-Smith 1983, 1989a; Woddis 1986; Campanelli and Kaplan 1996; Gilroy and Skaife 1997; Gilroy and Hanna 1998; Gilroy 1998; Coulter 1999, 2006a, 2006b; Slater 1999; Rosal 2007; Hurlbut 2011; Potash 2011; Wadeson 2002; Potash, Bardot and Ho 2012; Kalmanowitz, Potash and Chan 2012). Achieving an international perspective requires an understanding of the dichotomies and discrepancies between these two polarities. This chapter considers strengths and differences that are currently contributing towards a future global community of art therapy and acknowledges the ever-increasing need to integrate these 'camps' of art therapy difference (Coulter 2006a). 'Healing the split' is the job of the art therapist (Nowell-Hall 1987).

Conflicting origins of art therapy

Both UK and US art therapy claim early art therapy history, and it is clear that at a similar time a parallel growth of the profession was occurring. When both countries were in post-war circumstances, the rehabilitative use of art on either side of the Atlantic was documented (Hogan 2001). The term 'art therapy' was first coined by UK art educator Adrian Hill (Hill 1945) and in the US Margaret Naumburg was practising progressive education, calling her work with art a form of 'symbolic speech' (Naumburg 1958). Rubin's historic research of art therapy video footage includes an exploration of recent international growth and the historical contributions made by many art therapists and others over time (Rubin 2004).

Some would say that Jung was the first 'art therapist' because he was the first therapist to document the use of visual art in the consulting room while examining transference, and influenced early art therapy development in the UK. However, claims about the therapeutic arts pre-date any of these developments (Hogan 2001). From a global perspective, conflicting claims about the origins of art therapy practice or who should be regarded as the first 'art therapist', or where the more substantial knowledge base is located, does not help 'heal the split' between the US and UK 'camps' of art therapy difference. Bias is coloured by where one trained, from whom and what influences or prominent personalities impact on a specific training programme or country.

Polarised 'camps' of art therapy

Generally, art therapy in the US has a psychological emphasis, whereas in the UK there is a psychodynamic emphasis, 'the richness of the object-relations approaches and in-depth work on transference and countertransference... leaves me feeling envious that my American training did not focus more deeply on these aspects of art therapy' (Hagood 1994: 56). In the UK, art therapy is regulated by the Health Professions Council (HPC), a semi-independent body set up in 2001 that ensures both training and professional standards are maintained, whereas in the US, the American Art Therapy Association (AATA) and the Art Therapy Credentials Board (ATCB) regulate accreditation and certification. Clearly, the situation in the US is more complex than that of the UK.

One significant difference between the US and UK training standards is that US trainees are required to gain competence in the area of art therapy assessment. They also acquire skills in statistical reasoning including familiarity with the concepts of reliability and validity, and must be familiar with a selection of assessment tools, instruments and procedures used in evaluation and appraisal (Betts 2012). Furthermore, this training is linked to the formulation, administration and documentation of specialist treatment goals, as well as psychiatric diagnoses. The use of the Diagnostic and Statistical Manual (American Psychiatric Association 2013), theories of psychopathology and a basic knowledge of psychopharmacological medications are also required. Arguably, such knowledge is useful for the development of art therapy, possibly contributing, along with successful marketing and promotion, to US acceptance of the profession. Art assessment techniques are delivered as part of programmes packaging for private health schemes that have funding constraints and usually a limited number of sessions. To validate service delivery, US art therapists also invest heavily in researching effectiveness.

For the US art therapist, delivering visual art assessment tasks is the preferred procedure when the agency structure allows provision for this before treatment commences. UK art therapists tend to steer away from structured assessment regimes preferring to see what the client does with the art materials, placing as much value on a client's resistance to engage in this process. Sitting with unconscious processes and attempting to understand resistance and transference is part of the essential work in UK art therapy. On assessment, UK art therapist Edwards writes:

> [the client] will usually be invited for an initial assessment appointment... to establish whether or not art therapy is the most suitable form of therapy and to arrive at a shared understanding of the problems the client wishes to address.
>
> (Edwards 2004: 74)

To emphasise this point, a generalisation is that a UK art therapist might be viewed more as an 'art psychotherapist' with an interest in psychodynamic theory, whereas US art therapists are more grounded in a spectrum of psychological perspectives.

Although both work with unconscious processes, US art therapy works more towards a client's conscious realisation whereas UK art therapy provides the client opportunity to be immersed in unconscious processes. For UK art therapy the client's conscious understanding is not the goal whereas in the US, art therapy results are at times measured and analysed and time constraints are imposed in order for treatment to continue. To varying degrees, both work towards a conscious integration of issues but this becomes more important for US art therapists if treatment funding is to continue. Both orientations have merit – both 'camps' have produced speciality and excellence. In the US there is a training pre-requisite of at least four courses in psychology as well as at least five studio courses in visual art, whereas in the UK visual art is still the preferred requirement, although other first degrees are also accepted. Both countries require pre-course practical experience in a relevant work setting, but how rigorously this is enforced requires further research. This inconsistency in what is a 'sound basis' for art therapy was raised by Levick (1989: 59) and 'in researching such (inconsistent) perceptions of art therapy in Korea, Park and Hong (2010) found that the profession could gain more credibility if, among other factors, it had a unified curriculum' (Potash, Bardot and Ho 2012: 144).

Training

Arguably, US training has more emphasis on cultural and social diversity than its UK counterpart. Furthermore, a more social emphasis is taken in the US in educating trainees for possible roles in social justice, advocacy and conflict resolution work. In the UK these areas are often taken up by artists working in the arts and health movement rather than by art therapists. Thus an area of creative and interesting practice is sometimes lost to art therapists in the UK, because of an overtly narrow psychodynamic clinical focus.

Personal therapy during training is mandatory in the UK, demonstrating the trend towards the profession being that of 'art psychotherapy', where opportunity is built in to address less conscious material that may emerge. It is a further requirement that participation in non-directive psychodynamic training groups is an essential part of training accreditation. These groups focus on exposing the trainee art therapist to processing and developing an awareness of less conscious material (Waller 1993; Rosal 2007). In the US, personal therapy is strongly recommended but not enforced; the understanding and use of assessment techniques is essential and participation in non-directive psychodynamic groups is largely unheard of, although understanding more directive group art therapy dynamic experiences are included. When US-trained art therapist Maralynn Hagood was exploring the status of UK art therapy research (Hagood 1990), her suggestion was for a 'transatlantic dialogue' between US and UK art therapy in order to learn from each other and to expand the repertoire of theoretical models used in each country (Hagood 1993).

At present, UK and US training standards influence international professional promotion, regardless of local culture, and different education and health systems. For countries outside the established 'camps' of UK and US difference, there is an ever-increasing need for a more generalised, flexible international art therapy training guideline document.

Currently, in the absence of an agreed position for the global education of art therapists, training pioneers are faced with three options:

1   To adopt either a US or UK training model, so that approval and support is gained from at least one 'camp', which may be better than disapproval from both 'parent' nations (Coulter 2006a). For example, Taiwanese art therapy followed US standards (Lu 2006), whereas Singaporean standards began with a British accreditation process (Coulter 2006b).
2   To ignore US and UK training standards and develop a training model that is unique to the local culture, health care system and educational establishments, possibly adapting this within another more established therapy or counselling training programme so that the term 'art therapy' is obscured or over-ridden. In Australia, for example, other professions such as psychology and occupational therapy, as well as private training programmes, include or claim to offer training and supervision in 'art therapy' within another course title.

3 To compromise a training model to encompass the best of both US and UK training standards, so that overseas recognition is hard to achieve – there is no approval from either art therapy 'parent' nation. For example, Australia originally attempted this (Calomeris, Hogan and Coulter 1992), but the compromised qualification was not easily recognised outside Australia (Coulter 2006a). For example, in a compromised training model, group work training may be both a directive and non-directive approach, offering a phase of directive work, followed by a non-directive experience. Arguably, offering both gives maximum skills to the trainee to be confident in both techniques. Increasingly, such difference is being appreciated on some training programmes in both the UK and US (Rosal 2007). An enlightened position might be to define a more integrative 'transatlantic' theoretical framework for new training programmes (Hagood 1993, 1994), 'a challenge to the global education of art therapists is to define standards to determine minimally expected content areas of knowledge... there is a need to create a curriculum that... is culturally applicable and relevant' (Potash, Bardot and Ho 2012: 144).

Standards and policies from overseas do not transfer easily to the political and social systems of another country. The integration of the transatlantic 'camps' is being further researched 'in order to ensure world-wide sustainable art therapy training programs, we will need to find the careful balance between globalisation of standards and the unique value of local traditions' (Potash, Bardot and Ho 2012: 149). Emerging global trends increasingly integrate art therapy into new cultural perspectives that make provision for cultural flexibility (Hurlbut 2011) and it may be that an international training model will eventually be established to provide a departure point from which other countries can develop more flexible and culturally sensitive programmes; 'a truly international standard cannot simply be a Western one imposed on the rest of the world, but rather one that has input from many different cultures' (Potash, Bardot and Ho 2012: 149).

Until the 1990s, UK training standard requirement was a one-year post-graduate diploma, whereas US standards demanded a two-year Master's degree. The first training programme established in Australia in 1989 followed UK training standards, but the national association then made a decision to adopt the Master's degree training level requirement of the US (Harvey 1991). Other countries – Israel, South Africa, Japan, Singapore, Taiwan – have made a similar decision and more recently the UK postgraduate diploma in art therapy qualification was replaced by a Master's degree following debate about whether the basic qualification should remain a diploma, with an MA being a professional development undertaken after a period of clinical practice, leading to an advanced practitioner status.

UK and US art therapy training, standards and theoretical philosophies and practices are influencing the establishment of art therapy training programmes in Asia. Taiwan and Singapore have established training programmes modelled on

US and UK training standards respectively and there is increasing interest from other countries such as India, Thailand, Cambodia, mainland China, Malaysia, Indonesia and Hong Kong.

If there is no art therapy training already established in the art therapist's country of origin, then this is less problematic. However, if a course is later established that conflicts with the training standards of the local art therapists, there can be challenges for which one is unprepared. For example, in South Africa, UK-trained art therapists were marginalised because the government chose to only recognise art therapists with a US Master's degree.

The international dysfunctional family of art therapy

As mentioned above, currently, polarisation of art therapy continues either side of the Atlantic and inherent professional differences and theoretical divisions remain largely unaddressed. Although there are elements of individual professional respect, and ever-increasing opportunities for dialogue (Rosal 2007; Coulter 2006b; Spring 2007; Burt 2011; Gilroy, Tipple and Brown 2012; Potash, Bardot and Ho 2012), each 'camp' understandably regards itself as the seat of art therapy excellence and both are equally justified to hold this view historically, professionally, academically and culturally. On either side of the Atlantic art therapy is a respected profession that is well established and both 'camps' have produced specialist art therapists of excellence.

The analogy is of two parents who are aware of each other but whose communication could be more prevalent and effective. Historically each 'camp' has justified its existence, fought for professional recognition and until quite recently, tended to deny the existence or accepted the merit of the other. Neither 'parent' knows much of the other and neither takes much responsibility for the 'off-spring' they have created. They were never married yet bore children whom neither parent wishes to claim. These 'children' are other countries – for example, Taiwan, Australia, New Zealand, Israel, South Africa, Japan, Korea, Singapore, India, Thailand – that continue to try to establish art therapy, some more successfully than others, and which have a desire for communication and a cross-fertilisation of ideas. However, they are destined purely by geographic location to be related to but not part of US or UK 'camps'. Art therapists who find themselves working in isolated locations look to established professional organisations, current literature and prominent colleagues for support and validation of their work. Their situation demands examples from which to draw in establishing educational programmes, national associations, employment, pay scales and networking contacts within their own country. It may also require consultation in setting up seminars, engaging speakers or trainers to come from overseas or supportive documentation to gain licensing or certification.

In Australia, transatlantic differences affected all aspects of establishing a professional association: the drafting of a Constitution; membership criteria; registration and training standards; and eventually ethical guidelines and standards of practice. The founding committee, a combination of UK and US art therapists (Coulter 2006a) had to be considerate and respectful, harnessing the challenge of negotiation and compromise in its decision-making processes (Coulter-Smith and Cowie 1988; Coulter-Smith 1989a). The only way forward was to embrace difference – to be open and flexible to learn more about the other, despite initial entrenched positioning (Coulter 2006a).

Being in a position that demands compromise, flexibility and consideration of opposing models and standards, the pioneering art therapist risks marginalisation from transatlantic 'camps' because the revised position integrates and values the best of both. It is a compromise that is unappreciated. Transatlantic differences remain unresolved and despite increasing awareness and attempts to integrate polarities, the window is small in terms of a generally compromised and divided international community of art therapy.

International developments

The establishment of INGAT (The International Networking Group of Art Therapists) was originally proposed to provide a forum for international communication amongst geographically isolated art therapists (Coulter-Smith 1989b) who were interested in a global exchange that promoted and encouraged art therapy growth and development (Coulter-Smith and Stoll 1989). In the spirit of international promotion of art therapy, the Australian art therapy association convened the first international conference in 1989 (Hogan 1989a). During this conference, an international educators' forum took place at which both US and UK art therapists contributed and challenged the Australian training guidelines (Coulter 2006a). This early Australian experience was later echoed by Hagood's suggestion for a 'transatlantic dialogue' (Hagood 1993) and continues as a current discourse (Potash, Bardot and Ho 2012) despite genuine attempts to reconcile differences (Spring 2007; Gilroy, Tipple and Brown 2012; Kalmanowitz, Potash and Chan 2012).

Those who appreciate the pioneering aspects of art therapy development outside the US and UK have documented their research (Betensky 1971; Woddis 1986; Hogan 1989b; Campanelli and Kaplan 1996; Gilroy and Hanna 1998; Edwards 2004; Westwood 2012; Potash, Bardot and Ho 2012). However, consultation with local art therapists does not always take place for such research. In instances where local art therapists are not consulted, the history of art therapy can become biased, misinformed and written from fleeting impressions by transatlantic 'camp' representatives. This attitude is arguably parochial. It does not enhance a better understanding of the global challenges that pioneering the profession requires – dealing with limited resources, cultural diversity and addressing controversial political, economic issues and dilemmas. Pioneers of art therapy are often working alone, but need to accurately record their experiences rather than rely on outside impressionistic accounts. Although caught up in an isolated professional challenge, these art therapists are part of an unfolding existential narrative that is often hard to identify, understand or appreciate. In time, this becomes the professional art therapy history of a country.

The original purpose of INGAT as an international support for isolated art therapists was never realised. In fact the predominant activity of INGAT has been mainly for US art therapists to travel sharing their skills and knowledge. In most instances supporting isolated art therapists and establishing forums for communication and exchange has been arguably secondary to personal self-promotion.

Art therapy in Asia

Recent natural disasters have fuelled an interest in art therapy and trauma. Relief agencies engaged in servicing victims of natural disasters are becoming increasingly aware of the benefit of art in post-trauma recovery (Malchiodi 2006; Bovornkitti and Garcia 2006; St Thomas and Johnson 2007; Alfonso and Byers 2012). This growing awareness has influenced educational institutions in the planning of art therapy training. Until recently the only available option for Asian students wishing to pursue an art therapy career was to train overseas. During the 1980s and 1990s, the majority of Asian students studied in the US and more recently there is growing interest in Australian programmes. In Hong Kong there has been a UK influence (Potash 2011) with short introductory training courses being conducted for many years at Hong Kong University, fuelling interest from allied health, educational and other rehabilitative agencies. There is also an active professional art therapy association.

The first art therapy MA in Asia was launched in Taiwan in 2005 (Lu 2006) and the first in south-east Asia in Singapore in 2006 (Coulter 2006b). Both programmes participated in the integration of a Western art therapy-training model into an Eastern context – Taiwan was a US-based programme and Singapore was a UK-accredited programme. Singapore is a multi-cultural society with students from both Asian and European backgrounds, who have a broad range of religious, social, clinical, cultural and spiritual beliefs and backgrounds. Innovative teaching strategies helped integrate Western ideas and notions into an Eastern context. For example, based on UK training requirements, the Singaporean integration of Western notions of object-relations and attachment theory into a local medical context that favoured directive cognitive techniques was challenging. The introduction of an infant observation and seminar, even though not a standard part of UK art therapy training, was an effective way to teach this Western concept in a culturally sensitive way. Students participated in this weekly observational practicum visiting a young child, for one hour each week, and observing the child's relationship to significant and insignificant objects and people. The child's role within the family determines their emerging cultural identity and this could be related to and discussed in a weekly seminar discussion group. Although this course content was later revised when US course content was introduced, the training programme continues to be a rich blend of UK and US theory and clinical application, in an Asian context.

Although Taiwanese pioneering art therapists adapted their US standards and their US training experience to the local cultural context (Lu 2006), in Singapore, Western programme leaders were less familiar with the local culture and medical and clinical contexts (Coulter 2006b), disadvantaging the adaptation of UK and US theory and practice. In both situations, despite local and overseas input, the 'transatlantic split' of polarised art therapy origins is maintained and the unspoken discourse is perpetuated.

If art therapy is to be effectively practised globally, the profession must be able to accommodate Eastern thinking and cultural values that offer art therapy a rich and varied contribution to Asian clinical practice (Coulter 2006b). After all, it was Jung's tour of Asia that strongly influenced his later writings and theories. For example, Jung's notion of opposites making up the whole, such as the masculine versus feminine, or introversion versus extroversion, come directly from the Asian concepts such as Yin and Yang (Jung 1964: 290) as well as the therapeutic adaptation of the concept of 'mandala' from Eastern philosophy (Jung 1964: 213–17). We live in a time when Western appreciation of Eastern culture is gaining increasing respect, understanding and interest. There is a rise in the appreciation of Asian health practices such as acupuncture, massage, yoga and herbal remedies. Asian culture offers the field of art therapy a rich wealth of ideas and concepts that are likely to challenge Western theoretical models in the future. McNiff inspires consideration for a worldwide perspective of art therapy as he poses such questions as 'how do art therapists trained in North America, Europe and Australia operate in Korea, China and Japan where it is common to suppress personal emotions which are fundamental to the art therapy experience?' (McNiff 2012: 15). Kalmanowitz, Potash and Chan highlight Eastern concern for the whole versus the Western concern for the individual: 'Eastern traditions point to holistic health by reminding us that separation is contrived and that all aspects of life influence each other' (Kalmanowitz, Potash and Chan 2012: 40). Current established UK and US art therapy 'camps' need to listen, consider and sometimes accept alternate views that differ and challenge their culture. The task is not to impose a Western profession into an Asian context, but to adapt and integrate the complexity of art therapy theory into a society that has ancient complex philosophies and traditions of its own that are equally important: 'Western health is largely... focused on specifics without attention to the whole... educators will need to honor the dominant health beliefs in the country' (Potash, Bardot and Ho 2012: 147). Eastern societies have values and beliefs that require respect and integration (Kalmanowitz, Potash and Chan 2012).

An international perspective for art therapy

US and UK art therapists have rubbed shoulders over the years. Gilroy and Skaife (1997) felt 'the networking of two imperialist countries, ourselves and the US, in different parts of the world with only scant acknowledgement from each of the work of the other' was significant, and that 'the nature of art therapy practice in America was profoundly different, so much so it was hardly recognisable as the same profession in Britain' (Gilroy and Skaife 1997: 58). Rosal also encapsulates current theoretical and practical differences in her objective account about differences between UK and US art therapy group work (Rosal 2007). Hurlbut has recently reviewed and summarised the activities of the international networking group of art therapists (Hurlbut 2011) and Potash, Bardot and Ho ask the still pertinent questions: in parts of the world where there are no national associations or the ones that exist have not developed such standards, what course topics should be offered? Should we be beholden to standards set by associations beyond our borders? How do we integrate local cultural values? (Potash 2011; Potash, Bardot and Ho 2012: 144).

Art therapists from both sides of the Atlantic have appreciatively written about their discovery and exposure to 'new' or 'different' perspectives of the other (Hagood 1993; Betensky 1971; Woddis 1986, Coulter 2006a), but the fact that generations of art therapists continue to struggle to sustain a global stance highlights a sense of unclear definition of purpose. When there is a global disaster, art therapy is often there to assist, but this is usually a US-influenced model. As noted above, US training has a more social and cultural emphasis and is extrovert, marketable and more portable than UK art therapy. You are less likely to find a UK art therapist practising in a makeshift tent beside an earthquake disaster zone or a landslide-devastated area, because UK art therapy requires a secure space, a frame of safety. However, UK art therapists may miss opportunities because of an unwillingness or inability to compromise a less flexible position.

Much UK art therapy requires a considerable length of time to focus on the relationship, transferential issues and all that comes with the in-depth work that unconscious processing demands. US art therapy is robust, energetic and resilient. It can adapt to different cultural situations more readily and therefore has greater accessibility to a broader audience as it is packaged for portability, expediency and effectiveness, whereas UK art therapy is not packaged and has a focus on unconscious processing and is therefore by its very nature, less flexible. Both 'camps' can learn something from the other (Hagood 1993; Rosal 2007; Coulter 2006a).

Where art therapists live outside the UK or US 'camps', there is a motivation for greater international discourse, 'given that the currently available standards are from the West, educators will need to reconsider... as art therapy takes shape across borders' (Potash, Bardot and Ho 2012: 149). US academics are pursuing the location of student art therapy internships and post-training projects overseas, but UK art therapy follows Health Professions Council (HPC) training requirements and is not so flexible. Art therapy would benefit greatly if broader international standards could be determined that considered registration, training and standards of clinical practice.

International registration

Currently there is no international mechanism in place to recognise an art therapy qualification globally. To gain professional registration is to be clinically endorsed as an art therapist practitioner, but not all countries recognise art therapy nor do they have designated 'art therapist' positions or a clinical registration process. Depending on where the art therapist trained, clinical registration can require undertaking further supervised hours. Some countries provide statutory registration for approved training programmes, such as the ANZATA in Australia and New Zealand, the HPC in the UK and the ATCB in the US. Eligibility for UK registration is automatic, once one completes a state-endorsed training programme, but this credentialled qualification is only valid if the art therapist remains in Britain. Once the UK-trained art therapist resides outside Britain, their professional endorsement is no longer valid: they '… will not be on the HPC Register and therefore the membership category open to [them] is Associate International' (Huet 2010). In order to describe themselves as a 'registered art therapist', overseas students need to complete art therapy training where their clinical registration remains valid after they return to their homeland, migrate overseas or relocate to a professionally isolated part of the world. At present, US training offers more flexibility for this option but ATR registration is not automatic. On completion of training from an AATA approved programme, 1,000 supervised post-training hours are required (approximately 100 hours of clinical supervision is required; with one-half or 50 hours of supervision with an American registered art therapist, an ATR).

Variance depends on the relocation, but qualifications are scrutinised and may not be considered of equivalent value to existing standards in a new country. Even if there is a registration process in place, an overseas art therapy qualification may not be immediately recognised as relevant to that country. Endorsement of an international art therapy registration/credentialling that appreciates current variations, yet accepts difference, would mean art therapists could relocate between countries without the risk of their qualification being declared invalid. Such a system would provide greater opportunities for cross-cultural research and fertilisation for non-competitive collaboration on international projects. For example, both UK- and US-registered practitioners were originally eligible for automatic registered endorsement in Australia that accommodated overseas-trained practitioners to relocate. At the recent Coalition of Art Therapy Educators meeting in 2011 in Washington DC, the American Art Therapy Credentials Board (ATCB) announced the consideration of an international credentialling system. It is expected that culturally isolated art therapists will welcome this decision. As geographic barriers are crossed, a global view of the profession is enhanced, promoting a greater appreciation of cultural diversity and a better understanding of differing views that begin to integrate and enrich future growth of the profession.

Outside the UK and US, there is an increasing cross-fertilisation of ideas taking place (Coulter-Smith and Rosal 1985; Gilroy and Hanna 1998; Sedgewick 1991; Jones 1991; Hagood 1993; Lu 2006; Coulter 2006b; Kalmanowitz, Potash and Chan 2012). There is a growing interest, exchange of ideas and increasing acceptance of difference within the UK and US art therapy literature. Recent development welcomes an increase of collaborative art therapy texts as US and UK authors have exposure to the other's viewpoint (Rubin 2001; Malchiodi 2003; Hogan 2003). International pressure demands global dialogue, respectful acceptance and worldly consideration (Coulter-Smith 1989b; Hagood 1994; Rosal 2007; Potash 2011; Hurlbut 2011).

A more mutual dialogue is starting to take place (Spring 2007; Burt 2011; Gilroy, Tipple and Brown 2012; Potash, Bardot and Ho 2012). Consistent with their openness to new ideas from an extroverted and flexible position, US art therapists are keen to initiate and support a 'transatlantic' exchange. In 1999, the British Association renamed its journal the International Journal of Art Therapy, conveying an awareness of the need for a broader international dialogue.

International debate is increasingly taking place via the cyberspace revolution. Globally enlightened art therapists are making international connections, locating supervision support and debating issues through discussion forums and Internet alliances such as Art Therapy Without Borders, Linkedin and Facebook. It is through such initiatives that an integration of disparate concepts can begin to occur. The potential is there to expand and be innovative even in areas of specialisation, 'by learning from art therapy programs around the world, understanding the challenges to designing new programs and developing the profession, we can enhance the overall quality of art therapy education, which will ultimately benefit clients and professionals in every country' (Potash, Bardot and Ho 2012: 149–50).

Conclusion

Transatlantic polarities have determined our art therapy origins; however, it is the global art therapy community that will determine the future of our profession. International art therapy perspectives require ongoing flexibility, the ability to be open and respectful of a broad range of models and sensitive to an ever-increasing multi-cultural awareness, especially to eschew reductive interpretation that is not culturally sensitive.

Despite a narrowing of the 'gap' through enhanced dialogue between US and UK art therapy 'camps', the family of art therapy nevertheless remains arguably somewhat dysfunctional. Other countries, the 'children' and 'adolescents' of art therapy, wait for initiatives of repair and reconciliation to originate from the 'parent nations' of art therapy; however, this is perhaps an unrealistic and unreasonable expectation. Although UK and US art therapy 'parent nations' are related, the integration of an expanded repertoire of knowledge and mutual respect from these entrenched 'camps' of difference is questionable. Hagood's vision of a 'transatlantic dialogue' is inspiring but is it realistic? Perhaps it is time for countries outside the UK and US to initiate discourse and work towards a more unified international art therapy community. Any support towards favouring one art therapy 'camp' will perpetuate division in theory and practice.

Academic origins provide a secure base from which a sense of purpose is maintained and strengthened, but it is the challenges art therapists face when working in isolation, away from professional supports, that is going to bring art therapy into the twenty-first century. The vision of an international community of art therapy that is able to respect difference, acknowledge and cater for cultural diversity and has the potential to inspire a more integrated global future for the profession should be our goal.

Bibliography

Alfonso, G.A. and Byers, J.G. 2012. Art Therapy and Disaster Relief in the Philippines, in D. Kalmanowitz, J.S. Potash and S.M. Chan (eds) *Art Therapy in Asia: To the Bone or Wrapped in Silk*. London: Jessica Kingsley Publishers, pp. 269–82.

American Psychiatric Association. 2013. *Diagnostic and Statistical Manual of Mental Disorders* (DSM-5). Arlington, VA: American Psychiatric Association.

Betensky, M. 1971. Impressions of Art Therapy in Britain: a Diary. *American Journal of Art Therapy* 10(2), 75–86.

Betts, D. 2012. Positive Art Therapy Assessment: Looking Towards Positive Psychology for New Directions in the Art Therapy Evaluation Process, in G. Gilroy, R. Tipple and C. Brown (eds) *Assessment in Art Therapy*. London: Routledge, pp. 203–18.

Bovornkitti, L. and Garcia, B.J. 2006. An Introductory Course on Art Therapy. *Programme and Abstracts Book*. Bangkok, Thailand: Silpakorn University, 17–21 March.

Burt, H. (ed.) 2011. *Art Therapy and Postmodernism: Creative Healing Through a Prism*. London: Jessica Kingsley Publishers.

Calomeris, S., Hogan, S. and Coulter, A. 1992. Recommended Guidelines for Australian Art Therapy Training Standards. Australian National Art Therapy Association (ANATA).

Campanelli, M. and Kaplan, F.F. 1996. Art Therapy in Oz: Report from Australia. *The Arts in Psychotherapy* 23(1), 61–7.

Coulter, A. 1999. History and Current Training Models for Art Therapists in Australia. Unpublished keynote address, 6th International Annual Conference of Art Therapy, Korean Art Therapy Association, 28–31 October.

Coulter, A. 2006a. Art Therapy in Australia: the Extended Family. *Australian and New Zealand Journal of Art Therapy* 1(1), 8–18.

Coulter, A. 2006b. Art Therapy Education: No More Lip-Service to Cultural Diversity! Panel presentation, International Networking Group of Art Therapists: Education Development, Current Practice and Research, American Art Therapy Association Conference, 16 November.

Coulter-Smith, A. 1983. Report from the Antipodes. *BAAT Newsletter* December, 10–11.

Coulter-Smith, A. 1989a. Art Therapy in Australia. Unpublished paper, panel presentation for the 20th Annual Conference of the American Art Therapy Association, San Francisco, USA, 18 November.

Coulter-Smith, A. 1989b. The Extended Family: an International Art Therapy Development. Unpublished proposal for the 20th Annual Conference of the American Art Therapy Association, San Francisco, USA, January.

Coulter-Smith, A. and Cowie, J. 1988. Core-Curriculum: Masters of Arts in Expressive Therapy – Art Therapy. Brisbane College of Advanced Education, 13th October.

Coulter-Smith, A. and Rosal, M. 1985. Introductory Art Therapy. Network for Exploring Creativity in Therapy Through the Arts (NECTA Queensland) newsletter, January, 2, 4.

Coulter-Smith, A. and Stoll, B. 1989. International Networking Newsletter. Conference handout, International Networking Group of Art Therapists, launched at the 20th Annual Conference of the American Art Therapy Association, San Francisco, USA.

Edwards, D. 2004. *Art Therapy*. London: Sage Publications.

Gilroy, A. 1998. On Being a Temporary Migrant to Australia: Reflections on Art Therapy Education and Practice, in D. Dokter (ed.) *Arts Therapists, Refugees and Migrants: Reaching Across Borders*. London: Jessica Kingsley Publishers, pp. 262–77.

Gilroy, A. and Hanna, M. 1998. Conflict and Culture in Art Therapy, in A.R. Hiscox and A.C. Calisch (eds) *Tapestry of Cultural Issues in Art Therapy*. London: Jessica Kingsley Publishers, pp. 249–75.

Gilroy, A. and Skaife, S. 1997. Taking the Pulse of American Art Therapy: a Report on the 27th Annual Conference of the American Art Therapy Association, November 13th–17th, 1996, Philadelphia. *Inscape* 2(2), 57–64.

Gilroy, A., Tipple, R. and Brown, C. (eds) 2012. *Assessment in Art Therapy*. London: Routledge.

Hagood, M.M. 1990. Reflections: Art therapy Research in England – Impressions of an American Art Therapist. *The Arts in Psychotherapy* 17(1), 75–9.

Hagood, M.M. 1993. Letter to the Editor. *The Arts in Psychotherapy* 20(4), 279–81.

Hagood, M. M. 1994. Letters. *Inscape* 4, 56.

Harvey, D. 1991. Report from W.A. *Newsletter of the Australian National Art Therapy Association* 3(2), 5–6.

Hill, A. 1945. *Art Versus Illness*. London: Allen and Unwin.

Hogan, S. 1989a. Doing It Metaphorically. *Art Monthly* 26, 28.

Hogan, S. 1989b. Letters: Art Therapy in Australia. *Inscape* Spring, 24.

Hogan, S. 2001. *Healing Arts: the History of Art Therapy*. London: Jessica Kingsley Publishers.

Hogan, S. (ed.) 2003. *Gender Issues in Art Therapy*. London: Routledge.

Huet, V. 2010. Email with CEO Re: BAAT Membership, November.

Hurlbut, G. 2011. Going Global: a Profile of International Art Therapy Trends in 2010. Presented at the 44th Annual Conference of the American Art Therapy Association, Washington DC, July.

Jones, M. 1991. New Zealand: International Reports. *Newsletter of the International Networking Group of Art Therapists (INGAT)* 1(1), 7–8.

Jung, C.G. 1964. *Man and His Symbols*. London: Aldus Books.

Kalmanowitz, D., Potash, J.S. and Chan, S.M. (eds) 2012. *Art Therapy in Asia: to the Bone or Wrapped in Silk*. London: Jessica Kingsley Publishers.

Levick, M.F. 1989. On the Road to Educating the Creative Arts Therapist. *The Arts in Psychotherapy* 16(1), 57–60.

Lu, L. 2006. Introduction to Graduate Program of Art Therapy in Taipei Municipal University of Education, Taiwan. Panel presentation: International Networking Group of Art Therapists: Education Development, Current Practice and Research, American Art Therapy Association Conference, 16 November.

Malchiodi, C.A. (ed.) 2003. *Handbook of Art Therapy*. New York: Guilford Press.

Malchiodi, C.A. 2006. Keynote Address. The Use of Holistic Arts Therapies Symposium: Art in Hospitals, Hong Kong.

McNiff, S. 2012. Foreword, in D. Kalmanowitz, J.S. Potash and S.M. Chan (eds) *Art Therapy in Asia: To the Bone or Wrapped in Silk*. London: Jessica Kingsley Publishers, pp. 13–20.

Naumberg, M. 1958. Art therapy: Its Scope and Function, in E.F. Hammer (ed.) *The Clinical Application of Projective Drawings*. Springfield, IL: C.C. Thomas, pp. 511–17.

Nowell-Hall, P. 1987. Art Therapy: a Way of Healing the Split, in T. Dalley, C. Case, J. Schaverien, F. Weir, D. Halliday, P. Nowell-Hall and D. Waller (eds) *Images of Art Therapy: New Developments in Theory and Practice*. London: Tavistock Publications, pp. 157–87.

Park, K. and Hong, E. 2010. A Study on the Perception of Art Therapy Among Mental Health Professionals in Korea. *The Arts in Psychotherapy* 37(4), 335–9.

Potash, J.S. 2011. Building a Sustainable Art Therapy Program in Hong Kong. Presented at the 44th Annual Conference of the American Art Therapy Association, Washington DC, July.

Potash, J.S., Bardot, H. and Ho, R.T.H. 2012. Conceptualizing International Art Therapy Education Standards. *The Arts in Psychotherapy* 39, 143–50.

Rosal, M.L. 1985. The Use of Art Therapy to Modify the Locus of Control and Adaptive Behavior of Behavior Disordered Students. Unpublished doctoral dissertation, University of Queensland, Brisbane.

Rosal, M. 2007. A Comparative Analysis of British and US Group Art Therapy Styles, in D. Spring (ed.) *Art in Treatment: Transatlantic Dialogue*. Springfield, IL: C.C. Thomas, pp. 35–51.

Rubin, J.A. 2001. *Approaches to Art Therapy: Theory and Technique*. Second edition. New York: Brunner/Routledge.

Rubin, J.A. 2004. *Art Therapy Has Many Faces*. A video and DVD. Pittsburgh, PA: Expressive Media, Inc.

Sedgewick, C. 1991. Letters to the Editor. *Newsletter of the Australian National Art Therapy Association* 3(1), 2–3.

Slater, N. 1999. Keynote Address (unpublished). Tenth Annual Conference of the Australian National Art Therapy Association, Coming Full Circle: An Unfolding Journey, Brisbane, Queensland, Australia.

Spring, D. (ed.) 2007. *Art in Treatment: Transatlantic Dialogue*. Springfield, IL: C.C. Thomas.

St Thomas, B. and Johnson, P. 2007. *Empowering Children through Art Expression: Culturally Sensitive Ways of Healing Trauma and Grief*. London: Jessica Kingsley Publishers.

Wadeson, H. 2002. Confronting Polarization in Art Therapy. *Art Therapy: Journal of the American Art Therapy Association* 19(2), 77–84.

Waller, D. 1993. *Group Interactive Art Therapy: Its Use in Training and Treatment*. London: Routledge.

Westwood, J. 2012. Hybrid creatures: Mapping the Emerging Shape of Art Therapy Education in Australia, Including Reflections on New Zealand and Singapore. *Australian and New Zealand Journal of Arts Therapy* 7(1), 15–25.

Woddis, J. 1986. Reflections: Judging by Appearances. *The Arts in Psychotherapy* 13(2), 147–9.

A critical glossary of key terms informing art therapy

Susan Hogan

amplification A technique derived from Carl G. Jung in which the mood-tone or symbolic content of a picture is entered into in an imaginative way. For example, the therapist might ask (looking at a picture of a boat at sea) how it feels in the boat, or where the boat is going or whether the boat has a voice. Originally, the term referred to the symbolic quality of dreams:

> Compared to free association, amplification is a more narrowly defined, more controlled and more focussed type of association where one attempts to search for analogies that would expand the symbol in question.
>
> (Laine 2011: 129)

Irene Champernowne, an early pioneer of art therapy in Britain, for example, talked about 'dreaming the dream onwards on paper' (Hogan 2001: 240) and advocated 'entering into the language' of her clients' art works. She wrote, 'it is possible to accept the material in the state of the subject [the same mood-tone] at the moment, and discuss it from the experimental point of view, rather than from the intellectual interpretation of the symbols used' (1949, cited Hogan 2001: 271). This is a useful elicitation technique.

analogy 'An agreement, likeness, or correspondence between relations of things to one another; a partial similarity in particular circumstances on which a comparison may be based' (Macquarie Dictionary 1981: 103); for example, the analogy between a heart and a piston pump. It's an 'illustration of an idea by means of a more familiar idea that is similar or parallel to it in some significant features, and thus said to be analogous to it. Analogies are often presented in the form of an extended simile' (Baldick 2001: 12).

biological determinism This is the idea that shared behavioural norms, and the social and economic differences between groups (primarily races, classes and sexes), arise from inherited inborn distinctions. Certain sets of social relations have existed and evolutionary theory was (and is) used to justify them. In the nineteenth century, the application of evolutionary theories was simply a matter of analogy. Equated through supposed likeness were women, criminals, children, beggars, the Irish and the insane – all of whom were lacking in social power and were likened to 'primitives' or 'savages'. Biological determinism has changed shape over time, but is still evident in psychiatric discourses, especially in relation to gender 'norms'.

countertransference (Read 'projection' first) The therapist's projection to the client, which is a potentially distorting aspect of treatment. The term is also used to mean 'the analyst's emotional attitude towards the patient, including his response to specific items of the patient's behaviour' (a reflection upon which may be therapeutically useful in illuminating the therapist's understanding of the client) (Rycroft 1968: 25).

discourse Debate, or communication of thoughts in words, the term has a specific meaning within cultural theory. This is Foucault's idea of discursive practice, which is a highly organised and regulated set of practices and statements that serve to create and maintain definitions, say of 'madness' or 'femininity'. This has a history and a set of rules which distinguishes it from other discourses establishing both links and differences. In other words, the term has been used to denote any coherent body of statements that produces a self-confirming account of reality by defining an object of attention and generating concepts with which to analyse it (e.g. medical discourse, legal discourse, aesthetic discourse). The specific discourse in which a statement is made will govern the kinds of connections that can be made between ideas, and will involve certain assumptions about the kind of persons(s) addressed' (Baldick 2001: 68–9).

The literary theorist Catherine Belsey defines 'discourse' eloquently thus:

> A *discourse* is a domain of language-use, a particular way of talking (and writing and thinking). A discourse involves certain shared assumptions which appear in the formulations that characterise it. The discourse of common sense is quite distinct, for instance, from the discourse of modern physics, and some of the formulations of the one may be expected to conflict with the formulations of the other. Ideology is *inscribed* in discourse in the sense that it is literally written or spoken *in it*; it is not a separate element which exists independently in some free-floating realm of 'ideas' and is subsequently embodied in words, but a way of thinking, speaking, experiencing.
>
> (Belsey 1980: 5; original emphasis)

We can see in this definition that here 'discourse' is embodied in ways of experiencing and that as a particular 'domain of language-use' (thinking, talking and experiencing) it resembles a paradigm, and moves beyond the small 'd' discourse 'language-in-use' concept that the theorist Gee describes (1999: 7).

displacement A psychoanalytic idea used to describe the 'process by which energy (cathexis) is transferred from one mental image to another... for instance in dreams one image can symbolise another' (Rycroft 1968: 35).

embodied image Arguably, any image which carries with it a strong mood-tone is an embodied image; art can become imbued with another person's feelings in a tangible manner, or at least what appears to be a tangible manner. As the writer Tolstoy put it:

> Art is a human activity consisting in this, that one man consciously, by means of external signs, hands on to others feelings he has lived through, and that others *are infected by these feelings and also experience them.*
>
> (cited Harris 1996: 2; my emphasis)

Joy Schaverien (2011) suggests that, 'no other mode of expression can be substituted for it', and that 'in the process of its creation, feeling becomes "live" in the present' (2011: 80). In Chapter 8 I discussed how we feel other people's emotions; sometimes we can even feel engulfed by them. However, the intended meaning of the painter does not necessarily hold a privileged position, so art therapists must always be circumspect about whether they really are experiencing what was intended, and seek clarification from the person who created the art work. This is because we bring our own experience and 'habitus' (our embodied way of being) to the experience of viewing an art. Art objects in general are inherently open to multiple meanings and interpretations. Context too is important in how we see art works (Hogan 1997).

empathy 'This is the ability to identify [with] and thereby understand another person's feelings or difficulties' (Wood 2011: 81). Art therapists would wish to demonstrate an empathetic response to the art works produced in sessions.

feminist This is a much maligned and misused term. Feminism is the principle of advocating the social, political and other rights of women as equal to those of men. Feminism is necessarily interested in the question of equality (Hogan 2011). In academic writing, feminism refers to a mode of analysis that seeks to examine the function of sex in societal relations. This mode of analysis sees the construction of sex (or writers may use the term 'gender') as historically and geographically situated and subject to change. In terms of feminist art therapy, this is primarily an enhanced awareness of women's issues and misogynist discourses (particularly negative psychiatric discourses about women's inherent inborn 'instability'). Sometimes, when using directive art therapy, it is possible to introduce exercises that can help participants reflect on their sex and sexual orientation. For example, I offer a workshop in which I ask men and women to bring in two images from any source (newspapers, art books, magazines, etc.), of a man if they are a man, and of a woman if they are a woman, or if they regard themselves as gay, lesbian or transgender, they may reflect that in their choice of images. I ask them to bring in one image they like and another that makes them feel uncomfortable. These images form the basis of the session, and it is an opportunity to look at how women, 'gay' people and men are represented, and to explore how participants feel about these images which surround us in our daily lives.

Some art therapists work with women-only groups to readily allow women to explore unique aspects of their experience, such as pregnancy and childbirth (Hogan 2003, 2008, 2012a), or collective trauma such as breast cancer or rape (Malchiodi 1997), or the experience of ageing (Hogan and Warren 2012). However, maintaining a feminist awareness is, arguably, an important aspect of good practice in general and should form an integral part of training.

(Hogan 2011b: 87).

group resonance Members can show empathy towards each other by adopting a similar pictorial style or particular symbols or motifs, though this may be done quite unconsciously, and has been called 'group resonance' by Gerry McNeilly and others (1984, 2005). This is an idea (taken from physics and used metaphorically) to describe the way images can seemingly influence each other and 'resonate' or reverberate together. Certain themes can be held in the art works and they can be brought out over and over again and reworked. This process could take place over weeks or months. Richardson (2011) explains that 'resonance makes the group more than the sum of its parts, rather like the moment when the individual voices in a choir lend to a spine-tingling complex chord' (2011: 202).

hegemony Has been used to mean political prominence. In cultural theory, from the work of Gramsci, it is often used to mean what is taken for granted as 'common sense' or it refers to unquestioned assumptions. It is also used to refer to the dominant ideology. Taking the example of the concept of taste, Douglas writes:

Taste is always going to be harnessed to the *struggle for hegemony* in a particular community... although good taste claims to rest on universal principles, it is always challengeable; the challenge comes from those who wish to subvert the established order.

(Douglas 1994: 29; my emphasis)

This introduces the idea of a plurality of hegemonies linked to different 'community' interests, which is more sophisticated than suggesting one overarching oppressive hegemony.

icon According to semiology, an icon involves actual resemblance between the signifier and the signified; for example, a portrait signifies the person depicted less by arbitrary convention than by resemblance (Culler 1981); however, the resemblance could be analogous.

iconography 'The branch of knowledge concerned with pictorial or sculptural representations' or 'symbolical representation' (Macquarie Dictionary 1981: 865).

ideology Hadjinicolaou writes of ideology that:

the very function of ideology... is to hide the contradictions in life by fabricating an illusory system of ideas which shapes people's views and gives them a perspective on their experience of life... this system... extends to myths, taste, style, fashion, and the 'whole way of life' of a particular society.

(1978: 10)

In this example, ideology represents a false consciousness, a lack of awareness of ideas conditioning one's experience and actions. The term has also been used to describe a system of ideas appropriate to a specific social group such as 'bourgeois ideology' (Williams 1983: 157).

introjection A psychoanalytic concept that forms part of the idea of transference (hence its inclusion).

It describes the process by which the functions of an external object are taken over by its mental representation, by which the relationship with an object 'out there' is replaced by one with an imagined object 'inside'. The resulting mental structure is variously called an *introject*, an *introjected object*, or an *internal object*.

(Rycroft 1968: 77; original emphasis).

metaphor 'The figure of speech in which a name or descriptive term in transferred to some object to which it is not properly applicable' (Shorter Oxford English Dictionary 1973: 1315) or the 'comparison of one thing to another without the use of like or as' (dictionary.com). Henzell claims that for a metaphor to have real power, it must be concerned with more than simple truth or analogy: 'the comparison affected by it must scandalise current perceptions and so doing jolt them into a new frame of reference' (Henzell 1984: 23). He defines a metaphor as 'the illumination of one realm of related facts, associations, history, and orderings in terms of another. This is accomplished by the interaction of at least two conceptions of different things in one symbol which refers to them both' (Henzell 1984: 22). A simple example would be the idiomatic expression, 'to lay one's cards on the table' to denote frankness. Metaphors are used abundantly and eloquently in art therapy, as well as in literature: 'the road was a ribbon of moonlight' is a literary example (dictionary.com). The use of metaphor to produce new combinations of ideas is important in art therapy, where multiple metaphors can interlink to produce multifarious meanings.

motif 'A recurring subject or theme... a distinctive figure in a design' (Macquarie Dictionary 1981: 1118).

parataxic distortion This concept derives from the work of Harry Stack Sullivan and refers to a tendency to distort the perceptions we have of others. These distortions are the result of relating to another person, 'not on the basis of the real attributes of the other, but wholly or chiefly on the basis of the person we see in our fantasy' (Molnos 1998). Parataxic distortions result from the individual's propensity to shape their responses in relation to previous experiences; this may also serve as a defense against anxiety. It is a broader concept to that of 'transference'. See also 'habitus'.

projection Literally 'throwing in front of oneself' – hence its use in psychiatry and psychoanalysis to mean 'viewing a mental image as objective reality'. In psychoanalytic theory there are two further meanings. The first is 'a general misinterpretation of mental activity as events occurring to one as in dreams and hallucinations'. The other 'involves a process in which wishes or impulses or other aspects of the self are imagined to be located elsewhere in an object external to oneself' (Rycroft 1968: 125). Projection is often linked with reversal, in that the emotion or wish felt is denied, but asserted to belong to someone else.

reification A tendency to convert abstract concepts into entities. This tendency is applied to a complex and multi-faceted set of human capabilities. The 'shorthand' for these intelligences is then reified. Alternatively, sophisticated ideas about human interaction can be 'reificated' in the design of buildings. For example, a ranked lecture theatre with a built-in lectern is a physical design that illustrates assumptions about the transmission of knowledge.

representation In cultural theory, images and texts are not viewed simply as 'mirrors' which reflect reality. Rather, representations are seen as conventions and codes which articulate practices and forms that condition our experience.

resonance (see group resonance)

scapegoat transference (see also transference) Joy Schaverien describes the concept of transference, that is, the idea of the magical transferability of attributes and states, as the main pivot of psychoanalytical theory. Schaverien argues that the biblical scapegoat may be seen as representing a 'ritualised transference' – the goat having become a talisman, in that it is magically invested with the power of the sins (1987: 74–5). When the goat is killed his sins are absolved. A similar process takes place in art therapy when there is a transference of attributes and states to an object which, subsequently empowered, becomes a talisman. Once an object is experienced as a talisman, any act of resolution in relation to it becomes significant and might be seen as an act of 'disposal' (1987: 75).

Schaverien points out that 'scapegoating' can occur in groups, that a person is punished or ostracised for something which is not their own fault; for example:

> for exhibiting or expressing behaviours which those doing the rejecting might fear, or need to display themselves. The group fantasy may be that once this individual is removed, everyone else will relate harmoniously. The bad is all invested in one person.
>
> (1987: 80)

However, if recognition of transference can take place prior to 'disposal', then Schaverien argues that disposal can be positive rather than negative. Making an art work can enable 'acknowledgement' to take place, since the art work has undeniably been made by the client – though such acknowledgement may be fleeting (1987: 86).

Schaverien describes the destruction of the art object as a potentially 'meaningful act [which] offers a genuine opportunity to enact the scapegoating process in full. Keeping the art object is also a meaningful act which offers the solution of a different type of disposal'. The client, she argues, 'has dominion over the picture or art object, in a way that would never be possible with a person' (1987: 87).

sign In a sign, the relationship between the signifier and the signified is arbitrary and conventional; for example, a red cross (usually on a white background) denotes a first aid kit in the UK.

simile The explicit comparison of two unlike things; for example, 'she was like a rose'.

surrealist The word 'surrealistic' has acquired an idiomatic popular meaning, replacing the rather 1970s 'zany' in conversation. It can refer to iconoclastic images: images that jolt us out of our usual lazy sensibilities. Examples of iconic surrealistic images are perhaps Meret Oppenheim's fur-covered cup, saucer and spoon, Salvador Dali's melting clocks or René Magritte's 'Ceci n'est pas une pipe' ('This is not a pipe') or one of his floating bowler hats. The surrealist artistic movement dates from the 1920s; artists sought to apply the idea of 'free association' from psychoanalysis to art, harnessing thought 'freed from logic and reason' (Breton 1924, cited Hogan 2001: 94). First a technique called 'automatic writing' was developed and then these ideas were applied to images. Surrealism was a contributing influence to the development of modern art therapy (Hogan 2001).

symbol 'A material object representing something immaterial; an emblem, token or sign… Something that expresses, through suggestion, an idea or mood which would otherwise remain inexpressible or incomprehensible; the meeting point of many analogies' (Macquarie Dictionary 1981: 1720). 'Something that stands for, represents, or denotes something else (not by exact resemblance, but by vague suggestion, or by some accidental or conventional relation); esp. a material object representing or taken to represent something immaterial or abstract'; e.g. a wedding ring can be a symbol of marriage (Shorter Oxford English Dictionary 1973: 2220).

In psychoanalytic theory, symbolism is seen as arising out of an interpsychic conflict between the repressing tendencies [of the unconscious mind] and the repressed: 'only what is repressed is symbolised; only what is repressed needs to be symbolised…' (Rycroft 1968: 162). Furthermore, the object or activity symbolised is theorised as 'always one of basic, instinctual, or biological interest' (1968: 163). Therefore, the word 'symbolic' is used in a particular way by psychoanalytically-orientated writers.

It is not necessary to get bogged-down in the fundamentally reductive psychoanalytical theory of symbolism here. However, symbolic representation is immensely important in all forms of art therapy (not just psychoanalytically-oriented work), as feeling states and ideas which would be difficult or impossible to articulate verbally can be depicted in symbols and metaphors.

Symbols are often 'mysteriously indeterminate' with many possible meanings, or multiple meanings. Baldick speaks of literary symbols, but his point applies equally to images when he suggests that it is:

> usually too simple to say that a literary symbol 'stands for' some idea as if it were just a convenient substitute for a fixed meaning; it is usually a substantial image in its own right around which further significances may gather according to differing interpretations.
>
> (Baldick 2001: 252)

Thus symbols offer a rich and complex mode of communication.

transference The 'process by which a patient displaces onto his analyst [or art therapist] feelings, ideas, etc., which derive from previous figures in his life' via a process called displacement. In this process the client relates to the therapist as if the therapist 'was a former object in his life'. In psychoanalysis these are called object-representations [the mental representation of an object] acquired by earlier introjections' (Rycroft 1968: 168). Or put more simply, clients 'tend to re-experience emotional reactions which were originally directed towards members of their own families [or significant others]… in relationship to their doctor' (Tredgold and Woolf 1975: 22). These feelings are projected onto the therapist, and to the image. Broadly, the term can be used to describe the client's emotional attitude towards their therapist (Rycroft 1968: 168). In art therapy the client's demeanour towards their art work is of crucial importance, as well as their feelings about their therapist. However, seeing all aspects of the therapeutic relationship in terms of shifting transference is potentially reductive in my view.

unconscious Being unconscious is not realising the existence or occurrence of something, being 'temporarily insensible' (Shorter Oxford English Dictionary 1973: 2406). In psychoanalytical theory, unconscious processes refer to psychic material, which is only rarely accessible to awareness and which is repressed or pre-conscious (the latter may arise into consciousness more easily). It is believed that such psychic material can have a profound influence upon behaviour: 'when used loosely, the unconscious is a metaphorical, almost anthropomorphic concept, an entity influencing the SELF unbeknownst to itself' (Rycroft 1968: 173). In the 1920s Freud renamed the conscious mind the 'ego' and the unconscious mind the 'id' (a potentially useful distinction), the id being associated with 'instinctual' energy and the gratification of basic needs, the 'ego' being the more cultivated, civilised and socialised aspect of the psyche. Rycroft discusses why the use of the term unconscious is potentially problematic:

> First it can be and is used to obliterate a number of other distinctions, e.g. voluntary and involuntary, unwitting and deliberate, unself-conscious and self-aware. Secondly, it can be used to create states of sceptical confusion;

if a person [patient] accepts the general proposition that he may have unconscious motives, he may then find himself unable to disagree with some particular statement made about himself, since the fact that it does not correspond to anything of which he is aware does not preclude the possibility that it correctly states something of which he is unaware. As a result he may formally agree to propositions (interpretations) without in fact assenting or subscribing to them.

(1968: 173; my emphasis)

As discussed in the main text, it is potentially problematic for art therapists to offer interpretations for precisely these reasons: that the therapist's view may be hard to resist, especially if unconscious motivations are invoked. Rycroft also discusses the potential problem that a client may 'entertain an indefinite number of hypotheses about their unconscious motives without having any idea how to decide which of them are true' (1968). It makes much more sense, I'd maintain, for any interpretation of an art work to be undertaken by the art-therapy participant, as thoughts and feelings reach his or her awareness. The other, very serious, reason for avoiding focusing on 'unconscious' motivations for clients' behaviour is, as Rycroft suggests above, that it is simply too crude, and can distract from the more helpful task of enabling clients to explore their psychological motivations and complexities. Anyway, it is not my intention to try to re-convert the psychoanalytically inclined here, so much as to point out the conceptual pitfalls implicated with the use of this term. Making assumptions about what might be unconscious in art or discourse is potentially problematic as has been discussed in the main text. In Chapter 13 I discuss the contribution of Pierre Bourdieu, who has highlighted another way to think about what we 'unconsciously' bring with us, and called this habitus. This is an 'embodied history, internalised as a second nature and so forgotten as history – is the active presence of the whole part' (Bourdieu 1990: 56). It conjures up our habitual ways of being that are not necessarily in our conscious minds, or even in our consciousness. With an increasing emphasis on embodiment in art therapy, Bourdieu's ideas may be useful to us.

Bibliography

Baldick, C. 2001. *Concise Dictionary of Literary Terms.* Oxford: Oxford University Press.
Belsey, C. 1980. *Critical Practice.* London: Routledge.
Culler, J. 1983. *On Deconstruction: Theory and Criticism.* London: Routledge and Kegan Paul.
Douglas, M. 1994. The Construction of the Physician, in S. Budd and U. Sharma (eds) *The Healing Bond.* London: Routledge, pp. 23–41.
Gee, J.P. 1999. *An Introduction to Discourse Analysis: Theory and Method.* London: Routledge.
Hadjinicolaou, N. 1978. *Art History and Class Struggle.* London: Pluto.
Harris, R. 1996. *Signs, Language and Communication.* London: Routledge.

Henzell, J. 1984. Art, Psychotherapy and Symbol Systems, in T. Dalley (ed.) *Art As Therapy: an Introduction to the Use of Art as a Therapeutic Technique*. London: Tavistock Publications, pp. 12–23.

Hogan, S. (ed.) 1997. *Feminist Approaches to Art Therapy*. London: Routledge.

Hogan, S. 2001. *Healing Arts: the History of Art Therapy*. London: Jessica Kingsley Publishers.

Hogan, S. 2008. Angry Mothers, in M. Liebmann (ed.) *Art Therapy and Anger.* London and Philadelphia: Jessica Kingsley Publishers, pp. 197–210.

Hogan, S. 2011a. Feminist Art Therapy, in C. Wood (ed.) *Navigating Art Therapy: a Therapist's Companion*. London: Routledge, pp. 87–8.

Hogan, S. 2011b. Postmodernist but Not Postfeminist! A Feminist Postmodernist Approach to Working with New Mothers, in H. Burt (ed.) *Art Therapy and Postmodernism: Creative Healing Through a Prism*. London: Jessica Kingsley Publishers, pp. 70–82.

Hogan, S. and Warren, L. 2012. Dealing with Complexity in Research Findings: How Do Older Women Negotiate and Challenge Images of Ageing? *Journal of Women and Ageing* 24(4), 329–50.

Laine, R. 2007. Image Consultation, in J. Schaverien and C. Case (eds) *Supervision of Art Psychotherapy: a Theoretical and Practical Handbook*. London: Routledge, pp. 119–37.

Laine, R. 2011. Amplification, in C. Wood (ed.) *Navigating Art Therapy: a Therapist's Companion*. London: Routledge, p. 14.

The Macquarie Dictionary. 1981. Chatswood: Macquarie University.

Malchiodi, C. 1997. Invasive Art: Art as Empowerment for Women with Breast Cancer, in Hogan S. (ed.) *Feminist Approaches to Art Therapy.* London: Routledge, pp. 49–64.

McNeilly, G. 1984. Directive and Non-directive Approaches in Art Therapy. *Inscape: Journal of Art Therapy* Winter, 7–12.

McNeilly, G. 2005. *Group Analytic Art Therapy*. London: Jessica Kingsley Publishers.

Richardson, L. 2011. Resonance, in C. Wood (ed.) *Navigating Art Therapy: a Therapist's Companion*. London: Routledge, p. 201.

Rycroft, C. 1968. *A Critical Dictionary of Psychoanalysis*. London: Thomas Nelson and Sons.

Schaverien, J. 1987. The Scapegoat and the Talisman: Transference in Art Therapy, in T. Dalley, C. Case, J. Schaverien, F. Weir, D. Halliday, P.N. Hall and D. Waller (eds) *Images of Art Therapy: New Developments in Theory and Practice*. London: Tavistock, pp. 74–108.

Schaverien, J. 2011. Embodied Image, in C. Wood (ed.) *Navigating Art Therapy: a Therapist's Companion*. London: Routledge, p. 80.

Shorter Oxford English Dictionary. 1973. Oxford: Oxford University Press.

Tredgold, R. and Wolff, H. 1975. *UCH Handbook of Psychiatry*. London: Duckworth.

Williams, R. 1981. *Keywords: a Vocabulary of Culture and Society*. London: Fontana.

Wood, C. 2011. Empathy, in C. Wood (ed.) *Navigating Art Therapy: a Therapist's Companion*. London: Routledge, p. 81.

Online resources

Dictionary.com (n.d.) http://dictionary.reference.com/browse/metaphor (accessed 23/11/11).

Molnos, A. 1998. A Psychotherapist's Harvest. http://www.net.klte.hu/~keresofi/psyth/a-to-z-entries/parataxic_distortions.html (accessed 23/11/11).

Index